MARY KATHLEEN GLAVICH, SND

GOSPEL THEATER FOR THE WHOLE COMMUNITY

92 plays for education and worship

TWENTY THIRD 23rd
PUBLICATIONS

Dedication

To the Most Reverend Richard G. Lennon,
bishop of Cleveland,
for his Christlike leadership

Twenty-Third Publications
A Division of Bayard
One Montauk Avenue, Suite 200
New London, CT 06320
(860) 437-3012 or (800) 321-0411
www.23rdpublications.com

The Scripture passages contained herein are from the *New Revised Standard Version of the Bible*, copyright ©1989, by the Division of Christian Education of the National Council of Churches in the U.S.A. All rights reserved.

ISBN-10: 1-58595-563-9
ISBN 978-1-58595-563-3
Library of Congress Catalog Card Number: 2005935874
Printed in the U.S.A.

Contents

The Miracles of Jesus

The Parables of Jesus

The Paschal Mystery of Jesus

Sunday and Feast Day Gospels

Index of Themes

Introduction

Community Gospel Theater contains plays for ninety-two events from the gospel accounts of the life of Jesus. It is a new edition of my books *Acting Out the Gospels* and *Acting Out the Miracles and Parables*, both favorites among catechists and teachers. The playlets are a boon for many forms of religious education. Because they are short and ready-made, they are ideal for whole community catechesis, such as the Generations of Faith program. Learners can put on the plays for the assembly, or members of the whole group can perform them. Gospel playlets have long been an effective tool in traditional religion classrooms where teachers know that people learn more from what they do than from what they hear or see. Home schoolers, too, can benefit from the playlets as they bring stories about Jesus to life and make them more memorable.

You might incorporate the playlets into sessions or lessons on related topics. Or you can use them as an alternative to having learners merely reading or listening to the religion text or the Bible. Certainly having the learners themselves write gospel plays is an interesting, fun, and effective learning activity, but it consumes a lot of time. The material accompanying each playlet, as well as the plays themselves, provide an original approach.

The ready-made plays in this book are based directly on Scripture. These brief plays can be used in a session as

- a lively introduction,
- a method of developing a Bible story,
- a review activity,
- a culminating activity, or
- a lead into a prayer experience.

They can be presented
- for another class or other group,
- as part of a program for families and other guests, or
- within a liturgical or paraliturgical service.

The playlets are suitable for learners of any age for several reasons. The gospel stories themselves are simple and so is their vocabulary. Most of them will already be familiar to your learners. Furthermore, the faith sessions (the context of the playlets) provide you with the necessary preparation and follow-up that suit the playlets to the learners' developmental stage.

Most of the wording of the playlets is based on the New Revised Standard Version of the Bible. The playlets for events that appear in more than one gospel account are a blend of those accounts. Where dialogue is described in the Scriptures or merely implied, it has been supplied.

Each playlet in this book can be easily duplicated for the actors and others involved in staging it. The number of characters in a group marked (+) can be more or fewer according to the size of the group, to allow as many as possible—adults and children—to participate.

Helpful Features

Catechists and teachers, especially "novice" producers and directors, should not miss "Ten Tips for Putting on Playlets" below. The suggestions included there are important for smooth performances that will be rewarding for everyone.

Certain features in the book alert you to the most appropriate time or use for each playlet. A chart on page 208 lists Sunday or feast day gospels in each liturgical cycle that have a corresponding play in this book. It facilitates preparing liturgies enhanced by a play or helping learners derive more from the Sunday liturgy. The information that precedes each play also cites the Sunday or feast day of that gospel. Each gospel event is explained briefly under "Background Notes." These notes clarify what took place, supply background information, and indicate the event's significance. Themes for each gospel play assist you in correlating the play with the topics being studied. In addition, for each play discussion questions are suggested for before and after the performance. Some questions focus on the main message of the Scripture passage. Others are intended to help learners explore concepts that they might find puzzling or might overlook. Most importantly, some questions lead learners to relate the gospel events to themselves and their world. Choose or adapt the questions to the age level and needs of your learners.

In addition, the book offers two means for reinforcing the message. For each gospel event you'll find a prayer—a traditional prayer, reflection, imaginative prayer, or other form—that can be prayed any time during the session. Also included are activities that can be carried out by a family, a group, or individuals of different age levels. For some activities it will help to have a model or sample prepared ahead of time.

Community Gospel Theater will be an invaluable aid to all catechists and teachers in providing the variety and involvement that are essential ingredients of good teaching. The playlets will enable you to teach creatively without undue time spent preparing plays. Moreover, your learners will encounter the Scriptures and Jesus in an enjoyable way, through an experience they will remember more than reading a page in a book.

Ten Tips for Putting on Playlets

1. Make a copy of the playlet for each participant who has a speaking part or a major role. Write their names on the copies and highlight, or have the participants highlight, all of their parts, including stage directions.

2. Allow as many learners (of all ages) as possible to participate in the playlets. The number of characters marked (+) can be adjusted to the size of your group.

3. Assign parts or list the characters on the board or on a large sheet of paper so that volunteers can sign up for parts before the formal session begins. They might have time to practice and even to memorize their lines.

4. Make an identification sign, sandwich board, or headband for each character.

5. Prepare the props that are suggested for some of the playlets. Some of the props are everyday items that are easily accessible. Others—such as trees, fire, clouds, and other larger props—can be painted on a backdrop or made of construction paper. Bags of coins, loaves of bread, and other objects might also be made of construction paper. Printed signs indicating the setting would also be helpful, particularly if the location changes during the playlet. For example, for the Good Samaritan play make a sign that says "Inn." Draw scenery on the blackboard or on butcher paper to serve as the backdrop. If possible, have the actors wear simple costumes, such as a head piece for an apostle, a veil for Mary and other women, and so on. Inexpensive clothes can be bought at secondhand stores. If you have time, you can fashion tunics or skirts out of remnants, burlap, or other materials.

6. Arrange to have the actors rehearse together while the rest of the group is engaged in another activity. An assistant might take the group to another room for practice.

7. Encourage the actors to follow these basic acting principles:

    • Look up from the scripts as much as possible.

    • Speak so as to be heard and understood.

    • Avoid having your back to the audience.

    • Use expression in interpreting the lines.

    • Be creative in adding movements and gestures.

8. Before the playlet begins, have the characters introduce themselves to the audience, especially if they are not wearing any identification.

9. Affirm the group and individuals for a job well done. You might have the group evaluate its performance.

10. Make sure that each person has a speaking role at some time and is not always just a member of the crowd.

Caution: Avoid putting on a play only for the sake of putting on a play. With proper introduction and follow-up, a play is a meaningful educational experience.

The Announcement of John's Birth

Themes

- Advent
- the infancy narratives
- John the Baptist
- openness to God
- need for faith

Background Notes

Elizabeth and Zechariah were righteous people who were childless, like Abraham and Sarah of the Old Testament. While Zechariah was praying, God revealed startling news to him. Zechariah and Elizabeth would have a son who would be great in God's sight.

The day John's birth was announced was special for Zechariah. Out of eight hundred priests in his division, he was chosen by lot to offer incense that day in the Holy Place of the Temple. The many people present suggest that he was carrying this office out during the evening hours.

The angel Gabriel appeared to Zechariah and said, "Do not be afraid." This is just what he would say to Mary six months later. These words often preface a redemptive act of God. Gabriel's words to Zechariah followed the formula for a birth announcement commonly used in Scripture. The angel foretold that John would be a Nazarite dedicated to God as Samson was. God empowered him to be the forerunner of Jesus and help bring about the messianic age. Like Elijah, he announced the Lord. He was a great prophet. Zechariah was left speechless by the good news—either because he lacked faith or because he was overcome by joy.

For Discussion

Before the play: Who are angels? Which angels have you read or learned about? What is their role? When is a good time to pray to your guardian angel?

After the play: How is this event similar to the announcement of Jesus' birth? How is it different? What other times has God done the impossible? in the life of Jesus? in your life? How else does God speak to us besides through angels?

Activity

Show younger learners or a mixed group how to make an angel from a paper plate. Slit the plate stopping a half-inch from the center. Make another slit opposite this. Draw a neck and head above the center connecting to the slits. Cut around this so the top part of the plate separates. Pull the ends of the bottom half together to form a cone and staple it. Use the top part of the plate or half of a lace paper doily to make wings and glue them on. Draw a face on the angel and decorate its robe. Alternate activity: Draw an angel with a cartoon balloon coming from its mouth. In the balloon write what an angel might say to you today.

Invite older learners to look up information about the Jewish Temple. If you can obtain a picture, have them draw their own or make a simple model.

Prayer

Invite learners to think of a special prayer intention. This may be something personal or something as universal as world peace.

O God, you heard the prayers of Zechariah and Elizabeth and gave them a son. This was a miracle because they were elderly. Give me the grace to trust you to do miracles for me, too. Give me strong faith so that in times of need I may turn to you for help. Then let me keep praying even though it seems you are not listening. I believe that you can do the impossible. Please surprise me, especially by...

CAST: **NARRATOR, ZECHARIAH, ANGEL GABRIEL, PERSONS 1, 2, 3 (+)**

PROPS: TABLE FOR ALTAR, INCENSE

THE ANNOUNCEMENT OF JOHN'S BIRTH LUKE 1:5–25

Zechariah kneels before table with incense. Persons 1, 2, 3 kneel praying at a distance.

Narrator   Zechariah was a priest. He and his wife Elizabeth were good, holy people. They were very old and had never had any children. One day Zechariah was chosen by lot to burn incense in the Temple. People prayed outside.

Angel Gabriel enters and stands at right of altar. Zechariah gasps, trembles, and stands with hands up.

Angel   Do not be afraid, Zechariah, for your prayer has been heard. Your wife Elizabeth will bear you a son, and you will name him John. You will have joy and gladness, and many people will rejoice at his birth, for he will be great in the sight of the Lord. He must never drink wine or strong drink. Even before his birth he will be filled with the Holy Spirit. He will turn many people of Israel to the Lord their God. He will prepare people for the Lord.

Zechariah   How will I know this is so? For I am an old man, and my wife is getting on in years.

Angel   I am Gabriel. I stand in the presence of God. I was sent to announce to you this good news. But now, because you did not believe my words, (*shaking finger at Zechariah*) you will be unable to speak until the day these things occur. (*Angel exits*)

Person 1   What's taking Zechariah so long? He should be finished by now.

Person 2   Maybe he's ill. He's pretty old.

Zechariah rises and walks slowly in a daze toward the people.

Person 1   Here he comes.

Persons 1, 2, 3 rise. Zechariah gestures to the place he left and to his mouth. He points to heaven.

Person 3   Why doesn't he speak?

Person 2   I think he's had a vision.

Narrator   Zechariah learned to trust God's messages. The angel's words came true. Zechariah and Elizabeth had a son known as John the Baptist.

The Annunciation of the Lord

FOURTH SUNDAY OF ADVENT: YEAR B

Themes

- Advent
- the infancy narratives
- obedience
- openness to God
- Mary
- the identity of Jesus
- the Holy Spirit
- spiritual life

Background Notes

The announcement of the immediate coming of the Messiah was made to Mary, a virgin in Nazareth. The angel Gabriel greeted Mary with words of great praise. He disclosed that God had chosen her to bear a son who is the Son of God and who should be named Jesus, which means "God saves." The words Gabriel used to describe Mary's son, such as "Son of the Most High," signified God's redeeming presence in the Old Testament. Mary was espoused to Joseph, who was of the family of David. Because Joseph was Jesus' legal father, it was through him, not Mary, that Jesus would trace his lineage.

Mary accepted God's will for her and merited her name, which in Hebrew means "exalted one." In trust and obedience she agreed to be a virgin-mother, the mother of the Savior. She stands as a model for all who are called to bring forth Christ into the world and to further his kingdom.

For Discussion

Before the play: What does it mean to you when we say that God became a human being? Why do you think God chose Mary to be the mother of Jesus? Why was being God's mother a difficult thing for Mary to do?

After the play: What were some privileges God gave Mary because she was the Mother of God? How is Mary your mother too? How can you show your love for and desire to imitate Mary? What is the best way?

Activity

Mary brought forth Jesus, the Light of the World. Invite your learners to make a Mary candle. Younger learners might decorate a white candle with an "M" for Mary. You might tie blue ribbon around it and put sequins on it. Light the candle on her feast days and on Saturday, which is a day dedicated to Mary.

Older learners could make their own candles from sheets of beeswax. Inexpensive kits are available at craft stores. Or they might make a mural with scenes from the annunciation.

Prayer

Pray the Angelus together.

THE ANGELUS

*The angel of the Lord declared unto Mary
And she conceived of the Holy Spirit.
Hail Mary...*

*Behold the handmaid of the Lord.
Be it done to me according to your word.
Hail Mary...*

*And the Word was made flesh
And dwelt among us.
Hail Mary...*

*Pray for us, O holy Mother of God,
That we may be made worthy
of the promises of Christ.*

Let us pray: Pour forth, we beseech you, O Lord, your grace into our hearts, that we to whom the incarnation of Christ, your Son, was made known by the message of an angel, may by his passion and death be brought to the glory of his resurrection, through the same Christ our Lord. Amen.

CAST: NARRATOR, GABRIEL, MARY

THE ANNUNCIATION OF THE LORD LUKE 1:26–38

Mary is sitting on the stage, doing some work or praying.

Narrator   The angel Gabriel was sent from God to a town of Galilee called Nazareth. He went to the home of a virgin engaged to a man named Joseph, of the house of David. The virgin's name was Mary.

Gabriel enters and goes to Mary. Mary gasps and looks frightened.

Gabriel   Hail, favored one! The Lord is with you.

Mary puts her hand over her heart and tilts head, looking puzzled.

Gabriel   (*raises hand*) Do not be afraid, Mary, for God is very pleased with you. Now, you will conceive and bear a son. You will name him Jesus. He will be great and will be called the Son of the Most High. The Lord God will give him the throne of his ancestor David. He will reign over the house of Jacob forever. His kingdom will have no end.

Mary   How can this be, since I am not yet married?

Gabriel   The Holy Spirit will come upon you. The power of God will overshadow you. And so the child to be born will be holy. He will be called the Son of God. Your older relative Elizabeth is also pregnant. Although she is past the age for having children, she has been pregnant for six months. For nothing will be impossible with God.

Mary   (*bowing*) Behold, I am the servant of the Lord. Let it be done to me according to your word.

Gabriel exits.

Narrator   Because Mary was open to doing God's will, she became the mother of God. Her son, Jesus, saved the world. We try to be like our mother Mary and like Jesus by doing what God wants.

The Visitation

FOURTH SUNDAY OF ADVENT: YEAR C

Themes

- the infancy narratives
- Mary
- John the Baptist
- service
- the poor
- service

Background Notes

Mary's union with God prompted her to selfless action. Hastening to assist her elderly relative Elizabeth, she undertook a journey of about ninety miles. When the two women met, Elizabeth recognized the great blessing that had come to Mary. The baby in her womb leapt, a sign of messianic joy. Jesus was the reason for John's greatness and mission in life. John was filled with new life, the life of the Spirit. Tradition holds that at that moment John the Baptist was freed from sin.

Mary's hymn of praise is called the Magnificat, from the Latin for the opening words. The Church prays the Magnificat every day in evening prayer. In this canticle, Mary reflected on her role as handmaid favored by God. Then she recalled the great themes of salvation history: the surprising reversal as God acted on behalf of the poor and needy. The rich and powerful were brought low, while the poor and humble were raised. Mary closed her song by proclaiming that God has kept the promise made to Abraham. Israel, a servant, has been favored.

For Discussion

Before the play: Can you describe a time when you experienced God's love through a person who did something special for you? What were some hardships Mary faced in going to visit Elizabeth? Why did she go?

After the play: What was the relationship between Jesus and John? What are some hard things you have done out of love for and service to the members of your family? What else could you do for them?

Activity

Because Mary brought Jesus to Elizabeth, she was the first Christopher, which means "Christ bearer." Have the younger children trace their shoes onto construction paper and cut out the footprints. In the middle of each one they can write one practical way of showing Jesus' love for another.

Older learners might decide how they can share the gospel in a concrete way.

Prayer

Pray the Magnificat by having the learners say it together, or separate the group into two sides and have the sides read alternate verses (verses are separated by /).

THE MAGNIFICAT

My soul magnifies the Lord, and my spirit rejoices in God my Savior,/ for he has looked with favor on the lowliness of his servant. Surely, from now on all generations will call me blessed;/ for the Mighty One has done great things for me, and holy is his name./ His mercy is for those who fear him from generation to generation./ He has shown strength with his arm; he has scattered the proud in the thoughts of their hearts./ He has brought down the powerful from their thrones, and lifted up the lowly;/ he has filled the hungry with good things and sent the rich away empty./ He has helped his servant Israel, in remembrance of his mercy,/ according to the promise he made to our ancestors, to Abraham and to his descendants forever.

CAST: NARRATOR, MARY, ELIZABETH

PROPS: POT AND LADLE OR BROOM, TWO CHAIRS

THE VISITATION   LUKE 1:39–56

Elizabeth is off to the side, stirring a pot or sweeping the floor. Two chairs are in the center of the stage.

Narrator   After the angel Gabriel appeared to her, Mary traveled quickly to a town of Judah in the hill country. She was going to help her elderly relative Elizabeth, who was pregnant.

Mary enters and goes quickly toward Elizabeth. She pretends to open a door and steps inside.

Mary   Elizabeth, dear! How are you?

Elizabeth   (*surprised*) Ah? (*puts her hand on her stomach*) Mary!

Mary and Elizabeth hug.

Elizabeth   (*excitedly*) Blessed are you among women, Mary, and blessed is the fruit of your womb. Why should I be so blessed, that the mother of my Lord comes to me? As soon as I heard the sound of your greeting, the child in my womb leaped for joy. Blessed are you who believed that the Lord's words to you would be fulfilled.

Mary   My soul magnifies the Lord, and my spirit rejoices in God my savior. For he has looked with favor on the lowliness of his servant. Surely, from now on all generations will call me blessed. For the Mighty One has done great things for me, and holy is his name.

(*Optional*) His mercy is for those who fear him from generation to generation. He has shown strength with his arm; he has scattered the proud in the thoughts of their hearts. He has brought down the powerful from their thrones, and lifted up the lowly; he has filled the hungry with good things, and sent the rich away empty. He has helped his servant Israel, In remembrance of his mercy, according to his promise he made to our ancestors, to Abraham and to his descendants forever.

Elizabeth   Zechariah will be home soon. He can't speak, you know, ever since he found out about our baby. He'll be glad to see you too! How long can you stay?

Mary   About three months.

Elizabeth   Wonderful! Now tell me about yourself and all the things that have happened.

Mary and Elizabeth sit down.

Narrator   Mary helped Elizabeth during the last months before the birth of Elizabeth's son. Then she returned home to prepare for her own child. We pray to be as generous and selfless as Mary was.

The Birth of John

Themes
- Advent
- the infancy narratives
- John the Baptist

Background Notes

John was not named after his father, as was the custom. He who was to be the messenger of God was named by God. When Zechariah affirmed the name John, he regained the power of speech. Everyone was filled with wonder, and Zechariah praised God. The first part of his canticle (song) was modeled on Jewish circumcision ceremonies. The second part linked John to the Savior. It gave his identity in relation to Jesus. The hopes and promises of the Jewish forefathers would soon be fulfilled. The dayspring would dawn to save people from darkness. Zechariah's song is prayed everyday in the morning praise of the Liturgy of the Hours, the official prayer of the Church.

For Discussion

Before the play: Do you know why you received your name? Who gave you your name? What does your name mean?

After the play: What was John's mission going to be? What is God asking you to do? What are some reasons you have for blessing the Lord as Zechariah did?

Activity

Use these instructions to have younger learners make "name plates." Fold a sheet of drawing paper in half lengthwise and write or print your name along the fold so that it sits on the fold. Draw a line outlining the sides and tops of your name about a quarter of an inch away from the letters. With the paper still folded, cut along this line. Along the fold, cut away the underside of the letters. Open the paper to see the design your name forms. Paste it on another sheet of paper and decorate it.

Older learners can each look up the meaning of their name, and write a short poem or story about it.

Prayer

Canticle of Zechariah (excerpt)
Blessed be the Lord God of Israel,
*   for he has looked with favor on his people*
*   and redeemed them.*
He has raised up a mighty savior for us
*   in the house of his servant David.*
And you, child, will be called the prophet
*   of the Most High,*
*   you will go before the Lord*
*   to prepare his ways,*
*   you will announce salvation to his people*
*   through the forgiveness of their sins.*
By the tender mercy of our God,
*   the dawn from on high will break upon us.*
God will give light to those who sit in darkness
*   and in the shadow of death.*
The dawn will guide our feet into
*   the way of peace.*

Cast: Narrator, Zechariah, Elizabeth, Persons 1, 2, 3 (+)

Props: Paper, pencil, doll or blanket for baby

THE BIRTH OF JOHN Luke 1:57–78

Narrator When Elizabeth and her husband Zechariah were very old, she bore a son. Now she was no longer ashamed that she had no children, and she thanked God. Eight days after her son was born, neighbors and relatives came for a Jewish celebration. On that day the baby would be given a name.

Zechariah, Elizabeth carrying a baby, and Persons 1, 2, 3 enter.

Person 1 Let's name him Zechariah.

Person 2 Yes, he should be named after his father.

Elizabeth No, he is to be called John.

Person 3 But none of your relatives has this name.

Persons 1, 2, 3 turn to Zechariah, point to baby, and raise their hands questioningly. Zechariah motions as if writing and extends his hand. Person 2 brings pencil and paper. Zechariah writes. Person 1 looks over his shoulder.

Person 1 Zechariah wrote, "His name is John."

Person 3 I don't believe it. How strange.

Zechariah Blessed be God!

Person 2 (*excitedly*) He can speak now!

Person 1 What can this mean?

Person 3 Let's get out of here.

Person 2 What will this child become?

Zechariah (*takes baby from Elizabeth*) Blessed be the Lord God of Israel,
for he has looked with favor on his people and redeemed them.
He has raised up a mighty savior for us
in the house of his servant David.

(*holding up baby*) You, my child, will be called the prophet of the Most High.
You will go before the Lord to prepare his ways.
You will announce salvation to his people
through the forgiveness of their sins.
By the tender mercy of our God,
the dawn from on high will break upon us.
God will give light to those who sit in darkness and in the shadow of death.
God will guide our feet into the way of peace.

Narrator The child of Zechariah and Elizabeth was John the Baptist, the great prophet. He prepared the people for Jesus. Let us always be prepared to welcome Jesus.

The Birth of Jesus (January 1)

OCTAVE OF CHRISTMAS, SOLEMNITY OF MARY, MOTHER OF GOD: YEARS A, B, C; CHRISTMAS MASS AT MIDNIGHT: YEARS A, B, C; CHRISTMAS MASS AT DAWN: YEARS A, B, C

Themes

- Christmas
- the infancy narratives
- identity of Jesus
- Mary
- the good news
- obedience to law
- poverty

Background Notes

In the Scriptures, the birth of the Savior is told in the context of the Roman Empire. Mary and Joseph were good citizens responding to a call for a worldwide census. People had to return to their own towns to register. Because Joseph was of the House of David, he traveled to Bethlehem, about ninety miles from Nazareth. Joseph and Mary found shelter and privacy in a room where people kept livestock. The stable was probably the back room of a house. There Mary gave birth to Jesus. She wrapped him in swaddling clothes, long strips that Palestinians used so that their children would grow straight and strong. The newborn boy, who would someday be the bread of life, was placed in a manger, a feeding trough. He was Mary's firstborn, the first of many others—his future followers.

Angels announced to shepherds the good news of the child's birth. Shepherds were poor people whose job was that of the patriarchs: to guard and guide. In the angels' proclamation they referred to Jesus as Savior, Messiah, and Lord. The news was especially exciting for the shepherds because the Messiah appeared in humble surroundings, like one of them.

For Discussion

Before the play: How does your family celebrate Christmas? Why is this such a great feast? Who are some of the people in the Christmas story? What part do they play?

After the play: Why do you think the Son of God chose to be born in a stable? How does Jesus come to us today? How can we make room for Jesus in our lives?

Activity

Invite learners to design a Christmas card for someone special. Use these instructions for making a tryptich (three-part picture). Fold a large sheet of drawing paper into three equal parts. With the paper folded, cut a curve at one end to form the top of a church window. Open the paper and in each section draw a Christmas scene: Jesus, Mary, and Joseph in the stable; the shepherds with angels; and the three kings. Alternate activity: Make a baby Jesus by drawing facial features on a peanut shell and wrapping it with a small piece of material. Or place the baby in half of a walnut shell.

Younger and older learners might like to make these cards and gifts for children in a hospital, or for homebound persons in the parish.

Prayer

Gather the learners around the manger. Sing a religious Christmas carol such as "Silent Night," "O Come, All Ye Faithful," or "Hark, the Herald Angels Sing."

CAST: NARRATOR, MARY, JOSEPH, INNKEEPER, ANGEL 1, ANGELS (+), SHEPHERDS 1, 2 (+)

PROPS: DOLL OR BLANKET FOR BABY, BOX FOR MANGER, SHEPHERDS' STAFFS, SCROLL FOR INNKEEPER, CLOTHS FOR SWADDLING, COTHES IN BASKET OR BAG, TWO CHAIRS

THE BIRTH OF JESUS LUKE 2:1–20

Shepherds are on one side of the stage. Half of them are sleeping. Innkeeper is on other side, writing on a scroll.

Narrator In those days a decree went out from Emperor Augustus that all the world should be registered. This was the first census, when Quirinius was governor of Syria. So all went to their own towns to be registered. Joseph also went from the town of Nazareth in Galilee to Judea, to the city of David called Bethlehem. He was of the house and family of David. He went to be registered with Mary, to whom he was engaged. Mary was expecting a child.

Mary and Joseph enter, walking slowly. They stop at "door" and Joseph knocks. Innkeeper comes to door.

Innkeeper Yes?

Joseph Would you have room for two more, my wife and me?

Innkeeper Sorry, but the house is filled.

Joseph We'd appreciate even a small space. My wife is going to have our child any day now.

Innkeeper (*shaking head*) Sorry. Wish I could help. (*pause*) Wait. There's the stable in the back.

Joseph That would be fine.

Innkeeper Come with me.

Mary and Joseph go to center of stage with the Innkeeper. Joseph helps Mary to a chair.

Joseph (*to Innkeeper*) Thank you, sir.

Innkeeper Good night. (*exits*)

Mary It's almost time, Joseph.

While Narrator speaks, Joseph, with his back to the audience, takes the doll and cloths from the basket. He gives them to Mary. She wraps the doll in the cloths and sets it in the manger.

Narrator While they were there, the time came for Mary to have her child. She gave birth to her firstborn son. She wrapped him in swaddling clothes and laid him in a manger.

Angel 1 enters and stands before the Shepherds. Shepherds gasp and shield their faces. The sleeping ones awake and rub their eyes.

Angel 1 Do not be afraid. For see, I bring you good news of great joy for all the people. For this day in the city of David a Savior is born. He is the Messiah, the Lord. This will be a sign for you: you will find a child wrapped in swaddling clothes and lying in a manger.

Angels enter and join Angel 1.

Angels Glory to God in the highest and on earth peace among those whom he favors! (*exit*)

Shepherd 1 (*to Shepherd 2*) Let us go now to Bethlehem and see what has taken place. The Lord has made this known to us.

Shepherds run to Mary and Joseph.

Shepherd 2 (*to Mary and Joseph*) We have come to see the child. We were watching our flocks, and angels appeared. They told us that a savior was born in Bethlehem. They said we would find him in a manger.

Mary lifts the baby and holds him. Shepherds kneel around the family.

Joseph (*to Mary*) What an amazing story! (*Mary smiles and nods*)

Shepherds rise.

Shepherd 1 Well, we had better go back to our flocks now. Glory to God for this wonderful thing!

Shepherd 2 Blessed be God, who is rich in love and mercy!

Shepherds exit.

Narrator Let us always thank God for loving us so much and for becoming a human being like us. May we never forget how amazing this is.

The Visit of the Magi

EPIPHANY: YEARS A, B, C

- Advent/ Christmas
- the infancy narratives
- the good news
- the identity of Jesus
- missionary work
- Gentiles

Background Notes

The story of the Magi confirmed that Jesus was the Messiah who would be born in David's city. *Magi* was a term for people skilled in supernatural knowledge and power. They weren't kings. The gospel's Magi from the East were probably from Mesopotamia, the center of astrology. A popular belief was that a new star appeared whenever a person was born. When the star appeared that night, the Magi went to the Jewish people to find out about the Messiah. The Jewish prophets told them that the king was to be born in Bethlehem. Once the Magi reached Jerusalem, the star guided them to the house where Jesus was.

The Magi prostrated themselves before Jesus. The three presents they brought have led to the belief that there were three Magi. Tradition has named them Caspar, Melchior, and Balthasar. Their gifts are interpreted as symbols of the child's roles: gold, for a king; frankincense, for God; and myrrh, a sweet-smelling resin used in anointing for burial, to signify Jesus' death.

The feast of Epiphany (manifestation of God) is called Little Christmas. We celebrate it on January 6 or, in the United States, on a Sunday between January 2 and 8. Some people exchange gifts on this day. Priests may give an Epiphany house blessing in which they write a code like 20 + C + M + B + 07 above the door. The letters represent the Magi; the numbers, the year; and the crosses (like compass points), all nations.

For Discussion

Before the play: In a nativity scene we usually see three kings nearby. Whom do they represent? What nationality of people did Jesus come to save? What kind of king is Jesus, whom the Magi came to honor?

After the play: What gifts did the Magi give to Jesus? What gifts can you give to God? What part of the story of the Epiphany tells us about the conflict and suffering Jesus will face?

Activity

Invite young learners to cut out a star from yellow paper and on it print "Wise men still seek him." Add glitter. Alternate activity: Make star-shaped cookies or a star-shaped cake.

Older learners may discuss who the "magi" of today might be, that is, those seeking truth, seeking Jesus.

Prayer

Gathered around a nativity scene, hold a prayer service for missionaries.
- Sing "We Three Kings."
- Pray: *God, may people everywhere come to know you. Bless missionaries as they work to spread the Good News of your love. Bless their efforts with success. We pray today especially for missionary work in the countries of* (learners name countries).
- The learners place donations for the missions and/or promises of good deeds as a gift in a basket in front of the nativity scene.

CAST: NARRATOR, MARY, MAGI 1, 2, 3, KING HEROD, PRIESTS 1, 2 (+), SCRIBES 1, 2 (+), MESSENGER

PROPS: STAR; CHAIR; DOLL OR BLANKET FOR CHILD; THREE GIFTS TO REPRESENT GOLD, FRANKINCENSE, AND MYRRH

THE VISIT OF THE MAGI MATTHEW 2:1–12

Priest 1 and Scribe 1 are on stage.

Narrator   Jesus was born in Bethlehem of Judea, in the days of King Herod. Later, Magi, wise men from the East, came to Jerusalem.

Magi enter and go to Priest 1 and Scribe 1.

Magi 1   Where is the newborn king of the Jews?

Magi 2   We saw his star at its rising and have come to pay him homage.

Priest 1   I don't know anything about him.

Magi exit.

Priest 1   (*to Scribe 1*) We'd better tell King Herod about this.

Priest 1 and Scribe 1 exit.

Narrator   When King Herod was told, he was greatly troubled, and all Jerusalem was, too.

King Herod, Priest 1, and Scribe 1 enter.

King Herod   Have all the chief priests and the scribes come here?

Priest 1   Yes, my King.

Priest 1 and Scribe 1 exit. Priests and Scribes enter and stand before King Herod. Messenger enters and stands in back.

King Herod   Tell me, please, where is the Messiah to be born?

Priest 2   In Bethlehem of Judea.

Scribe 2   For a prophet wrote, "And you, Bethlehem, land of Judah, are by no means least among the rulers of Judah. From you shall come a ruler who is to shepherd my people Israel."

King Herod   Go. That's all I wanted to know.

All except Messenger exit.

King Herod   (*to Messenger*) Come here.

Messenger goes to King Herod.

King Herod   Find those Magi from the East and have them come here. Don't let anyone know I sent you.

Messenger   Yes, O King. (exits)

King Herod   (*pacing back and forth*) A new king who will take my place! I must get rid of him.

Messenger and Magi enter.

King Herod (*to Magi*) Thank you for coming. Naturally I'm interested in the new king. When did you see the star appear?

Magi 1 We believe the star appeared on the night of the child's birth. The child must be one or two years old by now.

King Herod Go to Bethlehem and search carefully for the child. When you have found him, bring me word. I want to go and pay him homage.

Magi 1 We'll be glad to.

Magi bow, and King Herod and Messenger exit. Magi walk a little way.

Magi 3 (*excitedly*) Look! There's the star again!

Magi 1 It's moving ahead of us.

Magi 2 To guide us to the newborn king.

Mary enters with child and sits in the background. Magi continue to walk.

Magi 1 It stopped moving.

Magi 2 It's right above this house. Let's see who lives here.

Magi go to Mary, "knock" on door.

Mary Come in.

Magi enter and kneel.

Magi 3 Hail to the new king!

Magi 2 We bring you gifts from our country.

Magi 1 Gold. (*presents gold*)

Magi 2 Frankincense. (*presents frankincense*)

Magi 3 And myrrh. (*presents myrrh*)

Mary smiles, accepts the gifts.

Narrator The Magi were warned in a dream not to return to Herod, so they went back to their country by another way. When Herod realized that the Magi had tricked him, he was furious. He had all boys two years and under who lived in and around Bethlehem killed. But Mary, Joseph, and Jesus escaped to Egypt. This story of the wise men from the East teaches us that God came to save people of all nations. God asks us, too, to teach them about Jesus.

The Presentation

SUNDAY IN THE OCTAVE OF CHRISTMAS: YEAR B

Background Notes

In obedience to the Jewish Law, Mary and Joseph took Jesus to Jerusalem to offer him to God. In this ceremony the firstborn son was consecrated to the Lord. This ceremony celebrated the Passover when the angel of the Lord did not slay the firstborn of the Israelites. Mary and Joseph gave the offering of the poor: a pair of turtledoves. Now in the Temple was a devout man named Simeon. He was inspired by the Spirit to come to the Temple when Jesus was there. The Spirit had revealed to Simeon that he would not die until he had seen the Savior. As all rabbis did when blessing children, Simeon took Jesus into his arms and blessed God. His canticle declared universal salvation. As Simeon blessed the parents, he predicted the child's destiny and foretold that Mary would share in Jesus' redemptive suffering. The Church, too, experiences his suffering and sorrow. Simeon, symbol of old Israel, having witnessed the fulfillment of God's promises, could depart in peace.

Anna, a holy widow, also recognized the Messiah and gave thanks to God. From that day she proclaimed the good news to all who waited for salvation. Simeon and Anna were members of the *anawim*, a small group of Israel's faithful people who had kept God's promise alive.

Today we no longer need to hope for a savior. We live in the time following his life, death, and resurrection. With Simeon we are grateful and happy that God sent a savior. Simeon's canticle is also a prayer for the dying.

For Discussion

Before the play: When was the first time you went to church? Why did you go? What are some Catholic rules and customs your family follows?

After the play: Why did Mary and Joseph take Jesus to the Temple? What Catholic rituals are part of a baby's becoming a child of God? How were Simeon and Anna rewarded for being faithful to God? What sorrows did Mary have to endure because she was the mother of Jesus?

Activity

Both younger and older learners might write a paragraph or draw a picture of a time when they recognized God in their lives.

Prayer

Pray Simeon's Canticle. Pray that all those who do not yet know Jesus may come to hear and accept the Good News. This would include people in mission countries as well as people in the learners' families.

SIMEON'S CANTICLE

Master, now you are dismissing
your servant in peace,
according to your word.
For my eyes have seen your salvation,
which you have prepared
in the presence of all people.
It is a light for revelation to the Gentiles
and for glory to your people Israel.

CAST: NARRATOR, MARY, JOSEPH, SIMEON, ANNA

PROPS: DOLL OR BLANKET FOR BABY, TWO BIRDS IN A CAGE

THE PRESENTATION LUKE 2:22–38

Mary and Joseph enter. Joseph carries the birds, and Mary holds the baby.

Narrator It was a Jewish law that every boy should be offered to God soon after birth. A lamb or two birds would be offered as a sacrifice. Mary and Joseph brought baby Jesus to Jerusalem to present him to the Lord. A holy man named Simeon was waiting there for the savior of Israel. The Holy Spirit let him know that he would not die until he had seen the Messiah. On the day that Mary and Joseph came to the Temple, the Spirit led Simeon there.

Simeon enters, goes to Mary and Joseph, and, smiling, takes the baby into his arms.

Simeon (*with great joy*)

Blessed be the God of Israel!
Master, now you can dismiss your servant in peace,
according to your word.
For my eyes have seen your salvation,
(*raises baby in front of him*)
which you prepared for all peoples.
He is a light for revelation to the Gentiles,
and for glory to your people Israel.

Mary (*surprised*) What amazing things to say about my son!

Joseph (*to Mary*) Remarkable! I wonder how he knows.

Simeon (*putting his hand on Mary's and Joseph's heads*) May God bless you both and make you good parents. (*turns to Mary*) This child is destined for the fall and rise of many in Israel. He will be a sign that will be opposed, so that the secret thoughts of many people will be revealed. A sword will pierce your heart, too. (*places baby in Mary's arms*)

Narrator Anna, a prophetess who was eighty-four years old, was in the Temple. She had moved there long ago after her husband died. She never left the Temple but fasted and prayed there night and day.

Anna enters and goes to Mary and Joseph.

Anna (*raising arms*) Thanks be to our great and good God! May I hold your baby?

Mary gives Anna the baby.

Anna (*smiling and rocking the baby*) Wait until the others hear. They will be so glad that our redeemer has finally come.

Narrator Simeon and Anna had been faithful to God. They were rewarded by seeing the Messiah they had longed for. They remind us to stay close to Jesus, to obey God's commands, and look for God's presence in our lives.

The Boy Jesus in the Temple

Sᴜɴᴅᴀʏ ɪɴ ᴛʜᴇ Oᴄᴛᴀᴠᴇ ᴏғ Cʜʀɪsᴛᴍᴀs: Yᴇᴀʀ C

Themes

- the infancy narratives
- the identity of Jesus
- obedience
- Mary
- ministry

Background Notes

Jewish people were obliged to travel to Jerusalem for three major feasts: Passover, Pentecost, and Tabernacles. Passover was celebrated for eight days in honor of the Exodus. When Jesus was twelve years old, Mary and Joseph brought Jesus to Jerusalem for the Passover. This marked the year before he officially reached manhood. The visit foreshadowed Jesus' going to Jerusalem for Passover at the end of his life, where he would undergo his own passover from death to life. On the way home, Mary and Joseph discovered that Jesus was missing. In a caravan men and women often traveled separately. Probably Mary assumed Jesus was with Joseph, and Joseph thought he was with her. They searched for Jesus for three days—a time period symbolic of the days between Jesus' death and resurrection.

Mary and Joseph found Jesus in the Temple, talking to the teachers. He explained to them that he was fulfilling his mission: his Father's work. Jesus was not referring to his father Joseph, but he was calling God his Father for the first time. He claimed divine sonship. The gospel says that Mary and Joseph did not understand what Jesus meant. Mary must have thought with sorrow of her future separation from him. She pondered the mystery she was sharing in.

Jesus returned to Nazareth with his parents. Under their guidance, he grew in all ways to perfect manhood. He was always ready to do his Father's will.

For Discussion

Before the play: Did your parents ever lose you or one of your brothers or sisters? How do you think they felt? How did they react when they found their missing child?

After the play: Why did Jesus stay behind in Jerusalem? What do you think Jesus might have done to help Mary and Joseph when they returned to Nazareth? How can you imitate Jesus' obedience?

Activity

Encourage your learners to talk about ways they can be of help to their families.

Prayer

Jesus, when you were my age, you obeyed Mary and Joseph even though you were God. By doing this you showed me how important you consider obedience. When we obey our parents, we are obeying our heavenly Father. The fourth commandment is "Honor your father and mother." Thank you for my family. Through their love and care you show your love for me. Help me return that love. Give me your grace to obey my parents, especially when what they tell me to do is hard or is something I don't understand. This is what you ask me to do today as a child in my family.

You might invite the children to reflect on the time when it was most difficult for them to obey. Encourage them to resolve to try harder and to trust in the Holy Spirit for help.

Cᴀsᴛ: Nᴀʀʀᴀᴛᴏʀ, Jᴇsᴜs, Mᴀʀʏ, Jᴏsᴇᴘʜ, Rᴇʟᴀᴛɪᴠᴇ (+), Uɴᴄʟᴇ, Jᴏʜɴ, Tᴇᴀᴄʜᴇʀs 1, 2 (+)

Pʀᴏᴘs: Cʜᴀɪʀs ғᴏʀ Jᴇsᴜs ᴀɴᴅ Tᴇᴀᴄʜᴇʀs

THE BOY JESUS IN THE TEMPLE LUKE 2:41–52

Jesus is seated on a chair off to the side. Teachers are seated around him.

Narrator   Jewish people went to Jerusalem every year for the feast of Passover. Mary and Joseph went, too. When Jesus was twelve, he went with them. On the way home, at the end of the first day of travel, Mary and Joseph missed Jesus.

Joseph enters, Mary enters a little later and catches up to him.

Mary   (*worried*) Joseph, isn't Jesus with you?

Joseph   (*shaking head*) No, Mary. I haven't seen him since we left. He's probably with his cousins. Don't worry. He must be somewhere in this caravan.

Mary   Let's look for him.

Relative 1 enters.

Mary   (*to Relative 1*) Have you seen Jesus?

Relative 1   (*shaking head*) No, not all day. (*exits*)

Uncle enters.

Joseph   (*to Uncle*) We're looking for our son. Has he been with you?

Uncle   No, sorry. I haven't seen him. Let me ask John. (*calls*) John, please come here a minute.

John enters running and goes to Uncle.

Uncle   (*to John*) Son, Joseph here is looking for Jesus. Was he playing with you and the others today?

John   No, Dad. He wasn't with us.

Mary   (*wringing hands*) Joseph, I'm frightened. We had better go back to Jerusalem to look for him.

Uncle and John, Mary and Joseph exit.

Narrator   Mary and Joseph searched for Jesus all over Jerusalem for three days. Finally they found him in the Temple sitting among the teachers.

Teacher 1   (*to Jesus*) Yahweh is a mighty God.

Teacher 2   Yes. We must follow his commands carefully.

Jesus   True, but is it better to serve out of fear (*puts out hand*) or out of love? (*puts out other hand*)

Teacher 1   (*to Teacher 2*) How can one so young be so wise?

Mary and Joseph enter and see Jesus.

Mary   (*pointing to Jesus*) Look over there. He's with the teachers. It seems as if he is teaching them.

Joseph   I don't know what to say!

Mary and Joseph walk quickly to Jesus.

Mary   (*to Jesus*) Child, why have you treated us like this? Your father and I have been looking for you, worried to death.

Jesus   (*surprised*) Why? Did you not know that I must be in my Father's house?

Mary and Joseph look at each other.

Joseph   (*to Mary*) What does that mean?

Mary   I don't know.

Joseph   (*to Jesus*) It's time to go home now, Son.

Narrator   Jesus went with Mary and Joseph to Nazareth and was obedient to them. Mary prayed and reflected on all that Jesus had done and said. Jesus grew in wisdom and age and goodness. Let us pray for the grace to obey like Jesus, to listen to God and the people God has set in authority over us.

The Baptism of Jesus

SECOND SUNDAY OF ADVENT: YEARS A, B, C;
THIRD SUNDAY OF ADVENT: YEARS B, C;
SUNDAY AFTER JANUARY 6: YEARS A, B, C

Themes
- the identity of Jesus
- John the Baptist
- humility
- conversion
- mission of Jesus
- baptism
- the Holy Spirit

Background Notes

As the greatest prophet, John prepared people for the Messiah. He preached conversion and repentance, telling the people they needed to turn their hearts toward God. John claimed that the one to come would be mightier than he in the war against evil.

Jesus was sinless and had no need of repentance. Therefore he did not need to be baptized, either. But he had come to be humanity's representative. He identified himself with sinners, and his baptism was an acceptance of the human condition. Jesus' baptism was an acceptance of his mission as Messiah.

Jesus went into the water. When he came up, God declared that Jesus was "my beloved Son." In Christian baptism we, too, are claimed as sons and daughters of God. But, unlike John's baptism, our baptism actually gives us the gift of the Spirit.

In the synoptic gospels, the Trinity is manifested at Jesus' baptism. The Father (the voice), the Son (Jesus), and the Holy Spirit (the dove) are all present. Calling on the persons of the Trinity has been an essential part of the ritual of Christian baptism since apostolic times: "I baptize you in the name of the Father, and of the Son, and of the Holy Spirit."

For Discussion

Before the play: What do you know about your baptism—where it took place, who was there, whether you cried? What difference does baptism make in your life?

After the play: What did Jesus' baptism signify? How was John's baptism different from the baptism you received? How can you tell whether you are really repentant and converted? What might John the Baptist say to us today?

Activity

With younger learners read *Charles Caterpillar* by James Haas or another children's story whose theme is transformation.

Invite older learners to make a scrapbook about their baptism. The scrapbook could include photos, drawings, a copy of their baptismal certificate, and a reflection on the effects of baptism.

Prayer

- Invite the children to renew their baptismal vows and profession of faith by answering "I do" to the following questions:

  Do you reject Satan?
  And all his works?
  And all his empty promises?
  Do you believe in God the Father almighty, creator of heaven and earth?
  Do you believe in Jesus Christ, his only Son, our Lord, who was born of the Virgin Mary, was crucified, died, and was buried, rose from the dead, and is now seated at the right hand of the Father?
  Do you believe in the Holy Spirit, the holy Catholic Church, the communion of saints, the forgiveness of sins, the resurrection of the body, and life everlasting?

- Bless the students with holy water as a reminder of their baptism and their mission to be Christians.

CAST: NARRATOR, JOHN, JESUS, PRIEST, PERSON, CROWD (+), VOICE

PROP: LARGE SEASHELL

THE BAPTISM OF JESUS
MATTHEW 3:4–17, MARK 1:4–11, LUKE 3:7–22, JOHN 1:19–34

John is facing crowd that includes Person and Priest.

Narrator	John the Baptist preached in the desert of Judea. He wore clothing made of camel's hair and a leather belt around his waist. He ate locusts and wild honey. The people in the region were being baptized by John in the Jordan River as they repented their sins.
John	Repent, for the kingdom of heaven is near. Every tree that does not bear good fruit will be cut down (*makes chopping motion*) and thrown (*makes tossing motion*) into the fire.
Person	What should we do?
John	Whoever has two cloaks (*holds up two fingers*) should share with the person who has none. And whoever has food should also share.
Priest	Who are you?
John	I am not the Messiah. I am the voice of one crying out in the desert, (*cups hand next to mouth*) "Make straight the way of the Lord."
Person	I am a sinner. But I am sorry. Please baptize me.

Person "wades" to John, who "pours water" on Person with seashell.

John	(*to Crowd*) I baptize with water as a sign of repentance. Someone else more powerful than I is coming. I am not worthy to undo his sandal strap. (*points down*) He will baptize you with the Holy Spirit and fire. (*raises arms*)
Narrator	One day Jesus came from Galilee to John at the Jordan River to be baptized.

Jesus enters and goes to John.

John	(*surprised*) I need to be baptized by you. How is it that you are coming to me?
Jesus	Let it be so now, for it is in God's plan.

Jesus "wades" into the water toward John, who "pours water" on him.

Narrator	Suddenly the heavens opened, and the Spirit of God came down like a dove upon him.
Voice	(*loud and low*) This is my beloved Son with whom I am well pleased.

All look up in awe.

Narrator	With his baptism, Jesus accepted his mission and was filled with power to begin it. At our baptism we received the mission to continue Jesus' work. May we teach others about God and show them God's love.

The Temptation of Jesus

FIRST SUNDAY OF LENT: YEARS A, B, C

Themes

- temptation
- the identity of Jesus
- the mission of Jesus

Background Notes

The temptation story shows the humanity of Jesus. Jesus went to the desert, the place where, according to tradition, evil spirits dwell. He was there for forty days, which paralleled the forty-year sojourn of the Israelites in the desert. The temptations are in a different order in Matthew and Luke, but the scriptural answers to each are the same. The temptations test Jesus as Messiah. He was tempted to be a messiah of pleasure (turning stones to bread), a messiah of power (owning nations), and a messiah of fantastic feats (surviving a leap from the Temple parapet). Victoriously, Jesus rejected these temptations and embraced the role of true Messiah, the suffering servant. One day when Peter tried to dissuade him from the path of the cross, Jesus called Peter Satan.

The outcome of the battle in the desert was later affirmed in the exorcisms Jesus performed. As members of the Church face temptations, they look to Christ's example as he dealt with temptations against his mission.

For Discussion

Before the play: Who is Satan? Why is he against us? What is it like to be tempted?

After the play: What were Jesus' temptations? How did he overcome them? What are the greatest temptations for people today? for children today? What helps do we have to resist temptation?

Activity

Invite younger learners to do the following activity. On a piece of sandpaper draw a picture or a symbol of a time when someone might want to do something not good. Somewhere on the picture print "No!" Color the picture with crayon.

Older learners might discuss or role play some situations in which they face a moral choice.

Prayer

Pray the following litany with the children. They may add their own prayers. The response is "Lord, lead us not into temptation."

When there are things we would rather do than go to Sunday Mass...

When we see items in the store that we want but don't have the money to buy...

When telling the truth might get us or a friend into trouble...

When our younger brother or sister is driving us crazy...

When we have a chance to get even with someone...

When our parents won't let us do what others our age do...

When there is a movie or a magazine or a book that we know we shouldn't see...

When it is easy for us to cheat...

Let us pray. Lord, you did not give in to temptation. By your cross you conquered evil forever. Help us overcome temptation and do what is right. When we are tempted to do wrong, make us strong like you. More than anything we want to be good Christians and live with you forever. Sometimes it is hard for us to do what is right. We are weak. We need the power of your grace to help us resist temptation.

CAST: NARRATOR, JESUS, DEVIL, ANGELS 1, 2 (+)

PROPS: ROCKS

THE TEMPTATION OF JESUS MATTHEW 4:1–11, MARK 1:12–13, LUKE 4:1–13

Jesus kneels, praying.

Narrator   After his baptism, Jesus was led by the Spirit into the desert for forty days. He ate nothing during those days and was very hungry.

Devil enters and goes to Jesus. Jesus looks surprised.

Devil   (*picking up rock*) If you are the Son of God, command these stones to become loaves of bread.

Jesus   (*in a strong voice*) It is written, "One does not live by bread alone, but by every word that comes from the mouth of God."

Devil   Come with me.

Narrator   The devil then took Jesus to the Temple in the holy city and had him stand on the edge of the roof.

Devil   If you are the Son of God, throw yourself down. For it is written, "He will command his angels to guard you," and "With their hands they will bear you up so that you will not dash your foot against a stone."

Jesus   (*with a strong voice*) Again it is written, "Do not put the Lord, your God, to the test."

Devil shrugs and shakes head.

Narrator   Then the devil took Jesus to a very high mountain.

Devil   (*making a wide sweeping motion outward*) Look at all these kingdoms of the world and their splendor. All these I will give you, if you will fall down and worship me.

Jesus   (*shouting and pointing*) Away with you, Satan! It is written, "Worship the Lord your God, and serve only him."

Devil stomps out angrily.

Narrator   Angels came and waited on Jesus. When we are tempted, Jesus knows what we are going through. We can always turn to him for help.

Angels enter and bow before Jesus.

The First Apostles

SECOND SUNDAY IN ORDINARY TIME: YEAR B

Background Notes

The first disciples of Jesus were originally John's disciples. They accepted Jesus and called him Rabbi, the title of a teacher. Andrew and the other disciple (perhaps John) responded to Christ's invitation "Come and see." The two disciples probably spent the night with Jesus. The next day, Andrew brought his brother Simon to meet Jesus. Jesus changed Simon's name to Cephas. This name change signified that Simon was assuming a new way of life.

Nathanael was commonly identified with Bartholomew. When Jesus referred to a personal incident in Nathanael's life, Nathanael acknowledged him as Son of God and King of Israel. The angels ascending and descending on the Son of Man was a reference to Jacob's ladder. In a vision, the patriarch Jacob saw a ladder, a mediator between God and human beings. The "far greater thing" that Nathanael would see was the glory of God manifested in Jesus, our divine mediator connecting heaven and earth.

For Discussion

Before the play: How did you come to know about Jesus? Why do you think people were attracted to Jesus? Who were some of his closest followers? How did they show strengths and weaknesses?

After the play: What does it mean to be a follower of Jesus? Why have you chosen to follow Jesus? Have you brought anyone else to meet him? How could you introduce others to Jesus?

Activity

Invite younger learners to make an apostle out of a clothespin. Draw facial features and glue on material for the head covering and robe.

Have older learners choose an event from the gospels involving one or more of the apostles. Ask them to write it up as a news article.

Prayer

Read the following adaptation of "One Solitary Life" and have the children think about what Jesus means to them.

He was born in a small village. He worked in a carpenter shop until he was thirty. He then became a traveling preacher. He never held an office. He never had a family or owned a house. He didn't go to college. He had no credentials but himself.

He was only thirty-three when the public turned against him. His friends ran away. He was turned over to his enemies and went through the mockery of a trial. He was nailed to a cross between two thieves. While he was dying, his executioners gambled for his clothing, the only property he had on earth. He was laid in a borrowed grave.

Twenty centuries have come and gone, and today he is the central figure of the human race. All the armies that ever marched, all the navies that ever sailed, all the parliaments that ever sat, and all the kings that ever reigned have not affected life on earth as much as that one solitary life.

—Source unknown

CAST: NARRATOR, JESUS, JOHN, DISCIPLE, ANDREW, SIMON PETER, PHILIP, NATHANAEL

PROPS: TABLE, THREE CHAIRS, TREE OR DRAWING OF TREE ON BOARD

The First Apostles John 1:35–51

John, Andrew, and Disciple are standing, talking together.

Narrator   One day John was with two of his disciples.

Jesus enters and walks by. John stops talking and watches him pass.

John   (*gesturing toward Jesus*) Look, here is the Lamb of God!

Andrew and Disciple wave to John and run after Jesus. They follow him for a while. John exits.

Jesus   (*turning*) What are you looking for?

Andrew and Disciple look at each other.

Andrew   Rabbi...

Disciple   Teacher, where are you staying?

Jesus   (*laughing*) Come and see.

Jesus, Andrew, and Disciple walk on for a while, then sit at the table.

Narrator   They stayed with Jesus that day. It was about 4:00 in the afternoon.

Andrew and Disciple rise, wave, and leave. Jesus stands. Simon Peter enters. Andrew runs to him.

Andrew   Here you are. We have found the Messiah. Come on. You have to meet him.

Andrew grabs Simon Peter by the arm and they walk to Jesus.

Andrew   Jesus, this is my brother Simon.

Jesus and Simon shake hands.

Jesus   (*looking into Simon's eyes*) You are Simon, son of John. From now on you will be called Peter.

All exit.

Narrator   The next day Jesus decided to go to Galilee. He found Philip who lived in Bethsaida where Andrew and Peter lived.

Jesus enters from one side and Philip enters from another. Nathanael enters and stands at a distance under the tree.

Jesus   (*to Philip as they pass each other*) Follow me.

Philip turns around and walks with Jesus for a while.

Philip   Teacher, I would like someone to meet you.

Philip leaves Jesus and goes to Nathanael. Jesus sits.

Philip (*to Nathanael*) We have found the one about whom Moses and the prophets wrote. He is Jesus, son of Joseph, from Nazareth.

Nathanael Can anything good come out of Nazareth?

Philip Come and see.

Philip and Nathanael approach Jesus.

Jesus Here is a true Israelite who is a sincere man.

Nathanael How do you know me?

Jesus (*rising*) I saw you under the fig tree before Philip called you.

Nathanael (*excitedly*) Rabbi, you are the Son of God! You are the King of Israel!

Jesus Do you believe because I told you that I saw you under the fig tree? You will see greater things than this. Amen, amen, I tell you, you will see heaven opened (*raises hand*) and the angels of God ascending and descending upon the Son of Man.

Narrator We, too, are disciples of Jesus. May we learn to know and love him more each day and lead others to him.

All exit, Jesus' arm around Nathanael's shoulder.

The Call of the First Apostles

THIRD SUNDAY IN ORDINARY TIME: YEAR B

Background Notes

The three disciples who formed the inner circle (Peter, James, and John) appear in this account of the call of the first disciples. Two sets of brothers are involved: Peter and Andrew as well as James and John. As Jesus passed by, he called these men to follow him. The fishermen dropped everything to follow Jesus. Discipleship can demand renunciation of possessions and family ties. Jesus promised to make these disciples fishers of people, a hint of their apostolic authority and missionary work.

Ordinarily disciples choose their master. Here Jesus reversed the situation and chose his disciples. He didn't pick learned rabbis but fishermen. The four fishermen in this story owned their own nets and had other people working for them. They were apparently successful at their trade but were willing to sacrifice all in order to commit themselves to Jesus. Their nets did not hold them captive.

For Discussion

Before the play: Is there something that keeps you from being more like Jesus? Would it be hard to change? Why would you do it? Did you ever think of becoming a priest, a deacon, or a religious sister or brother? How do these people serve Jesus?

After the play: What did the apostles give up to follow Jesus? What role did they play in the Church? How does Jesus call people today? How can you be a fisher of people for Jesus?

Activity

Invite your younger learners to do the following activity. Fold a paper in half, draw a fish, and cut it out double. On one fish write a Good News message like "God loves you," "Jesus saves," or "Jesus lives." Put the fish together and punch holes about every inch around the edge. Use yarn to sew the fish together with an overcast stitch. When you are almost finished, stuff the fish with newspaper or cotton. Finish sewing around it and tie a knot. If you wish, glue on sequins and draw fins and scales. Give your fish to someone.

Have your older learners express in writing, art, or song what they would like to do with their lives.

Prayer

Invite the children to respond, "Jesus, I will follow you" to the following words of Jesus in the gospels.

Let your light shine before others. (Matthew 5:16)

Do not store up for yourselves treasures on earth...but treasures in heaven. (Matthew 6:19–20)

Love one another. (John 13:34)

Do not judge. (Matthew 7:1)

Ask, and it will be given you. (Matthew 7:6)

Do to others as you would have them do to you. (Matthew 7:12)

Go, sell your possessions, and give the money to the poor. (Matthew 9:21)

You ought to wash one another's feet. (John 13:14)

Forgive, if you have anything against anyone. (Mark 11:25)

Love your enemies and pray for those who persecute you. (Matthew 5:43)

Follow me. (Matthew 4:19)

CAST: NARRATOR, JESUS, PETER, ANDREW, JAMES, JOHN, ZEBEDEE, HIRED MEN 1, 2 (+)

PROPS: ROWS OF CHAIRS FOR TWO BOATS, NETS

THE CALL OF THE FIRST APOSTLES   MATTHEW 4:18–22, MARK 1:16–20

Peter and Andrew are in one boat. James, John, Zebedee, and Hired Men 1, 2 are mending nets in the other boat some distance away.

Narrator   The brothers Peter and Andrew were fishing one day on the Sea of Galilee. The brothers James and John were with their father, Zebedee, and some hired men mending their nets.

Jesus enters. Peter and Andrew cast a net into the sea while Jesus watches.

Hired man 1   Isn't that the young rabbi people have been talking about?

Hired man 2   Yes, it is. I wonder why he is here.

Jesus   (*calling to Peter and Andrew*) Follow me, I will make you fishers of people. You will tell others about God's kingdom.

Jesus walks on. Peter and Andrew climb out of boat and catch up to Jesus. They all walk over to the other boat.

Jesus   (*shouting*) James! John! Come follow me, and I will make you fishers of people.

The two brothers look up.

John   (*to his brother*) It's the new rabbi!

Jesus   Come follow me.

James   (*to Zebedee*) Father, we must go.

Zebedee   God be with you, sons!

James and John get out of boat, wave to Zebedee, and follow Jesus. Zebedee waves back.

Narrator   All the fishermen Jesus called immediately went off in his company, leaving their jobs and their homes. They became his apostles, the men Jesus chose to lead his Church. May we always show great love and respect for our Church leaders and follow their guidance.

The Call of Matthew

Themes

- the apostles
- discipleship
- conversion
- the mission of Jesus
- vocations

Background Notes

In the gospels of Luke and Mark, Matthew is called Levi. When Jesus called Matthew to follow him, Matthew left his tax collector's booth as promptly as the fishermen left their nets. As a tax collector, Matthew was considered a traitor, a social outcast, and a sinner. He collected taxes from his own people for the oppressor Rome. His profit was made by extorting more than was legally due. By choosing Matthew to follow him and by accepting his dinner invitation, Jesus underlined the fact that he came for sinners. The upright Jewish person did not associate or eat with sinners and Gentiles. But Jesus invited everyone to the messianic banquet. In particular he reached out to the marginalized people, those whom others ignored and preferred to forget. We all must admit we are sinners before we can go to Jesus.

Matthew's wholehearted commitment to Christ involved a conversion. He reoriented his life, choosing to forsake the wicked ways of the tax booth and to become a doer of good. In fact, Matthew became a leader in calling other sinners to hear the good news and change their hearts.

For Discussion

Before the play: Who are some people in the gospel whom others stayed away from? How did Jesus treat these people? Why didn't the Jewish people like tax collectors?

After the play: Why do you think Matthew followed Jesus so quickly? What does it feel like to be left out? When you see others left out, what do you do?

Activity

On a long sheet of paper write down ideas for how to reach out to someone. Choose one idea that you can do and do it!

Prayer

Jesus, following you has a price. You call us away from temptation and sin. Help us be truly sorry for offending God and other people. You may ask for forgiveness in silence. (Pause.) Give us the grace to change. May we be more like you: kind, unselfish, obedient, honest. Let us live a good Christian life, walking in your footsteps, bringing life and love to others.

Invite learners to speak to Jesus in their hearts about one thing in their lives they need to change to be better disciples.

CAST: NARRATOR, JESUS, MATTHEW, SINNERS 1, 2 (+), DISCIPLES 1, 2 (+), PHARISEES 1, 2 (+)

PROPS: TWO OR MORE TABLES, CHAIRS

THE CALL OF MATTHEW MATTHEW 9:9–13, MARK 2:14–17, LUKE 5:27–32

Matthew sits behind table.

Narrator   Matthew was a tax collector. Jewish people did not like Jewish men who collected taxes for their conqueror, Rome. Often these tax collectors gathered more taxes than they needed to. They kept some money for themselves. One day Matthew was sitting at the tax booth.

Jesus and Disciples enter. Jesus goes to Matthew.

Jesus   (*to Matthew*) Follow me.

Matthew stands and follows Jesus.

Matthew   (*to Jesus*) Master, please come to my house for dinner.

All walk to other table and sit. People enter and sit with Jesus and Disciples. Pharisees enter and sit apart.

Narrator   While Jesus was at table in Matthew's house, many tax collectors and sinners came and sat with Jesus and his disciples.

Pharisees 1, 2 stand and go to Disciples.

Pharisee 1   (*to Disciple 1*) Why does your teacher eat with tax collectors and sinners?

Jesus looks up at Pharisees.

Jesus   (*to Pharisees*) People who are well have no need of a physician, but those who are sick do. Go and learn what these words mean: "I desire mercy, not sacrifice." I have not come to call the righteous but sinners.

Pharisees return to places, shaking heads.

Narrator   Jesus shows us that it is good to reach out to people who are not accepted by others. They may become our good friends.

Rejection at Nazareth

Themes
- the mission of Jesus
- the suffering of Jesus

HOLY THURSDAY (CHRISM MASS): YEARS A, B, C;
THIRD SUNDAY IN ORDINARY TIME: YEAR C;
FOURTH SUNDAY: YEAR C; FOURTEENTH SUNDAY: YEAR B

Background Notes

The Jewish people met in local synagogues for prayer. The sabbath synagogue service in the first century seems to have included a reading from the Torah, a reading from the prophets, and a sermon on the meaning of the readings. Rows of people sat around the perimeter of the room, leaving the center empty for the speakers. Jesus acted as teacher by doing the reading and explaining it in such a way that people marveled at his wisdom. .

In Luke the passage Jesus read was a combination of Isaiah 61:1–2 and 58:6. These verses reflect the jubilee year, which is celebrated every fifty years. During this year fields lay fallow, persons returned home, debts were canceled, and slaves set free. In Jesus God has fulfilled his promise. His townspeople, however, lacked faith in him.

Just as prophets were rejected in the Old Testament times, so too was Jesus rejected. The people were offended and enraged when he implied that salvation was not only for them. Foreigners, too, would be welcomed into God's kingdom. The opposition Jesus experienced in Nazareth foreshadowed the rest of his life. But just as he escaped from death at the hands of his neighbors, in the end he was victorious over death through his resurrection.

For Discussion

Before the play: What did Jesus come to teach us? Who are some people who rejected him? Why do you think they did this? How do we reject Jesus today?

After the play: How do the phrases in Isaiah apply to Jesus? What would our mission statement include?

Activity

Your younger learners might enjoy this activity. Place a sheet of paper horizontally on a table. On it write "He has anointed me to bring good news to the poor." Tear around the edges of the paper and then outline the edges with brown crayon. Roll up each end until they meet in the middle. Tie your scroll together with yarn or ribbon.

Older learners can discuss what the prayer reflection means to them.

Prayer

Read the following reflection and prayer slowly with pauses.

The mission of Jesus is my mission. The Spirit of the Lord is upon me, because he has anointed me in the sacraments of baptism and confirmation. I am anointed to bring good news to the poor, to show needy people my love for them. God has sent me to to tell people who are imprisoned in mental or physical pain and suffering that God has conquered sin and death. God has sent me to give sight to the blind, to help people see that there is a loving God, that they are saved, and that they are to live as Christ taught.

Jesus, bless my efforts to carry on your work. Help the people whose lives I touch be open to the good news I bring by my words and deeds.

CAST: NARRATOR, JESUS, PERSONS 1, 2, 3 (+)

PROPS: AT LEAST TWO ROWS OF CHAIRS

REJECTION AT NAZARETH LUKE 4:16–30, MARK 6:1–6

Jesus and Persons are seated in two or more rows facing one another across a space.

Narrator Jesus had been teaching successfully in synagogues in Galilee. Then he returned to Nazareth, his hometown. On the sabbath he went as usual to the synagogue. There he was handed the scroll of the prophet Isaiah to read.

Jesus stands and moves to the center area. Person 1 hands him a scroll. Jesus opens the scroll horizontally.

Jesus The Spirit of the Lord is upon me,
because he has anointed me.
He has sent me
to bring good news to the poor.
He has sent me to proclaim release to the captives
and recovery of sight to the blind.
I'm sent to let the oppressed go free
and to proclaim the year of the Lord's favor.

Jesus rolls up the scroll, hands it to Person 1, and sits. All look at Jesus.

Jesus Today these words of Scripture have been fulfilled in your hearing.

Person 2 Jesus is such a wonderful teacher. Where did he get all this knowledge?

Person 3 Isn't this Joseph's son?

Jesus You will probably quote to me this proverb, "Doctor, cure yourself!" And you will say, "Do here also in your hometown the things that we have heard you did in Capernaum." Truly I tell you, no prophet is accepted in the prophet's hometown. When there was a famine in Israel there were many widows, but Elijah was sent only to the widow in Sidon. There were many lepers in the time of Elisha the prophet, but none of them were cleaned except Naaman the Syrian.

Persons look at one another with eyebrows raised. They frown.

Person 2 (*angrily*) How dare he speak this way to us!

Person 3 (*pointing*) Jesus, get out of our synagogue!

Person 2 (*shaking fist*) Get out of our town!

Persons (*standing and shaking fists*) Get out! Get out!

Persons gather around Jesus and move him off stage.

Narrator The people drove Jesus out of the town to the brow of the hill. They intended to hurl him off the cliff. But Jesus passed through their midst and went on his way. May we have the courage to speak the truth even when others do not accept it.

Nicodemus

FOURTH SUNDAY OF LENT: YEAR B;

TRINITY SUNDAY: YEAR A

Themes

- the mission of Jesus
- need for faith
- the Holy Spirit
- baptism

Background Notes

Nicodemus was a leader of the Jews, probably a member of the Sanhedrin, the Jewish council. When he called Jesus "rabbi," he accepted Jesus as a teacher. Since Jewish officials opposed Jesus, Nicodemus went to him under cover of the night in search of truth.

Jesus explained faith to Nicodemus. Through the Spirit we are born from above. Only if we are born from above can we have eternal life in the kingdom of God. We must become like children again. Faith calls for a spiritual rebirth, not a physical rebirth. (The word for spirit in Hebrew and in Greek also means wind.)

Later Nicodemus appeared in the gospels as someone who had seen the light. The chief priest and Pharisees tried to arrest Jesus while he was speaking in the Temple area during the Feast of Tabernacles. Nicodemus spoke out on his behalf, pointing out that Jesus should have a fair hearing before being condemned. Then, after the crucifixion, Nicodemus brought myrrh and aloes to anoint the body of Jesus.

For Discussion

Before the play: How is Jesus light for us? If you had a private meeting with Jesus, what questions might you have for him? How can you speak to Jesus today and grow in faith?

After the play: How does faith sometimes demand taking risks? When does the Holy Spirit work in us? How?

Activity

Invite younger learners to carry out this activity. On a sheet of black construction paper, put a dot halfway along the bottom edge. Fold in both sides of the paper up to this dot to create doors. Place a half sheet of yellow construction paper vertically on the table and neatly print, "God so loved the world that he sent his only Son." (John 3:16). You might use calligraphy (fancy lettering). Add symbols for Jesus to the yellow sheet, such as a cross, a chi-rho, a manger, and an empty tomb. Glue the sheet to the center of the black sheet so that the doors close over it.

Older learners might write their own conversations with Jesus.

Prayer

Lead the children in the following imaginative prayer:

Close your eyes and imagine that, like Nicodemus, you are going in the dark of night to the house where Jesus is. You are in search of some truths about life. There are some things you just don't understand. The stars are out, and it is a pleasant evening. You walk down a narrow deserted street and come to a small stone house. The door is open as though Jesus is waiting for you. Light is pouring out from it. Jesus is standing in the doorway. When he sees you, he smiles. He welcomes you in and has you sit down. He sits beside you. Looking at his kind, concerned face, you know you can talk to him about anything. Speak to Jesus now in your heart. You might ask him questions. You might talk about anything that is bothering you. You might ask his help, thank him, tell him you love him.

CAST: NARRATOR, JESUS, NICODEMUS

PROPS: TWO CHAIRS

NICODEMUS JOHN 3:1–21

Jesus is seated on one of two chairs.

Narrator The Pharisee Nicodemus was a leader of the Jewish people. One night he came to visit Jesus.

Nicodemus enters, looking over his shoulder.

Jesus (*stands*) Nicodemus! Welcome! (*gestures to chair*) Please, have a seat.

Nicodemus and Jesus sit.

Nicodemus Rabbi, we know that you are a teacher who has come from God. For no one can do the signs that you do if he were not from God.

Jesus Truly, I tell you, no one can see the kingdom of God without being born from above.

Nicodemus How can anyone be born after he or she is old? Can one enter a second time into the mother and be born again?

Jesus Truly, I tell you, no one can enter the kingdom of God without being born of water and Spirit. What is born of the flesh is flesh (*hits chest*) and what is born of the Spirit is spirit. (*points up*) Do not be astonished that I said, "You must be born from above." The wind blows where it chooses, and you hear it, but you do not know where it comes from or where it goes. So it is with everyone born of the Spirit.

Nicodemus How can these things be?

Jesus (*shaking head*) Are you a teacher of Israel, and yet you do not understand? We speak of what we know and testify to what we have seen, yet you people do not accept our testimony. No one has ascended into heaven except the one who descended from heaven, the Son of Man. (*points to self*) And just as Moses lifted up the serpent in the wilderness, so must the Son of Man be lifted up. (*raises hand*) Whoever believes in him may have eternal life.

Nicodemus (*nodding*) Ah, yes. Through Moses' serpent of bronze, God healed the people bitten by snakes. You say God will give us eternal life?

Jesus God so loved the world that he gave his only Son. May everyone who believes in him not perish but have eternal life. The light has come into the world, but people loved darkness because their deeds were evil. All who do evil hate the light (*puts up hand as to ward off light*) and do not come to the light, so that their deeds may not be exposed. But those who do good come to the light (*raises other hand facing up*) so that it may be seen that their deeds were done in God.

Nicodemus I see you are a wise teacher. I'd like to know more.

Jesus and Nicodemus stand. Nicodemus leaves.

Narrator Like Nicodemus, may we seek to learn more about God by praying, reading the Bible, and studying our faith.

The Blessing of the Children

TWENTY-SEVENTH SUNDAY IN ORDINARY TIME: YEAR B

Background Notes

The children whom the parents brought to Jesus for his blessing may have been infants or boys and girls less than twelve. When the disciples scolded the parents, Jesus rebuked his disciples for turning the parents away. Then he embraced the children and blessed them.

No other ancient religious or philosophical teachers made a point of receiving children this way. Writers in the time of Jesus presented children as examples of unreasonable behavior or objects to be trained. Jesus, however, regarded them as persons who could enter into a relationship with him and enter the kingdom of God. This particular story is the basis for infant baptism and early first communion.

Children were the little ones of society who had no rights or status in the ancient world. Jesus presented them as the model for his disciples, who had at least once argued about who was the greatest. His followers are to be simple and small, not self-important and power-hungry. They are to be dependent on the Father and open to accepting the gift of the kingdom. In Luke 10:21 Jesus observed that the Father revealed the mysteries of the kingdom not to the learned and wise but to the childlike.

For Discussion

Before the play: What are some words that describe children? Why do you think children were not afraid to come to Jesus?

After the play: What does this story tell us about Jesus? What must we be like if we wish to enter the kingdom of God? How can we treat others as Jesus did?

Activity

Use holy water to bless each other. With the water make the sign of the cross on the forehead and say, "God bless you, (Name)."

Prayer

Help the learners formulate a litany in which they ask for a childlike heart. Their prayer may take the form, "That we may be _____, we pray, O Lord." Some positive characteristics of a child that they might name are joyful, open, receptive, spontaneous, dependent, sinless, trusting, loving, full of wonder, simple, and eager to learn.

CAST: NARRATOR, JESUS, DISCIPLES 1, 2 (+), MOTHERS 1, 2, 3 (+), JACOB, CHILD 1, CHILD 2, CHILDREN (+)

PROPS: CHAIR, DOLLS OR BLANKETS TO BE BABIES

THE BLESSING OF THE CHILDREN
MATTHEW 19:13–15, MARK 10:13–16, LUKE 18:15–17

Jesus and Disciples are seated. Mothers enter holding Children by the hand or carrying babies. Mothers walk to Jesus. Children run.

Child 1   (*pulling Jesus' hand*) Come, play with us, Jesus.

Mother 1   (*hands on shoulders of Child 2*) Master, won't you bless my child?

Mother 2   (*holding out baby*) Jesus, touch my baby.

Mother 3   (*holding Jacob by the hand*) Please pray over my son Jacob.

Disciples stand and gesture to Mothers and Children to go away.

Disciple 1   (*to Mothers*) Leave him alone.

Disciple 2   Can't you see how tired he is?

Mothers and Children start to move away.

Jesus   (*beckoning to Children*) Come, children. (*to Disciples, sternly*) Let the little children come to me. Do not stop them, for the kingdom of God belongs to such as these. (*gestures to Children*) Truly, I tell you, whoever does not accept the kingdom of God as a little child will never enter it.

Jesus takes a baby in his arms. He puts his hand on Child 1's head. Children surround him. Mothers smile at Disciples.

Narrator   Jesus wants us near him as much as he wanted the children to come to him. Let us never be afraid to go to him and stay close to him.

The Cleansing of the Temple

THIRD SUNDAY OF LENT: YEAR B

Themes

- prayer
- the resurrection
- the identity of Jesus

Background Notes

This event happened at Passover when there were great crowds in Jerusalem. Animals needed for sacrifice were sold in the Court of Gentiles at the Temple: oxen, sheep, and doves. Moneychangers were there because Greek and Roman coins, which bore images, could not be used at the Temple. The whip Jesus used to clear the Temple was probably a symbol of authority, rather than for practical use. In John's gospel Jesus attacks the institutions, whereas in Mark, he attacks the dishonesty of the dealers. The event shows his zeal as a reformer. In Matthew's gospel, after the cleansing of the Temple Jesus stays there healing the blind and the lame.

Jesus referred to God as "my Father." He called the Temple a house of prayer. It was not meant to be a market. He said that the Temple was for all nations, an indication of the universality of God's love and salvation. His cleansing was a symbolic action. It implied that the Temple cult no longer had meaning. Prayer and faith were what mattered. The temple that Jesus predicted would be raised up after three days was himself. He was the new temple that replaced the Temple of Jerusalem. God was found in him.

For Discussion

Before the play: What do we do in church to show reverence? How do we behave there?

After the play: Why did Jesus drive the people out of the Temple? Why wasn't Jesus' anger sinful? When should we speak out against what is wrong? Can you give some examples of Christians who have done this?

Activity

Draw a picture of your church. Alternate activity: Make a model of your church using a box.

Prayer

Explain that on the way to the Temple for feasts, the people sang hymns. Invite the learners to pray the following pilgrim song with you:

> How lovely is your dwelling place,
>   O Lord of hosts!
> My soul longs
>   for the courts of the Lord;
> my heart sings for joy
>   to the living God.
>
> Even the sparrow finds a home,
>   and the swallow a nest for herself,
>   where she may lay her young,
> at your altars, O Lord of hosts,
>   my King and my God.
> Happy are those who live in your house,
>   ever singing your praise.
>
> For a day in your courts is better
>   than a thousand elsewhere.
> I would rather be a doorkeeper
>   in the house of my God
>   than live in the tents of wickedness.
> For the Lord God is a sun and shield;
>   he bestows favor and honor.
> No good thing does the Lord withhold
>   from those who walk uprightly,
> O Lord of hosts.
> Happy is everyone who trusts in you.

—Psalm 84:1–5, 10–12

CAST: NARRATOR, JESUS, DISCIPLES 1, 2 (+), MONEYCHANGERS 1, 2 (+), SELLERS OF DOVES 1, 2 (+), JEWISH PERSONS 1, 2 (+), OXEN AND SHEEP (+)

PROPS: TWINE FOR CORDS, BAGS OF COINS, BIRD CAGES, TABLES, CHAIRS

The Cleansing of the Temple

Mark 11:15–18, Matthew 21:12–13, Luke 19:45–46, John 2:13–22

Moneychangers are seated. Sellers of Doves stand behind tables. Cord and bags of coins are on a table. Jesus and Disciples 1, 2 enter and slowly walk toward tables.

Narrator   Because the feast of Passover was near, Jesus went to Jerusalem. In the temple area he found those who sold oxen, sheep, and doves. Moneychangers were also seated there.

Jesus picks up a cord and waves it in the air.

Jesus   Out! Get out of here! (*hits table with cord, pushes table over so coins spill*)

Moneychangers, oxen, and sheep exit in fear.

Jesus   (*angrily to Sellers of Doves*) Take these things out of here. Stop making my Father's house a marketplace! It is written, "My house shall be called a house of prayer, but you have made it a den of robbers."

Sellers of Doves exit.

Disciple 1   (*to Disciple 2*) Remember, Scripture says, "Zeal for your house will consume me."

Jewish Persons 1, 2 enter and go to Jesus.

Jewish Person 1   What sign can you show us for doing this?

Jesus   Destroy this temple and in three days (*holds up three fingers*) I will raise it up.

Jewish Person 2   This Temple has taken forty-six years to build, and you will raise it up in three days?

Jewish Persons 1 and 2 walk away, shaking heads.

Narrator   Jesus was speaking about the temple of his body. When he was raised from the dead, his disciples remembered that he had said this. They came to believe the Scriptures and the words Jesus had spoken.

  The Jewish Temple was a sacred place. Our church building is holy, for it is the house of God. We speak and act in it with reverence.

The Rich Young Man

Twenty-Eighth Sunday in Ordinary Time: Year B

Themes

- discipleship
- holiness
- riches
- the kingdom
- vocations

Background Notes

Jesus pointed to keeping the law as the way to enter the kingdom and attain eternal life. In addition, in Mark's gospel Jesus demanded that his followers give away their possessions to be saved. In Matthew, such extreme renunciation is not a mandate but a counsel of perfection for all people. In either case, Jesus reversed the Jewish concept that wealth is a sign of God's favor. It was a radical following of Jesus—the total commitment of heart and soul—that is, the way of salvation. We must find our security in Jesus and not in possessions. The motivation behind giving up possessions is not because they are evil, or that asceticism has value, but that we must show concern for the poor.

To illustrate how nearly impossible it is for the rich to enter heaven, Jesus posed a humorous comparison, an oriental exaggeration. He said it was like a camel, the largest animal in Palestine, passing through the eye of a needle. While riches can be used to perform much good, they could be spiritually dangerous. Crime might be involved in attaining them. They can distract us from developing our spiritual life and relationship with God. They can cut us off from other people. They might even lead to exploiting others.

The rich have a difficult time giving their possessions to the poor, but God can assist them. For the rich young man, it was too difficult. He was the only person in the gospels who refused to follow Jesus. He did not respond to Jesus' love. His riches possessed him.

For Discussion

Before the play: Would you like to be wealthy? Why? Why might someone who is rich have a hard time following Jesus?

After the play: What kept the young man from following Jesus? How did Jesus feel about him? What might keep us from following Jesus? In what ways can we help the poor?

Activity

Think about what you have that you could give to the poor. Decide on one thing, find out how to give it to an organization, and then donate it.

Prayer

Lord Jesus,
I offer you everything I have as a gift:
my liberty, my memory,
my understanding,
and my entire will.
Whatever I have and possess,
you have given to me.
To you, Lord, I now return it.
All is yours.
Do with it whatever you want.
Give me only your love and your grace.
I will be rich enough;
that is enough for me.

—St. Ignatius of Loyola

Cast: Narrator, Jesus, Rich Man, Disciples 1, 2 (+)

THE RICH YOUNG MAN MARK 10:17–31, MATTHEW 19:16–26, LUKE 18:18–27

Jesus and Disciples 1, 2 walk along. Rich Man enters, runs up to Jesus, and kneels before him.

Rich Man Good teacher, what must I do to inherit eternal life?

Jesus Why do you call me good? Only God is truly good. You know the commandments: "You shall not murder. You shall not commit adultery. You shall not steal. You shall not bear false witness. You shall not defraud. Honor your father and mother."

Rich Man Teacher, I have kept all these since my youth.

Jesus looks at him lovingly and puts his hand on the young man's shoulder.

Jesus You lack one thing. Go, sell what you own, and give the money to the poor. You will have treasure in heaven. Then come, follow me.

Rich Man lowers his head, shaking it. He rises and walks away from Jesus. Jesus watches sadly.

Jesus (*looking around at Disciples*) How hard it will be for those who have wealth to enter the kingdom of God.

Disciple 1 and Disciple 2 look shocked and puzzled.

Jesus Children, how hard it is to enter the kingdom of God. It is easier for a camel to go through the eye of a needle than for someone who is rich to enter the kingdom of God.

Disciple 1 (*to Disciple 2*) Then who can be saved?

Jesus For human beings it is impossible, but not for God. For God all things are possible.

Narrator Let's not allow anything to keep us away from Jesus: not wealth, other people, pride, laziness, or our sins.

The Withered Fig Tree

Themes

- prayer
- need for faith
- holiness

Background Notes

In Matthew's gospel the tree withered immediately after Jesus' curse. In Mark the disciples found it withered the next day. Mark notes that it was not the time for figs. Jesus appeared irrational in demanding fruit out of season. Some scholars explain that Jesus was really looking for the edible, nut-shaped knobs that appeared before the leaves. If there were no knobs, there would be no fruit.

In the Old Testament a tree stood for life, and figs, a very sweet fruit, for blessedness and fulfillment. The story is a parable-in-action. The withered tree might symbolize Israel whose piety was mere lipservice and produced no good deeds. Many Israelites did not heed the prophets' warnings to change their hearts. Many Israelites did not respond to the message of Jesus. They were failures. On the other hand, the tree might stand for the end of the Temple and its worship.

The tree was barren when Jesus needed fruit. This story recalled the parable of the Barren Fig Tree, in which the owner threatens to cast his barren tree into the fire. Other gospel references to fruit are: "Every good tree bears good fruit" (Matthew 7:17) and "By their fruits you will know them" (Matthew 7:20).

Jesus' action leads into a discussion of faith and prayer. His warning to Israel ends with words of hope. It's not too late to change.

For Discussion

Before the play: What would you do if you had an apple orchard, and one of your trees didn't bear any apples? What kind of "good fruit" are we human beings supposed to bear?

After the play: How can you bear good fruit? How will prayer help you? How many different types of prayer do you pray?

Activity

Use the following activity with your younger learners. Draw different kinds of fruit. Write a virtue inside each piece of fruit and then color the fruit. Cut out the pieces and put the fruit in a bowl. Each day pull one out and try to practice the virtue on it.

With older learners, ask them to share what the gospel passage means to them.

Prayer

O Lord, you who are all merciful,
take away my sins,
and enkindle within me the fire of your
Holy Spirit.
Take away this heart of stone,
and give me a heart of flesh and blood,
a heart to love and adore you,
a heart which may delight in you,
love you and please you,
for Christ's sake.

—St. Ambrose

CAST: NARRATOR, JESUS, PETER, DISCIPLES 1, 2 (+)

PROPS: FIG TREE, WITHERED FIG TREE

THE WITHERED FIG TREE MARK 11:12–14, MATTHEW 21:18–22

Jesus, Peter, and Disciples walk along.

Narrator One day Jesus and his disciples were leaving Bethany.

Jesus I'm hungry. Ah, I see a fig tree.

Jesus leaves Disciples and goes on ahead to the fig tree. He looks for figs.

Jesus There's nothing here but leaves. No fruit.

Disciple 1 (*to Disciple 2*) But it's not the season for figs.

Jesus (*pointing to tree*) May no one ever eat of your fruit again!

Jesus and Disciples exit.

Narrator Leaving Jerusalem early in the morning, Jesus and the disciples were walking along.

Jesus and Disciples enter.

Peter (*excitedly*) Rabbi, look! The fig tree that you cursed has withered away to its roots.

Jesus Have faith in God. Truly I tell you, if you say to this mountain (*gestures to the right*) "Be lifted up and thrown into the sea," and you do not doubt in your heart but believe that what you say will happen, it will be done for you. I tell you, all that you ask for in prayer (*folds hands*) believe that you will receive it, and it will be yours.

When you pray, forgive anyone who has hurt you. Then your Father in heaven (*points up*) may also forgive you your sins.

Narrator We can be good trees that bear good fruit if we pray, for then we have God's help.

The Samaritan Woman

THIRD SUNDAY OF LENT: YEAR A

Themes

- the identity of Jesus
- the mission of Jesus
- women
- evangelization
- spiritual life
- baptism
- the Holy Spirit

Background Notes

Jesus' conversation with the Samaritan woman was unconventional on several counts. First, she was a woman, and Jewish men didn't speak to women in public. Second, she was a Samaritan. The Samaritans were enemies of the Jewish people for two main reasons. First, during the Exile they had remained in a foreign nation and intermarried with their foreign neighbors. Second, they worshiped in their own temple on Mount Gerizim instead of in Jerusalem. (When the Samaritans' offer to help rebuild the Temple in Jerusalem had been rejected, they built their own temple.) Usually, the Jewish people avoided passing through Samaritan territory, which lay between Judea and Galilee. It was surprising, too, that Jesus asked the woman for water since, according to Jewish law, Samaritan utensils for eating and drinking were ritually unclean.

Jesus offered the woman living water, which is the Spirit sent by the risen Jesus, the gift that confers eternal life. Christians receive this gift through the waters of baptism. As Jesus conversed with the woman, she came to recognize him as prophet and eventually as the Messiah. He affirmed that he was the Messiah by stating, "I am he." The "I am" indicates divinity. It recalls the name Yahweh revealed to Moses: "I am who am."

The Samaritan woman became the first missionary. She spread the news about Jesus to her neighbors. They learned for themselves that Jesus is the Savior of the world. At the well, a Jewish place of courtship, Jesus replaced the five husbands in the woman's life.

For Discussion

Before the play: What do we use water for? Why is it a good symbol for the Holy Spirit?

After the play: What was unusual about what Jesus did? What was the living water he offered the woman? How did her neighbors come to believe in Jesus? How can we know him better?

Activity

Use this activity with younger learners. Make a cup out of clay and on the side of it etch a dove for the Holy Spirit with a pencil. Keep the cup as a reminder that Jesus gives us living water.

Have your older learners draw applications to their own lives. For example, how do they treat people whom they consider "different" from themselves?

Prayer

Carry out this prayer activity:

- Pour water from a pitcher into a glass.

- Have the learners recall how good, cool water tastes when they are hot and thirsty. Ask them to think back to a time when water tasted really good to them.

- Invite them to close their eyes and imagine that they are like an empty cup. God can fill them up with powerful divine life, with divine love. They can be refreshed and renewed.

- Suggest that they repeat over and over in their hearts: "My soul thirsts for God, for the living God" (Psalm 42:2). Allow at least a minute for this.

CAST: NARRATOR, JESUS, DISCIPLES 1, 2 (+),
WOMAN, SAMARITANS 1, 2 (+)

PROPS: PAIL OR WATER JAR, PACKAGE (FOR FOOD),
CHAIR

THE SAMARITAN WOMAN JOHN 4:4–42

Narrator   Passing through Samaria, Jesus and the disciples came to a town called Sychar. It was near the land Jacob had given to his son Joseph. Jacob's well was there. The Jewish people and the Samaritans did not get along. They would have nothing to do with one another.

Jesus and Disciples enter. Jesus goes to the chair and sits.

Jesus   I'm tired from this journey. Let me sit a while here at Jacob's well.

Disciple 1   Sure, Master. It's about noon. We'll go into town and buy some food. (*to other Disciples*) Come on.

Disciples exit. Woman with pail enters and goes to where Jesus is.

Jesus   Will you give me a drink?

Woman   (*surprised*) How is it that you, a Jew, ask a drink of me, a Samaritan woman?

Jesus   If you knew the gift of God and who it is that is saying to you, "Give me a drink," you would have asked him. He would have given you living water.

Woman   Sir, you have no bucket, and the well is deep. Where then can you get this living water? Are you greater than our ancestor Jacob, who gave us the well and with his children and his flocks drank from it?

Jesus   Everyone who drinks this water (*points to well*) will be thirsty again. But those who drink the water I will give them will never be thirsty. The water that I give will become in them a spring of water gushing up to eternal life.

Woman   Sir, give me this water, so that I may never be thirsty or have to keep coming here to draw water.

Jesus   (*gestures to town*)   Go, call your husband, and come back.

Woman   I do not have a husband.

Jesus   You are right in saying, "I have no husband." For you have had five husbands, (*holds up hand with fingers spread*) and the one you have now is not your husband. What you have said is true!

Woman   Sir, I see that you are a prophet. Our ancestors worshiped on this mountain. But your people say that the place to worship is in Jerusalem.

Jesus   (*stands*) Woman, believe me, the hour is coming when you will worship the Father neither on this mountain (*points down*) nor in Jerusalem (*points in distance*). Your people worship what you do not know. We worship what we know, because salvation is from the Jews.

Woman   I know that the Messiah is coming, the one called the Anointed. When he comes, he will tell us everything.

Jesus   (*pointing to self*) I am he, the one who is speaking to you.

Disciples enter with package.

Disciple 1   (*to Disciple 2*) Look. Jesus is talking to a woman.

Disciple 2   I don't believe my eyes!

Woman exits, leaving her pail.

Disciple 1   (*handing package to Jesus*) Rabbi, eat something.

Jesus   I have food to eat that you do not know about.

Disciple 2   (*to Disciple 3*) Could someone have brought him something to eat?

Jesus   My food is to do the will of the one who sent me and to complete his work.

Jesus opens package. He and Disciples sit down on the ground. Woman enters with Persons 1, 2.

Woman   (*to Persons 1, 2*) I'm sure he is the Messiah. He told me everything I have ever done.

Person 1   Let us go to see him.

Narrator   Jesus stayed with the Samaritans two days. Many more came to believe in him.

Persons 1 & 2 and Woman enter.

Person 1   (*to Woman*) We no longer believe because of your word.

Person 2   We have heard for ourselves and we know that this is truly the Savior of the world.

Narrator   Jesus offers us living water, too. We accept it whenever we celebrate the sacraments. We are given the strength and desire to go out and bring others to Jesus.

The Pardon of the Sinful Woman

ELEVENTH SUNDAY IN ORDINARY TIME: YEAR C

Themes

- sacrament of reconciliation
- forgiveness of sin
- conversion
- love
- sinners
- hypocrisy

Background Notes

The story of the Pardon of the Sinful Woman in Luke's gospel is very similar to the story of the Anointing at Bethany in the other gospels. The main difference is that the woman in Luke's story is a sinner who has been forgiven by Jesus.

Jesus was dining at the home of Simon, a Pharisee. He was probably reclining on a mat at a low table with his sandals off and his feet behind him. A woman who was known to be a sinner anointed Jesus' feet. She burst into tears, then dried his feet with her hair and anointed them. Simon said to himself that Jesus was no prophet or he would not let the woman touch him. Then Jesus showed he was a prophet by reading Simon's mind. He explained that the woman was forgiven, and she had shown more love than Simon himself. Simon should have shown Jesus the courtesies performed for a guest: a kiss of greeting, water for his feet, and oil for his head. Simon's stinginess was in sharp contrast to the woman's generosity.

Jesus told a parable that illustrates how a person who has been forgiven more, loves more. Jesus forgave the woman and gave her peace.

For Discussion

Before the play: How do you feel after you've done something wrong? What can you do to make up?

After the play: How was the woman different from Simon? How did she show love for Jesus? How do the steps of the sacrament of reconciliation help us toward conversion? How can we show love for Jesus?

Activity

Invite younger learners to do this activity. Put cologne, bath powder, or another fragrance on a few cotton balls. Set these in the center of a square of material and pull up the fabric to make a little bag. To close the sachet wrap yarn around the top and tie a bow. Put the sachet before a crucifix, another image of Jesus, or a Bible, which contains his Word.

Ask your older learners to think about someone whom they need to forgive or ask forgiveness of. What are some practical, simple ways they can use to show their desire for reconciliation?

Prayer

Lead the children to reflect on God's forgiveness.

Recall God's love in forgiving you just as he forgave the sinful woman. Think back to the times you have sinned and did not do as God wished. (Pause.) As soon as you were sorry, God offered you forgiveness. Time and again God forgave you for little sins and perhaps for big sins. Maybe God has forgiven you every day. Maybe God has forgiven you over and over for the same sins. No one can fathom the depths of God's mercy and great love. Spend some time now thanking God in your heart for being so good and for forgiving you repeatedly. (Pause.)
You might ask God now for the grace to show your love in return by avoiding sin. (Pause.) Whenever you do sin, you can trust that God loves you and will always accept you. Ask for the wisdom to return to God immediately.

CAST: NARRATOR, JESUS, SIMON, PERSONS 1, 2 (+), WOMAN

PROPS: TABLE AND FOUR CHAIRS, PLATES, FLASK FOR OINTMENT

THE PARDON OF THE SINFUL WOMAN LUKE 7:36–50

Table and chairs are in the center. Simon and Persons 1, 2 are seated.

Narrator Once a Pharisee named Simon invited Jesus to dine with him at his house.

Jesus enters and goes to Simon.

Jesus Hello, Simon.

Simon Jesus! I'm so glad you have come. Welcome to my table.

Jesus sits.

Simon (*offering Jesus a plate*) Here, have some of this fresh bread.

Narrator Now there was a woman in the city whom people avoided as a sinner. She learned that Jesus was at table in the house of the Pharisee. She came with an alabaster flask of ointment.

Woman enters with flask, goes behind Jesus, and weeps.

Simon You should not approach the Teacher.

Woman stoops and pretends to wipe Jesus' feet with her hair and kiss them.

Person 1 (*with shocked expression to Person 2*) She's wiping his feet with her hair.

Person 2 And kissing them.

Woman pretends to pour the ointment on his feet.

Simon (*aside*) If this man were a prophet, he would know that this woman is a sinner.

Jesus Simon, I have something to say to you.

Simon Teacher, speak.

Jesus Two people were in debt to a certain man. One owed five hundred days' wages, and the other owed fifty. When they could not repay him, he cancelled the debts for both of them. Now which of them will love him more?

Simon I suppose the one for whom he cancelled the greater debt.

Jesus You have judged rightly. (*turning and gesturing to Woman*) Do you see this woman? When I entered your house, you gave me no water for my feet, but she has bathed them with her tears and dried them with her hair. You did not give me a kiss, but since the time I came in, she has not stopped kissing my feet. You did not anoint my head with oil, (*gestures toward head*) but she has anointed my feet with ointment. (*gestures toward feet*)

   Therefore, I tell you, her many sins have been forgiven, so she has shown great love. But the one to whom little is forgiven loves little. (*to Woman*) Your sins are forgiven.

Person 1 (*to Person 2*) Who is this who even forgives sins?

Jesus (*to Woman*) Your faith has saved you. Go in peace.

Woman exits, walking backwards looking at Jesus.

Narrator God is always willing to forgive us. May we pray an act of contrition after we sin and celebrate the sacrament of reconciliation regularly. Then we will experience God's love in a new way.

The Anointing at Bethany

PASSION SUNDAY: YEAR B

Themes

- love for Jesus
- gratitude
- the death of Jesus

Background Notes

The details of this event differ from gospel to gospel. In Matthew and Mark, Jesus' head is anointed. It was the custom to anoint the heads of guests. In John, Jesus' feet are anointed. Matthew and Mark identify the host as Simon the leper. John identifies the woman as Mary, the sister of Lazarus, and Judas as the disciple who complains.

The perfume the woman used, which was made from a rare Indian plant, was valued at three hundred days' wages. It was sealed in an alabaster vase to keep the fragrance in. The vase had to be broken before the perfume could be used. Perhaps the woman hit it on the edge of the table. Jesus showed appreciation for the woman's generous gesture and defended it. He stated that she would always be remembered. This occurred in an age when women's actions went unnoticed, unrewarded, and unrecorded.

Jesus asserted that he would not always be there, whereas the poor would be. And he described the anointing as prophetic—a preparation for his burial. Bodies were anointed with spices and oil before being buried. Jesus never was anointed. His burial was hurried, and when the women did come to anoint him, he was already risen.

In Matthew and Mark the anointing occurred after the chief priests and elders had conspired to arrest Jesus and before Judas arranged the betrayal with them. The woman's extravagant act of love softened the unfolding of the tragic events that led to the end of Jesus' life, when his blood was poured out for us in another extravagant act of love.

For Discussion

Before the play: Did anyone ever laugh at you for your choices as a Christian? What are some things that Christians do or believe today that others might consider foolish?

After the play: How was the woman's gesture a great act of love? How was she different from Judas? What can we do to honor Jesus? When is anointing used in the Church today? Why?

Activity

Create a get-well card for someone. Write a personal message inside and then send it to the person with a promise of prayer.

Prayer

Invite the learners to think of one special way they can show love for Jesus soon. They might say a prayer, volunteer somewhere, or do something difficult for love of Jesus, such as changing a bad habit. You might discuss ideas and then allow several moments for the learners to decide what they wish to do. End by praying together the traditional Act of Love.

> *O my God, I love you above all things,*
> *with my whole heart and soul*
> *because you are all-good and worthy*
> *of all my love.*
> *I love my neighbor as myself for the love*
> *of you.*
> *I forgive all who have injured me,*
> *and I ask pardon of all whom I have*
> *injured. Amen.*

CAST: NARRATOR, JESUS, SIMON, PERSONS 1, 2 (+), WOMAN

PROPS: TABLE AND CHAIRS, JAR

THE ANOINTING AT BETHANY   MATTHEW 26:6–13, MARK 14:3–9, JOHN 12:1–8

Jesus, Simon, and Persons 1, 2 are seated at table.

Narrator   One day Jesus was at table in the house of Simon the leper in Bethany. A woman came with an alabaster jar of costly perfumed oil.

Woman enters. She "breaks" the top off the jar by hitting it against the table and "pours" the contents on Jesus' head.

Person 1   (*angrily*) What a stupid thing to do!

Person 2   (*to Woman*) Why this waste of perfumed oil?

Person 1   It could have been sold for more than three hundred days' wages.

Person 2   And the money given to the poor.

Jesus   (*putting up hand*) Let her alone. Why do you make trouble for her? She has performed a good service for me. The poor you will always have with you. You can show kindness to them whenever you wish. But you will not always have me. (*gesturing toward Woman*) She has done what she could. By pouring this perfume on my body, she has prepared me for burial.

Person 1   What does he mean?

Person 2   Why is the Master talking about his burial?

Jesus   Truly I tell you, wherever the gospel is proclaimed in the whole world, (*gestures widely*) what she has done will be told in remembrance of her.

Narrator   The fragrance of the perfume filled the house. And Jesus' words came true. We all know the story of the woman's beautiful act of love. May we imitate her overwhelming show of love for Jesus by serving him and his people.

Peter's Profession of Faith

TWELFTH SUNDAY IN ORDINARY TIME: YEAR C; TWENTY-FIRST SUNDAY: YEAR A; TWENTY-FOURTH SUNDAY: YEAR B

Themes
- the apostles
- faith
- the identity of Jesus
- Peter
- the Church

Background Notes

Although this story begins with what people think of Jesus, the focus is what the apostles think of him. Peter, as usual, was their spokesperson. While others, including King Herod, said that Jesus was a prophet returned to earth, Peter proclaimed that Jesus was the Messiah, the fulfillment of the Old Testament promises. In response, Jesus declared that his Church would be founded on Peter, whose name means "rock." The powers of death shall not overcome the Church. Jesus bestowed on Peter and his successors the power to lead the Church until the end of time. Whatever they declare lawful will be held lawful in heaven.

Jesus' warning not to tell others has been interpreted in different ways. It could be that he did not want people to follow him as the kind of Messiah they expected—a powerful, worldly ruler who frees them from their oppressors. In Matthew's account, Peter added that Jesus is the Son of the living God.

For Discussion

Before the play: Who do you believe Jesus is? Why was it hard for the Israelites to accept Jesus as their Messiah?

After the play: What special role do Peter and the popes have in the Church? In what ways is the present pope guiding the Church? How is your bishop guiding you?

Activity

Involve your younger learners in this activity. Peter is the rock on which our Church is founded, but we are living stones of this Church. Use permanent marker to write your name on a rock and add symbols of yourself: your favorite things, what you like to do. Add your rock to a pile of other rocks, building a wall if possible. Later use your rock as a paperweight.

Invite older learners to use the Internet to look up symbols for Jesus and the Church.

Prayer

Pray a litany for the Church, like the one below. The learners may add petitions.

Response: *Pray for us.*

Mary, Mother of the Church...
St. Peter...
The Apostles, first leaders of the Church...
All saintly popes and bishops...

Response: *Hear us, O Lord.*

That our Holy Father, Pope (Name), may be a good shepherd of the Church...
That our Church leaders may have the wisdom and courage to guide us well...
That the bishop of our diocese, Bishop (Name), may lead us with love...
That our pope and bishops may have good health and strength to carry out their responsibilities...
That they may be filled with the gifts of the Holy Spirit, to serve as Jesus did...
That all believers may come to unity...

Let us pray. Lord, you have given us leaders to guide us to holiness and to you. Give them the grace to always be true to you, and give us the grace to be open to their teachings. Amen.

CAST: NARRATOR, JESUS, PETER, DISCIPLES 1, 2, 3 (+)

Peter's Profession of Faith
Matthew 16:13–20, Mark 8:27–30, Luke 9:18–23

Jesus, Peter, and Disciples 1, 2, 3 walk along.

Narrator Jesus went with his disciples to the village of Caesarea Philippi.

Jesus Who do people say that the Son of Man is?

Disciple 1 Some say John the Baptist.

Disciple 2 Others say you are Elijah.

Disciple 3 And still others Jeremiah or one of the prophets.

Jesus stops and faces the Disciples and Peter.

Jesus (*pointing to Disciples*) But who do *you* say that I am?

Peter You are the Messiah, the Son of the living God.

Jesus puts his hand on Peter's shoulder.

Jesus (*to Peter*) Blessed are you, Simon, son of John! For flesh and blood has not revealed this to you, but my Father in heaven.
And I tell you, you are Peter, and on this rock I will build my Church, and the gates of the underworld will not prevail against it.

Disciple 1 What does Jesus mean?

Disciple 2 Why is he calling Simon Peter?

Jesus I will give you the keys of the kingdom of heaven. Whatever you bind on earth (*points down with right hand*) will be bound in heaven (*points up*); and whatever you loose on earth (*points down with left hand*) will be loosed in heaven (*points up*).
(*looking around at the Disciples*) Now I give you strict orders: Don't tell anyone that I am the Messiah. The Son of Man must undergo great suffering, and be rejected by the elders, chief priests, and scribes, and be killed, and on the third day be raised.

Peter (*to Disciple 1*) Why is Jesus talking about his death?

Jesus If any want to become my followers, let them deny themselves and take up their cross daily and follow me.

Narrator Peter became the head of the Church. He followed Jesus and led the early Church until, like his master, he was killed on a cross. Who is Jesus for you? Do you respond to him as though he were your Messiah, the living God?

The Transfiguration of Jesus

SECOND SUNDAY OF LENT: YEARS A, B, C

Background Notes

At the Transfiguration, Jesus was revealed in glory to Peter, James, and John, the three apostles privileged to be alone with him on other occasions. The Transfiguration anticipated the resurrection glory of Jesus and confirmed his role as Messiah. The account was rooted in some mystical experience the three disciples had. They did not perceive the impact of it until after the resurrection. The expression "six days" linked the event to Peter's confession of faith at Caesarea Philippi. The high mountain is traditionally held to be Mount Tabor.

Details of the story that are reminiscent of God's theophany on Sinai point to Jesus as the New Moses: the high mountain, the cloud, Moses' presence, and the tents. The apostles represent the new people of God. Moses and Elijah, who are present at the event, stand for the Law and the prophets. As such, they witness to Jesus. He is the fulfillment of the Law and the greatest prophet. They discuss Jesus' fate—that he is to suffer and die. The cloud and the mountain symbolize God's presence, and Jesus' dazzling appearance signifies the divine world. Tents were used during the Exodus. Peter's suggestion to make tents could refer to this journey to freedom or simply reflect his wish to prolong the experience.

The apostles fell to the ground in fear. They did not understand. The words of the Father confirmed Jesus' role as the Messiah and revealed his divine sonship. The Transfiguration may have been intended to strengthen the apostles' faith during the passion and death of Jesus.

For Discussion

Before the play: Where in the gospels is it shown that Jesus was God? When Jesus was put to death, why might his followers have doubted that he was God?

After the play: How does the Transfiguration story parallel Moses' experience on Mount Sinai? Why do you think the Transfiguration took place? How do we regard the suffering and death of Jesus?

Activity

Invite younger learners to do this activity. Make a postcard that Peter might have sent after the Transfiguration. On one side draw the mountain, the cloud, and Jesus, and on the other side write what Peter might have said about the experience.

Have older learners read Deuteronomy 5:1–2, 22–27, and compare Moses' experience to Jesus' transfiguration.

Prayer

O most merciful Redeemer,
friend and brother,
may we know you more clearly,
love you more dearly,
and follow you more nearly,
for your own sake.

—St. Richard of Chichester

CAST: NARRATOR, JESUS, PETER, JAMES, JOHN, MOSES, ELIJAH, VOICE

PROP: CLOUD

THE TRANSFIGURATION OF JESUS
MATTHEW 17:1–8, MARK 9:2–8, LUKE 9:28–36

Narrator Luke's gospel tells us that, eight days before the transfiguration, Jesus was praying with his disciples. He asked them, "Who do you say I am?" Then one day something happened to show them who he was.

Jesus, Peter, James, and John enter.

Jesus (*gesturing up*) My three friends, come up this mountain with me.

Jesus, Peter, James, and John walk around with difficulty as if climbing.

Narrator Jesus and the three apostles went up the high mountain by themselves. As Jesus prayed, he was transfigured before them.

Jesus extends his arms. Peter, James, and John kneel and shade their eyes.

Narrator The face of Jesus shone like the sun, and his clothes became dazzling white. Moses and Elijah appeared.

Moses and Elijah enter and go to Jesus, one on each side.

Narrator Moses and Elijah talked to Jesus. They spoke about the passion and death he would undergo in Jerusalem.

Peter Lord, it is good for us to be here. If you wish, I will make three tents here, one for you, one for Moses, and one for Elijah.

Narrator While Peter was still speaking, a bright cloud cast a shadow over them. From the cloud came a voice.

Voice (*loud and strong*) This is my beloved Son; with him I am well pleased. Listen to him!

Peter, James, and John fall to the ground face down and tremble. Jesus walks over to them and touches each one.

Jesus Get up and do not be afraid.

Peter, James, and John sit up, open their eyes, and rub them. They look around.

Narrator They saw no one else but Jesus.

Jesus Let's go down now.

Jesus, Peter, James, and John walk around.

Jesus Tell no one about the vision until after the Son of Man has been raised from the dead.

Narrator Jesus is God. Let us adore him, pray to him, make sacrifices for him, and obey him. Someday we will live with him forever.

Martha and Mary

SIXTEENTH SUNDAY IN ORDINARY TIME: YEAR C

Themes

- faith
- love for Jesus
- prayer
- spiritual life

Background Notes

Martha, Mary, and their brother Lazarus lived in Bethany, a town near Jerusalem. Jesus often visited these good friends.

This story illustrates the primary place of faith in the life of a Christian. Martha invited Jesus to her house but then was totally absorbed in the task of serving him and his companions. Meanwhile Mary, her sister, sat at the Lord's feet, listening to his teaching. This was the posture a disciple took while being taught by the master. A woman would not usually assume this posture. When Martha complained to Jesus that she was doing all the work, Jesus chided Martha for her busy-ness, her anxiety and worry. Perhaps she was doing more than was necessary. Jesus pointed out that focusing on him, as Mary was doing, was not only good but necessary. Valuing the person of Jesus and his message is the only thing that matters. However, we must balance prayer with love in action.

For Discussion

Before the play: Who were some of Jesus' friends? How do you show you are a friend of Jesus?

After the play: Why did Jesus praise Mary? Why is it important to pray? How do we serve Jesus today? What do you think happened at the end of this story?

Activity

Ask younger learners to do the following activity. Fold a sheet of drawing paper in half. On one half draw a picture of yourself listening to Jesus like Mary. On the other half draw yourself doing something for Jesus like Mary.

Invite older learners to do some research about the home life of Jewish families.

Prayer

Dear Jesus,
  help us spread your goodness every-
  where.
Fill our souls with your spirit and life.
Let us belong to you so completely
  that our lives may radiate yours.
Let us praise you in the way you love
  best:
  by shining on those around us.
Let us preach you without preaching,
  not by words, but by our example,
  by the catching force,
  the influence of what we do,
  the evident fullness of the love our
  hearts bear to you.

—adapted from John Henry
Cardinal Newman's prayer

CAST: NARRATOR, JESUS, DISCIPLES 1, 2 (+), MARTHA, MARY

PROPS: LARGE POT AND LADLE, DISHES, TABLE, CHAIRS FOR JESUS AND DISCIPLES

MARTHA AND MARY   LUKE 10:38–42

Martha stands in the center of the stage in front of chairs. Mary is in the background. Pot is on the floor, and dishes on the table. Jesus and Disciples enter.

Narrator Jesus entered the village of Bethany. A woman named Martha and her sister Mary welcomed him into their home.

Jesus Martha! How are you?

Martha (*excitedly*) Jesus! I'm fine. Welcome to Bethany. Dinner is almost ready. Won't you join us?

Jesus I would be happy to.

Mary (*going to Jesus*) Master, it is so good to see you!

Jesus and Disciples are seated. Mary sits at Jesus' feet. Martha goes to pot and stirs.

Mary What have you been doing, Jesus?

Jesus We've been teaching in towns as we journey to Jerusalem.

Martha sets table.

Mary Tell me. What did you teach at the last town you were in?

Jesus Well, someone asked me what to do to have eternal life...

Martha walks over to Jesus.

Martha (*hands on hips*) Lord, do you not care that my sister has left me to do all the work by myself? Tell her then to help me.

Jesus (*shaking head*) Martha, Martha, you are worried and distracted by many things. There is need of only one thing. Mary has chosen the better part, which will not be taken away from her.

Narrator Following Jesus means both serving him by acts of love and being with him in prayer.

Paying Taxes to Caesar

TWENTY-NINTH SUNDAY IN ORDINARY TIME: YEAR A

Background Notes

The Pharisees sought to trap Jesus in the matter of paying taxes. Beginning in 6 AD, the Romans exacted from the Jewish people a census tax, which the Jewish people resented. The tax had to be paid by a silver Roman coin. If Jesus supported the tax, he would alienate his people. If he said the tax shouldn't be paid, his enemies could report him to the governor as a rebel, like a Zealot. Jesus escaped the trap by using his wit. Coins bore the image of the emperor and were inscribed "Tiberius Caesar, son of the divine Augustus." They were his possession. Ironically, when Jesus asked for this coin, the Pharisees had one, though apparently Jesus did not. This means they already submitted to the emperor themselves and used his system of commerce.

By saying, "Give to Caesar the things that are Caesar's and to God the things that are God's," Jesus implied that loyalty to state and obedience to God did not have to contradict one another. It is up to us to apply this principle and determine what exactly belongs to "Caesar."

For Discussion

Before the play: What are some laws and rules that you follow? Why do you try to keep them? Why do your parents pay taxes?

After the play: How did the Pharisees try to get Jesus into trouble this time? Why were they always trying to trap Jesus? What do we owe God? What do we owe the government?

Activity

List as many people as you can whom you are to obey. (You might have a race to see who has the longest list!) Choose one person on your list and do something nice for him or her.

Prayer

Lord, help us give every person what he or she deserves. May we obey our parents and respect those who care for us. May we honor our religious leaders. May we be truthful and joyful with our friends and honest and helpful with our neighbors. May we show kindness and compassion to the poor. Above all, may we give you praise, glory, and love forever.

CAST: NARRATOR, JESUS, PHARISEES 1, 2, PHARISEES' DISCIPLES 1, 2 (+), CROWD (+)

PROPS: MONEY BAG, COIN

PAYING TAXES TO CAESAR   MATTHEW 22:15–22, MARK 12:13–17, LUKE 20:20–26

Narrator   The scribes and chief priests watched Jesus. They sent persons to try to trap Jesus by what he said. They could then hand him over to the governor.

Pharisees enter. Pharisees' disciples follow at a distance.

Pharisee 1   (*to Pharisee 2*) We must trap him in his speech.

Pharisee 2   Yes. If we make him look like a fool, his followers will leave him.

Pharisee 1   If we can get him to speak against the government, we might be rid of him.

Pharisee 2   I've got it. (*to Pharisees' disciples*) Come here.

Pharisees' Disciples walk up to Pharisees 1, 2.

Pharisee 2   Find Jesus. Ask him if it is lawful to pay taxes to Caesar. (*laughs wickedly*) That will catch him.

Pharisees 1, 2 exit laughing. Jesus and Crowd enter. Pharisees' Disciples go to Jesus.

Disciple 1   Ah, Teacher, we know that you are a truthful man and that you teach the way of God in truth.

Disciple 2   You are not concerned with anyone's opinion, for you do not regard a person's status.

Disciple 1   Tell us, then, what do you think? Is it lawful to pay the census tax to the emperor or not?

Disciple 2   Should we pay or should we not pay?

Jesus gives them a hard look.

Jesus   Why are you testing me? Show me the coin used for the census tax.

Pharisees' disciple 1 opens his money bag and takes out a coin.

Disciple 1   (*handing coin to Jesus*) Here. A Roman coin.

Jesus   (*holding up coin*) Whose head is this and whose inscription?

Disciples 1, 2   It is Caesar's.

Jesus   (*calmly*) Then repay to Caesar what belongs to Caesar and to God what belongs to God.

Pharisees' disciples 1, 2 gasp. They turn and walk away quickly.

Narrator   Jesus wants us to obey rightful authority: our parents, teachers, policemen, and anyone else set over us to care for us. We owe them obedience, honor, and gratitude.

The Woman Caught in Serious Sin

FIFTH SUNDAY OF LENT: YEAR C

Background Notes

The Pharisees used a woman's humiliation to try to ensnare Jesus. Having caught her in adultery, they brought her to him and asked if she should be stoned. If Jesus answered "No," he would be contradicting the Law of Moses, which prescribed death for her crime. If Jesus answered "Yes," he would depart from his own teaching of mercy. Instead, Jesus wrote on the ground. What he wrote and why remain a mystery. One theory is that Jesus was listing the sins of all those present.

Jesus cleverly invited those without sin to throw the first stone. Conscious of their sins and perhaps realizing how base was the trap they had laid, the Pharisees left, one by one. In St. Augustine's words, "There remained together great misery and great mercy." Jesus, the sinless one, freed the woman but with an admonition to sin no more. He gave her a chance to change her life.

For Discussion

Before the play: How do you feel when you are caught doing something wrong? How do you feel when you are forgiven?

After the play: What do you think Jesus wrote on the ground? Why? Why should we forgive others? How do we show we forgive others? How are Christians forgiven?

Activity

Invite your young learners to carry out this activity. Cut out a rock from grey or brown paper. On it write the name or names of people who have hurt you. Say a prayer for them and then tear the paper into bits. Burn the bits in a pail, or throw them away, as a sign of forgiveness.

Older learners can act out situations in which they have the chance to forgive someone or they need forgiveness.

Prayer

Ask the children to think of the sin they are most sorry for. Remind them that Jesus is just as willing to forgive them as he was the woman who had sinned. His mercy is without bounds. So is his love for us. Pray together an act of contrition. This could be the traditional formula, the formula in the new Rite of Penance, or one that you compose.

CAST: NARRATOR, JESUS, WOMAN, SCRIBES 1, 2 (+), PHARISEES 1, 2 (+), CROWD (+)

PROP: CHAIR

THE WOMAN CAUGHT IN SERIOUS SIN JOHN 8:2–11

Narrator Early one morning Jesus walked in the temple area.

Jesus enters. Crowd enters gradually. Jesus sits.

Jesus I am the light of the world. Whoever follows me will not walk in darkness.

Narrator Jesus was interrupted when some scribes and Pharisees brought a woman to him. She had been caught in adultery.

Scribes and Pharisees enter with Woman. Pharisee 1 and Pharisee 2 are on either side of her.

Pharisee 1 (*pointing to ground before Jesus, to Woman*) Stand there in the middle.

Woman stands before Jesus with her head down.

Pharisee 2 Teacher, this woman was caught committing a serious sin.

Scribe 1 In the law, Moses commands us to stone such women.

Scribe 2 Now what do you say?

Narrator They said this to test him, so that they could have some charge to bring against him.

Jesus bends down and writes with his finger on the ground.

Pharisee 1 Well, Jesus, what do you say?

Pharisee 2 Do we stone her or not?

Jesus straightens up.

Jesus (*looking around at them*) Let the one among you who is without sin be the first to throw a stone at her.

Jesus bends over again and writes. Scribes and Pharisees look at writing. One by one they leave. When Jesus and Woman are alone, Jesus stands up.

Jesus Woman, where are they? Has no one condemned you?

Woman No one, sir.

Jesus Neither do I condemn you. Go your way, and from now on do not sin again.

Woman walks away slowly, looking back at Jesus from time to time.

Narrator Jesus shows loving mercy for sinners. If we are Christians, people who are like Christ, we will have compassion on one another, for we are all sinners. Only Jesus and Mary are without sin.

Zaccheus, the Tax Collector

Themes

- sacrament of reconciliation
- conversion
- forgiveness
- the mission of Jesus

Background Notes

Jesus demonstrates that it is possible for a rich man to be saved. Zaccheus was a tax collector who collected taxes for the Roman oppressors. Tax collectors were allowed to keep for themselves any money collected above their quota. This practice led to greed and abuse of the people. To the Jewish people then, to be a tax collector was synonymous with being a sinner.

Zaccheus was so short that, in order to see Jesus passing by, he climbed a sycamore tree, a tree with a short trunk and wide branches. This act took ingenuity and humility. When Jesus invited himself to Zaccheus's house, the crowd objected. But Zaccheus responded with joy. He was open to Jesus, and his life was changed. He made restitution for his sins far beyond what was necessary. His whole household reaped the benefits. This story clearly shows that Jesus seeks out sinners. The good shepherd is always on the lookout for lost sheep.

For Discussion

Before the play: What are some physical shortcomings people can have? What are some other kinds of shortcomings? Name some people who were great despite their flaws.

After the play: How did Jesus reach out to Zaccheus? How was Zaccheus open to salvation? What actions did he promise to take as signs of his conversion? In what ways does Jesus reach out to us?

Activity

Invite young learners to take part in this activity. Put a drop of India ink or black paint near the bottom of a piece of paper. Using a straw, blow the ink or paint upward and outward to make a tree trunk and branches. When the tree is dry, add leaves and Zaccheus (or yourself!) peeking through them.

Older learners might prepare a scenario in which they welcome Jesus to their city and home.

Prayer

Have mercy on us, O God,
according to your steadfast love;
according to your abundant mercy
take away my sins.
Wash me thoroughly from my
*   wickedness*
and cleanse me from my sin.
Create in me a clean heart, O God,
and put a new and right spirit
*   within me.*

—Psalm 51:1, 2, 10

CAST: NARRATOR, JESUS, ZACCHEUS, PERSONS 1, 2, CROWD (+)

PROP: CHAIR OR LADDER FOR TREE

ZACCHAEUS, THE TAX COLLECTOR Luke 19:1–10

Crowd and Persons 1, 2 are on one side of stage facing the wings. Tree is on the other side. Zacchaeus stands between the Crowd and the tree.

Narrator   Once Jesus was passing through the town of Jericho. Now a man there named Zacchaeus was a chief tax collector and a rich man. He was not liked because of his job. Zacchaeus wanted to see who Jesus was, but he could not see him because of the crowd. He was too short.

Crowd looks offstage. Zacchaeus tries to look between people.

Person 1   (*excitedly*) I see him! I see him! He's coming!

Zacchaeus jumps up and down to see. He shakes his head and looks frustrated. He sees the tree, his face brightens, and he snaps his fingers. He runs to the tree and "climbs" up.

Narrator   From the sycamore tree Zacchaeus had a good view of Jesus.

Jesus enters and Crowd moves with him toward the tree. At the tree Jesus looks up.

Jesus   (*shouting*) Zacchaeus, hurry and come down, for I must stay at your house today.

Zacchaeus climbs down.

Zacchaeus   You don't mean it! How wonderful! I am honored. Come with me.

Jesus and Zacchaeus begin to walk off.

Person 2   (*angrily*) He has gone to be the guest of a man who is a sinner.

Zacchaeus stops.

Zacchaeus   (*to Jesus*) Look, half of my possessions, Lord, I will give to the poor. If I have stolen anything from anyone, I will pay back four times as much.

Jesus   (*to Zacchaeus*) Today salvation has come to his house because this man, too, is a son of Abraham. The Son of Man has come to seek and to save what is lost.

Jesus and Zacchaeus walk off, Jesus' arm around Zacchaeus.

Narrator   Jesus forgave Zacchaeus and made him a better man. Who knows what good we do when we forgive others who have hurt us, whether on purpose or unintentionally?

The Widow's Offering

THIRTY-SECOND SUNDAY IN ORDINARY TIME: YEAR B

Themes

- Lent
- the poor
- generosity
- holiness

Background Notes

In the Temple's Court of Women were thirteen horn-shaped chests for offerings, each labeled for a certain purpose, such as incense, doves, and oil. Jesus sat and watched people deposit money. A widow came. She was one of the truly holy Jewish people who contrasted with the righteous "pious ones." The widow put in two copper coins, the smallest coins in circulation. Jesus praised her generosity because the coins were all she had. She didn't even keep one of the two coins for herself. Her offering was more than everyone else's, for she gave her total security. She trusted God to care for her. The story of the widow's offering leads into the story of Christ's offering. He, too, gave his all.

For Discussion

Before the play: When do people contribute to the church? Do you use church envelopes? How much should we give to the church?

After the play: Why was the widow's offering great? Why do you think she was willing to give that much? What we can offer the church besides money?

Activity

Ask younger learners to each decide on at least one toy or article of clothing they can give to a poor child.

Invite older learners to choose how they might give of their time and talents to help their needy sisters and brothers. For example, they might hold a bake sale, or wash cars, or run a clothing drive.

Prayer

Ask the learners to take out a coin. Have pennies on hand in case they don't have change. Ask them what they observe about the coin, for instance, its size, shape, weight, what is imprinted on it. Ask what the coin is used for. Then guide the learners in the following reflection:

Each of us is like a coin that belongs to God. God made us, and we have value in God's eyes. Because God owns us, everything we are is for God's glory. Like money, our lives can be used in different ways. They can be used for good or for bad. Everything we do can be offered to God as a gift. We want to live in such a way that God is proud of us and happy that we are his. At the end of our lives we will return to God. Then we will realize whether our lives have been wasted or have been lived generously.

CAST: NARRATOR, JESUS, DISCIPLES 1, 2 (+), WEALTHY PERSONS 1, 2 (+), WIDOW

PROPS: CHAIR, LARGE BOWL FOR MONEY, TABLE FOR BOWL, BAGS OF MONEY, TWO SMALL COINS

THE WIDOW'S OFFERING MARK 12:41–44, LUKE 21:1–4

Chair is opposite bowl. Jesus and Disciples 1, 2 enter. Jesus walks away and sits down.

Narrator One day Jesus sat watching people put money into the temple treasury. Many rich people put in large sums of money.

Wealthy Person 1 enters, empties bag into bowl, and exits. Wealthy Person 2 enters, empties bag into bowl, and exits. Disciple 1 sees this.

Disciple 1 (*to Disciple 2*) Did you see that? Those people just gave to the treasury more money than I've made all my life.

Narrator A poor widow then came along with two small copper coins.

Widow enters and shyly puts two coins in bowl. She exits.

Jesus (*to Disciples*) Come here so I may tell you something.

Disciples go to Jesus.

Jesus I want you to know that this poor widow has put in more than all the other contributors to the treasury. For all of them have given out of their abundance, but she, from her poverty, has put in everything she had to live on.

Narrator We have an opportunity to give to God in church collections and collections for the poor and needy. We can be stingy, or we can be generous like the widow.

Water into Wine

Themes

- the identity of Jesus
- Mary
- sacrament of marriage

Background Notes

According to John's gospel, changing water into wine by a word was the first sign that Jesus worked to reveal his identity. Miracles are signs of God's presence and power. In Jesus' case, they are signs of the kingdom of God breaking into our world. Both a wedding feast and an abundance of wine are symbols of the messianic age. Jesus is the Messiah, the one who announces and makes present the reign of God. The water Jesus used for the miracle was reserved for ceremonial washings. It filled six jars, each holding twenty to thirty gallons. The wine that Jesus produced was not only plentiful but excellent, as the headwaiter attested. In Jesus is the fullness that satisfies every living creature.

The intercessory role of Mary was highlighted in this miracle. She relied on her son to help when the wine ran low, and as a result the newlyweds were spared embarrassment. Jesus' words to Mary were mysterious. He addressed her as "woman," just as he did later when she stood at the foot of the cross. Perhaps this title was a sign that she is a new Eve who brings forth new life as the Church does. The "hour" that Jesus spoke of was his glorification, the paschal mystery that achieved salvation. The miracle of wine, which occurred "on the third day," obviously foreshadowed that hour.

For Discussion

Before the play: How does Jesus feel about his mother? Why is Mary powerful? How has she helped you?

After the play: What in the Cana story shows that Jesus does things very well? Why do we pray to Mary? What are some favorite prayers and devotions to Mary?

Activity

Involve young learners in this activity. Make a water jar. Cover a small jar with brown construction paper. Use clear scotch tape to hold the ends together. Fold a piece of stiff paper in half so it stands. On one side write Mary's request to the servants: "Do whatever he tells you." Set the jar and sign somewhere at home where you will see it.

Invite each of the older learners to research one of the feastdays of Mary and make a brief presentation to the group.

Prayer

THE MEMORARE

Remember, O most loving Virgin Mary, that never was it known that anyone who fled to your protection, implored your help, or sought your intercession was left unaided. Inspired with this confidence, we turn to you, O Virgin of virgins, our Mother. To you we come, before you we stand, sinful and sorrowful. O Mother of the Word Incarnate, do not despise our petitions, but in your mercy hear us and answer us. Amen.

CAST: NARRATOR, JESUS, MARY, BRIDE, HEADWAITER, GROOM, DISCIPLES 1, 2, SERVANTS 1, 2, GUESTS (+)

PROPS: TUREEN OR PITCHER, LADLE, MUG, RED PUNCH OR PACKAGED DRINK

WATER INTO WINE JOHN 2:1–11

Jesus, Disciples, and Guests stand talking. Mary speaks to the Bride, and the Headwaiter to the Groom. Servants 1, 2 stand together.

Narrator   Jesus worked the first sign of his divine power at Cana in Galilee. Mary, Jesus, and his disciples were guests at a wedding there. The servants were probably the first to realize that there was a problem.

Servant 1   The wine has run out. What can we do?

Servant 2   I don't know. How embarrassing for the family!

Mary goes to Jesus. The Bride and Groom speak together.

Mary   (*to Jesus*) They have no wine.

Jesus   Woman, what concern is that to you and to me? My hour has not yet come.

Mary   (*walks over to Servants*) Do whatever he tells you.

Jesus   (*to Servants*) Fill those jars with water.

Narrator   (*while Servants fill the jars*) There were six stone jars standing there. The people used them for ritual washings. Each jar could hold about twenty-five gallons. The servants filled them to the brim.

Jesus   (*to Servants*) Now draw out some water and take it to the headwaiter.

Servant 1 ladles water into mug, takes it to the Headwaiter.

Servant 1   Sir, would you taste this wine, please?

Headwaiter takes a sip and goes to the Groom.

Headwaiter   (*to Groom*) But this wine is delicious! Everyone serves the good wine first and the cheaper wine when the guests have drunk a lot. But you have kept the good wine until now.

Disciple 1   (*to Disciple 2*) Did you see that?

Disciple 2   I think we can believe this man Jesus.

Narrator   Jesus worked his first miracle at the request of his mother Mary. When we have a special favor to pray for, let us ask Mary to add her prayers to ours.

The Calming of the Storm

TWELFTH SUNDAY IN ORDINARY TIME: YEAR B

Themes

- the apostles
- faith
- humanness of Jesus
- identity of Jesus

Background Notes

This miracle account reveals more clearly the identity of Jesus. His humanity shows in the fact that fatigue caused him to sleep through a bad storm. Yet he was able to subdue the wind and waves by a word. To the Jewish people the sea was considered life-threatening, a symbol of chaos and evil. In Hebrew Scriptures, the act of creation was described as God's conquest over the sea. God also had power to divide the Reed Sea during the Exodus. Consequently, when Jesus mastered the sea, he manifested divine power. He was raised up out of his sleep and conquered evil, as he one day would be raised up out of his tomb and triumph over evil forever. The story also calls for deeper faith on our part. After rebuking the sea, Jesus chided the disciples for their lack of faith. If we believe in Jesus, we trust him to care for us through all the storms of life, even when he appears to be sleeping.

For Discussion

Before the play: Why can we trust Jesus? When have you turned to Jesus for help and been answered?

After the play: Why was Jesus tired? How else did he show he was human? What are some storms you might have to weather?

Activity

Invite the young learners to draw a picture of a boat on a calm sea with a blue sky and sun shining. Fold over the ends of the picture to form doors. On the outside of these doors draw a storm at sea. Use your open-the-doors picture to tell someone the story of Jesus calming the sea.

Ask the older learners to write their own version of "Footprints," or illustrate it, or write a short poem based on it.

Prayer

Read the following reflection. Invite the children to think about it and talk to God about it.

One night a man had a dream. He was walking along the beach with the Lord. Across the sky flashed scenes from his life. In each scene he noticed two sets of footprints in the sand: one belonging to him, and the other to the Lord. When the last scene of his life flashed before him, he looked back at the footprints in the sand. He noticed that many times along the path of his life there was only one set of footprints. He also noticed that it happened at the very lowest and saddest times in his life. This really bothered him, and he questioned the Lord about it. "Lord, you said that once I decided to follow you, you'd walk with me all the way. But I have noticed that during the most troublesome times in my life, there was only one set of footprints. I don't understand why, when I need you most, you would leave me." The Lord replied, "My precious, precious child, I love you and I would never leave you. During the times of trial and suffering, when you saw only one set of footprints, it was then that I carried you."

—Anonymous

CAST: NARRATOR, JESUS, DISCIPLES 1, 2, 3, 4, 5, 6 (+)

PROPS: 4 OR MORE PAIRS OF CHAIRS, ONE BEHIND THE OTHER FOR A BOAT, CUSHION, SOUND-MAKERS FOR THUNDER AND WAVES (SHEET OF METAL OR DRUM FOR THUNDER; WAVES: RECORD WATER SPLASHING AND CREATE WAVES IN A TUB)

THE CALMING OF THE STORM
MATTHEW 8:23–27, MARK 4:35–41, LUKE 8:22–25

Jesus and Disciples stand near boat.

Narrator   The day had been long and busy. Jesus had preached to crowds of people. He had cured many of the sick. Evening had come and Jesus was tired.

Jesus   (*to Disciples*) Let us go across the lake to the other side.

Disciple 1   Fine. Our boat is docked right here.

Disciple 2   Jesus, why don't you try to get some rest in the back of the boat?

Jesus   That sounds like a good idea.

Jesus and Disciples board boat. Jesus lies in last seat with his head on cushion.

Narrator   The Sea of Galilee was known for its sudden storms. As the disciples' boat sailed along, a strong wind arose and blew down on the lake. Huge waves broke over the boat. But Jesus was sound asleep.

Sound of storm. Disciples rock back and forth.

Disciple 3   We're taking in a lot of water.

Disciple 4   We can't last much longer.

Disciples 5 and 6 stagger back to Jesus and shake him.

Disciple 5   Master, don't you care that the boat is flooded?

Disciple 6   Save us. We're going down.

Jesus wakes, stands, and extends his arm to the sky.

Jesus   Quiet now. (*extends his arm to the sea*) Peace! Be still! (*to Disciples*) Why are you afraid? Where is your faith?

Disciple 1   (*to Disciple 2*) Who can this be?

Disciple 3   (*to Disciple 4*) What kind of man is this?

Disciple 5   (*to Disciple 6*) Even the winds and the sea obey him!

Narrator   The disciples continued to wonder at the power of Jesus. He can calm difficult moments in our lives, also.

The Multiplication of Loaves

Background Notes

This miracle is the only one Jesus performed recorded in all four gospels. In fact, Matthew and Mark have two accounts of it. This story strikes familiar chords in Jewish and Christian hearts. It recalls the Exodus during which God fed the people of Israel with manna and quail in the wilderness and also brings to mind the bread miracles of the prophets Elijah (1 Kings 17:2–6) and Elisha (2 Kings 4:42–44). In this miracle Jesus is presented as the shepherd who spreads a banquet before us. The story also looks to the future. It prefigures the Last Supper, the Christian eucharistic celebration, and the messianic banquet. In John's gospel the story is followed by the discourse on the Bread of Life, which serves to heighten the miracle's eucharistic dimension.

Jesus had compassion on the hungry crowd. He took the little food the apostles provided and multiplied it to feed the people. His actions are described by the same words used in the account of the institution of the Eucharist. At the end when everyone was satisfied, there were twelve baskets left over. Twelve symbolizes fullness, completion.

This miracle was the Parable of the Yeast (about yeast going through the entire mass of dough) in action. The bread distributed through the crowd to nourish the people was like the growth and blessings of God's kingdom.

For Discussion

Before the play: What do we believe about the sacred bread and sacred wine at Mass? What are some of the other times in the gospel that Jesus showed power over nature?

After the play: How does this miracle prepare for and symbolize the Eucharist? How did Jesus have the apostles help him minister to the people at that event? How can we satisfy one another's hunger? What are some gifts we have that we might let God use?

Activity

Have young learners carry out this activity. In Israel a church marks where this miracle took place. In its floor is a mosaic of the loaves and fish. On paper draw five loaves and two fish. Outline them with heavy black crayon. Cut colored squares and triangles out of magazine pictures and glue them into your shapes. Use brown for the bread and different colors for the fish. Make the background different shades of one color.

Older learners might check websites with information about hunger in the world. One is www.povertyusa.org.

Prayer

Jesus, just as you multiplied the loaves and fish, today you feed all of us with the Eucharist. Make us one with you and with one another. Change us into yourself so that more and more we may bring your love to others through our words and actions. Help us appreciate more this miracle that occurs every day on our altars. As we take part in this holy meal, make us more worthy of eternal life in your kingdom, the heavenly banquet. Amen.

CAST: NARRATOR, JESUS, PETER, ANDREW, PHILIP, BOY, PERSONS 1, 2, CROWD (+), APOSTLES (+)

PROPS: FIVE PAPER LOAVES, TWO PAPER FISH, THREE BASKETS

THE MULTIPLICATION OF LOAVES
MATTHEW 14:13–21, MARK 6:30–44, LUKE 9:10–17 JOHN 6:1–15

Jesus stands before the Crowd, speaking to them.

Narrator Jesus had gone off with his apostles so they could be by themselves and rest a little. But a large crowd had followed Jesus. He taught them and healed the sick until evening.

Peter, Andrew, and Philip come to Jesus.

Peter It's very late and this is an out-of-the-way place.

Andrew Send the people away so they can get something to eat in the village.

Jesus They don't have to leave. Give them something to eat yourselves.

Philip Sixth months' wages would not buy enough bread for each of them to have a little.

Jesus How much bread do you have here?

Andrew (*presenting Boy*) There is a boy here who has five loaves of barley bread and two dried fish. But this will not be enough for all these people.

Jesus (*taking bread and fish from Boy*) Have the people sit in groups of about fifty.

Apostles arrange Crowd in groups. Jesus takes the bread and fish and looks up to heaven.

Jesus Thank you, Father, for the gift of this bread and fish that will feed us. (*handing bread and fish to the Apostles*) Here, pass out this food to the people.

Apostles distribute the bread and fish. The Crowd shares it. Then Apostles join Jesus to eat.

Narrator All the people there—the five thousand men, the women, and the children—had as much as they wanted to eat.

Jesus (*to Apostles*) Gather the leftovers. Let's not waste anything.

Apostles collect pieces in baskets.

Person 1 Look, they have filled twelve baskets.

Person 2 Surely this is the Prophet who is to come into the world.

Narrator Part of this miracle of the multiplication may be that the people in the crowd shared with one another. May we do the same in our daily lives.

The Large Catch of Fish

FIFTH SUNDAY IN ORDINARY TIME: YEAR C

Background Notes

In Luke's gospel the lake is a place for manifestations of power. This particular miracle happened when the fishermen trusted Jesus, a non-fisherman, who told them to put out their nets once more. Although they had caught nothing all night, suddenly there was an overwhelming number of fish available. In response to the miracle of the large catch, Peter fell to his knees before Jesus. All the fishermen, sensing that they were in the presence of the divine, left everything to follow him.

It was Peter's boat from which the Lord spoke. Peter first acknowledged Jesus' greatness and his own unworthiness. Also, the Lord addressed the words "You will be catching people" to Peter alone, using the singular. These features indicated Peter's vocation of leadership in the Church. The verb used for "will be catching" implied that it would be a lifelong ministry.

For Discussion

Before the play: What is the role of all the apostles? Why is Peter a special apostle?

After the play: How does Jesus show power over nature and people? What is the result of obeying Jesus? What does it mean to be "fishers of people"? How can we be recognized as followers of Jesus?

Activity

Invite younger learners to carry out this activity. On construction paper draw a large boat on the water. Glue or staple a net from a vegetable or fruit bag onto the ends of the boat so it hangs down. Draw and cut out a variety of fish from other sheets of paper and glue them onto the net.

Older learners might examine the vocations of priest, deacon, religious sisters and brothers. What other vocations or occupations are they interested in?

Prayer

Pray for Church leaders. Name them and invite everyone to respond "Pray for him (or her)." Begin with the pope, your bishop(s), priest(s), and deacons. Conclude: "Lord, please move the hearts of many more good people to serve as leaders in your church."

CAST: NARRATOR, JESUS, JAMES, JOHN, SIMON PETER, ANDREW, PARTNER, PERSONS 1, 2 (+), CROWD (+)

PROPS: TWO SETS OF CHAIRS FOR TWO BOATS, TWO NETS

THE LARGE CATCH OF FISH LUKE 5:1–11

Simon Peter, Andrew, and Partner are by one boat. James and John are by the other. They are washing nets. Jesus, near Simon Peter's boat, speaks to Crowd, which is pushing to get closer to him.

Narrator One day Jesus spoke to a crowd of people on the shore of Lake Gennesaret.

Jesus The kingdom of God is upon you.

Person 1 What did he say?

Person 2 I don't know. There are too many people around him.

Jesus gets into nearest boat and sits down.

Jesus Simon, would you please put out a little way from the shore?

Simon, Andrew, and Partner enter the boat and row.

Narrator Jesus taught the crowd from Simon's boat. When he finished, he spoke to Simon.

Jesus (*motioning to "sea"*) Simon, put out into the deep water and let your nets down for a catch.

Simon Master, we have worked all night long but have caught nothing. Yet if you say so, I will let down the nets.

Simon, Andrew, and Partner let down nets.

Simon Look at all the fish! There must be hundreds.

Andrew Where'd they come from?

Simon Who knows? Let's pull them in.

All tug at nets.

Partner The nets are going to break.

Simon gestures to James and John to come. They get in their boat and row.

Simon Help us take these fish in. Put half in your boat.

All take the nets into the boats.

John Hey, the boats are about to sink!

James Isn't this fantastic?

Simon (*falling on knees before Jesus*) Go away from me, Lord, for I am a sinful man!

Jesus (*to Simon*) Do not be afraid. From now on you will be catching people.

Narrator With that the fishermen brought their boats to land, left everything, and became followers of Jesus.

Walking on the Sea

NINETEENTH SUNDAY IN ORDINARY TIME: YEAR A

Themes

- need for faith
- identity of Jesus
- Peter

Background Notes

Jesus' power over the sea signified divinity to the Jewish people. This miracle recalled the Exodus during which God saved the Israelites by mighty deeds, such as leading them safely through the Reed Sea. The story takes place on Lake Gennesaret, which is subject to sudden storms. Jesus walked on the surface of the lake, enabled Peter to walk on it, and quieted the wind and the waves. This miracle, therefore, was a revelation of Christ's divinity to the apostles. He even identified himself by saying, "It is I," which is comparable to "I am," the name Yahweh revealed to Moses.

If the apostles in their boat stand for the Church, the story teaches that Jesus is present to assist his Church through any storm. In Matthew's account Peter was singled out, a sign of his responsibility in the Church as chief fisherman. As long as he had faith and kept his hand in Jesus' hand, Peter was able to do what he should as a leader.

For Discussion

Before the play: How is Jesus present in his Church today? When do you feel like you are sinking?

After the play: What sign of Jesus' divinity is in this story? How does Jesus reach out his hand to support us in difficult times? How does Jesus care for his Church?

Activity

On construction paper draw water with a boat on one half of it. On another sheet of paper draw and cut out Peter. Glue or staple a cardboard tag or a thick paper pulltab to the back of the Peter figure. Cut a slit next to the boat and insert the tag (or pulltab) so that you can move Peter up and down in the water.

Alternate activity: Make a diorama, a three-dimensional scene in a box. Turn a box on its side. Draw a storm inside on the back and sides of the box: clouds and lightning. From blue construction paper draw and cut out waves and glue them to the bottom of the box. On paper draw a boat, Peter, and Jesus, leaving a strip on the bottom that can be folded and glued so that the figures stand. Cut out the figures and glue them to the bottom of the box.

Prayer

My Lord God, I have no idea where I am going. I do not see the road ahead of me. I cannot know for certain where it will end. Nor do I really know myself, and the fact that I think that I am following your will does not mean that I am actually doing so.
But I believe that the desire to please you does in fact please you. And I hope I have that desire in all that I am doing. May I never do anything apart from that desire.

If I do this, you will lead me by the right road, though I may know nothing about it. Therefore will I trust you always, though I may seem to be lost and in the shadow of death. I will not fear, for you are ever with me, and you will never leave me to face my perils alone.
—Thomas Merton

CAST: NARRATOR, JESUS, DISCIPLE 1, 2, 3, (+), PETER, CROWD (+)

PROPS: PAIRS OF CHAIRS IN A ROW FOR BOAT

WALKING ON THE SEA MATTHEW 14:22–33, MARK 6:45–52, JOHN 6:16–21

Jesus, Peter, and Disciples face Crowd.

Narrator It is the end of a long day of teaching.

Jesus (*to Disciples*) You take the boat and go ahead to the other side of the lake. I'm going to say goodbye to the people and pray awhile.

Disciples board boat and row. Jesus waves to Crowd as it exits. Jesus walks to the far side of stage and kneels.

Narrator Sometime between three and six o'clock in the morning the disciples were in the middle of the lake. (*Disciples struggle to row*)

Disciple 1 We're hardly getting anywhere.

Disciple 2 Well, the wind is directly against us.

Jesus walks toward them.

Disciple 3 Say, what's that light?

Disciple 1 It looks like it's coming toward us.

Disciples It's a ghost! (*they scream*)

Jesus Take courage. It is I. Don't be afraid.

Peter Lord, if it's really you, command me to come to you on the water.

Jesus Come.

Peter climbs out of boat and walks toward Jesus.

Peter The wind! (*starts to sink*) Lord, save me! (*Jesus grabs hold of his arm*)

Jesus You of little faith! Why did you doubt?

Jesus and Peter walk to boat and climb in.

Disciple 2 Hey, the wind died down.

Disciples bow down before Jesus.

**Disciples
and Peter** Truly you are the Son of God.

The Tax Money in the Fish

Themes
- obedience to law
- Peter
- virtue

Background Notes

Every adult male over nineteen was obliged to pay a half-shekel temple tax annually for the upkeep of the Temple and the priests' salary. Just as Roman citizens were exempt from paying Roman taxes, we may think of Jesus and the apostles, as members of the kingdom of heaven, as exempt from the temple tax. But so as not to give scandal, Jesus arranges to pay the tax for himself and for Peter. The event reveals Jesus' sense of humor: Peter, a fisherman by trade and chief fisherman, finds tax money in a fish! The shekel is twice the temple tax, enough for Peter and Jesus. This story might have been used to settle a problem of the early Church regarding the temple tax.

For Discussion

Before the play: What is meant by scandal? What do you give during Mass as your offering for the Church?

After the play: How does this story show Jesus' sense of humor? His obedience to authority? What are some church regulations that we are obliged to follow?

Activity

Involve young learners in this fun activity. Draw and cut out several fish from stiff paper. Punch a hole in the top of each. Make slits in a cereal box or a box top covered with blue paper and insert the fish. Tie an opened paperclip to string and attach it to a stick as a fishing pole. See how long it takes to catch all the fish. Race with a friend. Alternate activity: Instead of punching a hole in the fish, put a paperclip on each one and tie a magnet onto the string to go fishing.

Invite older learners to think of a law they would like to change or propose to help a group of people.

Prayer

Lord, Jesus, you were obedient to all who had authority over you. Give us the grace to show respect and honor for government and Church leaders. May we obey their laws for our good and support them in their efforts to bring about a just and peaceful society. Above all, help us to obey you, our supreme and loving ruler.

CAST: NARRATOR, JESUS, PETER, TAX COLLECTORS 1, 2

PROPS: PAPER FISH WITH A PENNY TAPED TO IT, STRING TIED TO POLE

THE TAX MONEY IN THE FISH MATTHEW 17:24–27

Narrator Rome didn't tax its citizens because it received enough money from the foreign countries it conquered. Since the Jewish people were part of the Roman Empire, they had to pay taxes to Rome. In addition, each Jewish man paid a half-shekel tax every year for the upkeep of the Temple. When Jesus and his disciples entered Capernaum, the temple tax collectors came to Peter.

Peter walks alone. Tax Collectors 1, 2 come toward him. Jesus sits some distance away.

Collector 1 Doesn't your master pay the temple tax?

Peter Of course, he does. Wait a minute.

Peter goes into the house where Jesus is.

Narrator Before Peter can say a word about the tax, Jesus speaks to him.

Jesus What is your opinion, Simon? Do the kings of the world tax their citizens— or foreigners?

Peter Foreigners.

Jesus Then the citizens don't have to pay. But we don't want to offend these people. Go to the lake, drop in a line, and take in the first fish you hook. In its mouth you will find a coin worth enough for your temple tax and mine. Take it and give it to the authorities for you and me.

Peter If you say so.

Peter takes fishing pole and goes out.

Peter (*to Tax Collectors*) I'll be right back.

Peter catches fish and removes coin.

Peter (*to himself*) Now how did Jesus know this would be in the fish?

Peter goes to Tax Collectors.

Peter (*handing coin to Tax Collector 1*) Here, this is the temple tax for Jesus and me.

Collector 1 Thank you.

Collector 2 Have a good day.

Tax Collectors exit.

The Second Large Catch of Fish

THIRD SUNDAY OF EASTER: YEAR C

Themes

- Easter/ eternal life
- the identity of Jesus
- ministry

Background Notes

This miracle story has eucharistic overtones. It resembles the multiplication of loaves and fish that also occurred on the shore of the Sea of Tiberias (Lake Gennesaret). The apostles caught nothing all night. Then when they cast their net to the side of the boat as the man on shore directed, they made an enormous catch. With this miracle of abundance Peter recognized that the stranger was the Lord. Peter donned his cloak because Jewish etiquette required that greetings be made in proper attire. Then in a typically spontaneous way he jumped overboard and swam to Jesus.

Although Jesus has been cooking fish, he asked for some of the apostles' fish. This act symbolized the apostles' share in his mission. Why the gospel states the precise number of fish caught is a mystery. One theory is that 153 was how many species of fish there were known to be. This number then suggests the universal dimension of the Church's ministry. A simpler explanation is that the apostles, like any fishermen proud and excited by a huge catch, counted the fish and remembered the large number.

Because this was a post-resurrection appearance of Jesus, the apostles naturally were awed and puzzled by the mystery of his presence with them. They were slow to identify him and did not ask him to confirm that he was the Lord.

For Discussion

Before the play: What are some things that God provides for us in abundance?

After the play: How is this story like the multiplication of loaves and fishes? How do we share in Christ's mission? When is it hard to recognize the Lord when he comes in daily life?

Activity

Invite young learners to make this Christian symbol. The initials of the Greek words "Jesus, Son of God, Savior" (ICHTHYS) spelled *fish*, so a fish became a symbol for Jesus. Fold a sheet of construction paper in half. Draw a fish on one side and in it write "Jesus" or the Greek letters. Cut the fish out double. Punch holes around the edge about an inch apart and lace yarn around the fish. Stuff it with cotton or newspaper before you make the final stitch and knot the yarn.

Older learners might each make their own crossword puzzle, based on the Scripture reading. They can then exchange and solve each other's puzzles.

Prayer

Guide the learners to pray the Jesus prayer: "Lord Jesus Christ, Son of God, have mercy on me, a sinner." Sitting quietly, breathe in deeply and exhale slowly. After a few minutes, pray the words of this prayer in your mind: breathe in on the first phrase (Lord Jesus Christ), exhale on the second phrase (Son of God), slowly inhale with the third phrase (have mercy on me) and slowly let out your breath with the fourth phrase (a sinner).

CAST: NARRATOR, JESUS, PETER, THOMAS, NATHANAEL, JAMES, JOHN, DISCIPLES 1, 2

PROPS: EIGHT CHAIRS IN PAIRS FOR BOAT, CLOAK, BREAD, A FEW FISH, NET

THE SECOND LARGE CATCH OF FISH John 21:1–14

Peter, Thomas, Nathanael, James, John, and Disciples are seated away from the boat.

Narrator   After the resurrection some of the disciples were by the Sea of Tiberias.

Peter   (*standing up*) I'm going fishing.

Disciples   We'll go with you.

Disciples go to boat and sit in it. Peter pushes the boat off and then jumps in. All row.

Narrator   The disciples fished all night, but by the time dawn had come, they had caught nothing. Someone called to them from the shore.

Jesus enters.

Jesus   (*speaking loudly*) Children, have you caught anything to eat?

Disciples   No.

Jesus   Cast the net over the right side of the boat and you will find something.

Disciples cast their net to the right side of the boat.

Thomas   Look at all the huge fish!

Nathanael   Every fish in the sea must be here.

Disciples struggle to pull up net.

James   We can't even haul the net up.

John   (*to Peter*) It is the Lord!

Peter throws on cloak, jumps overboard, and swims to Jesus. The two talk for a while and then watch the others come in.

Thomas   We'll never be able to lift this net on board. Let's just tow it behind us.

Disciples row to shore, get out of boat, and join Jesus and Peter.

Nathanael   Look, he has some bread, and fish is cooking over a charcoal fire.

Jesus   Bring some of the fish you have just caught.

Peter goes to the boat and drags the net to shore.

Peter   All these big fish and the net isn't breaking! (*to John*) Let's count them.

Jesus   Come, have breakfast.

Jesus takes the bread, and passes it out to them. Then he serves them the fish.

Narrator   When the disciples counted the fish, they found that there were one hundred and fifty-three. No one asked the man who he was. They knew it was the Lord.

A Possessed Man

FOURTH SUNDAY IN ORDINARY TIME: YEAR B

Theme

■ the identity
of Jesus

Background Notes

In the gospels of Mark and Luke, exorcism was the first miracle that Jesus worked. An exorcism was an appropriate beginning to his ministry, since it signaled Jesus' ultimate victory over evil. Demons were powerless before him, even if, like the ones in this miracle, they knew his name (a way to have magical power over an enemy).

At Jesus' words a struggle ensued that underlined the gravity of the man's situation. Whether truly possessed or suffering from a disease attributed to demons, the man regained his health. Once more he was welcome in society and in the synagogue.

For Discussion

Before the play: What do you do when you feel like doing something wrong?

After the play: How can Jesus help us in our struggle against sin?

Activity

Make a poster with the caption "Stamp out evil." You might use photos and words from newspapers and magazines along with your own artwork.

Prayer

Pray the Our Father in which we ask to be delivered from evil.

CAST: NARRATOR, JESUS, MAN,
PERSONS 1, 2, CROWD

A Possessed Man   MARK 1:21–28, LUKE 4:31–37

Jesus stands facing the Crowd and Persons 1, 2.

Narrator   One sabbath Jesus was teaching in the synagogue in Capernaum. A man possessed by an evil spirit interrupted him.

Jesus   I say to you, God is a loving Father.

Person 1   (*to Person 2*) This Jesus is not like our other teachers.

Person 2   No, he teaches with authority.

Jesus   And so, my brothers and sisters...

Man enters, screaming.

Man   Ah! Let us alone! What do you want with us, Jesus of Nazareth? Have you come to destroy us? I know who you are...the Holy One of God.

Jesus   Be silent and come out of him!

Man shakes, falls down, screams, and then stops suddenly.

Person 1   (*to Man*) Are you all right?

Man   Yes, I'm fine.

Person 2   (*to Person 1*) What does this mean?

Person 1   Here is new teaching—with authority.

Person 2   He commands even evil spirits, and they obey him.

Narrator   Jesus' reputation spread quickly all through Galilee.

Demons Sent into Swine

Themes

- evangelization
- universal salvation

Background Notes

In this colorful miracle account Jesus saves a Gentile and makes him an evangelist. The possessed man lived among tombs, the place where demons were believed to live. The evil that possessed him caused him to hurt himself. When Jesus arrived, the demons, as usual, recognized him as the Son of God. Jesus learned that their name was Legion. At that time knowing someone's name was thought to give you power over them. A Roman legion consisted of 6,000 troops. Jesus sent "Legion" into a herd of swine, which immediately rushed into the sea. The earth was no place for demons when Jesus was there.

The cured man sat at Jesus' feet like a student. Ironically, the people, seeing the man sane again, feared Jesus' power and asked him to leave. When the man begged to go with him, Jesus told him to spread the news of his healing.

For Discussion

Before the play: People in Jesus' time thought that certain illnesses were caused by demons. How does sin keep us from loving God? How does it harm us?

After the play: Why may people reject Jesus? How can we proclaim the good things God has done for us?

Activity

Invite younger learners, according to age, to carry out one of the following activities. Make eleven strips of paper about 1" x 12". In the center of each strip write the name of a sin that binds people, such as lying. On the other side write one of the following words on each strip: "If the Son makes you free, you will be free indeed" (John 8:36). Glue or staple the strips together to form a chain so that the verse can be read on the outside of the links.

Have older learners write a news article based on the Scripture passage.

Prayer

Angel of God, my faithful guardian angel, God's love has entrusted me to your care. Be at my side every day, to light and guard, to guide me in God's way. Amen.

CAST: NARRATOR, JESUS, DISCIPLES 1, 2, MAN, SWINEHERDS 1, 2, PERSONS 1, 2, 3 (+)

PROP: BROKEN CHAINS

DEMONS SENT INTO SWINE MATTHEW 8:28–34, MARK 5:1–20, LUKE 8:26–39

Narrator One day Jesus and his disciples sailed across the Lake of Galilee. They came to the land of the Gerasenes, who were not Jewish. Jesus had just set foot on the shore when a man possessed by demons came toward him. For a long time this man had lived in burial caves. He did not wear clothes, and day and night he howled and cut himself with stones. When people tried to chain him, he broke out of the chains.

Swineherds stand at the side. Jesus and Disciples 1 and 2 enter. Man runs toward Jesus, cries out, and falls at his feet.

Man (*shouting*) Jesus, Son of the Most High God, what do you want with me?

Jesus Come out of the man, you evil spirit!

Man I beg you. Don't torment me.

Jesus What is your name?

Man My name is Legion, for there are many of us. Please do not send us away from here and into the depths of the earth. Send us into the pigs.

Jesus Go.

Narrator There was a herd of about two thousand pigs nearby. To the Jewish people, pigs were the most unclean animal. The demons went out of the man and into the pigs. The whole herd then rushed down the cliff into the lake and were drowned.

Jesus, Disciples, and Man walk to the side. Man sits at Jesus' feet. Swineherds walk to front. Persons 1, 2, 3 enter and stay at a distance.

Swineherd 1 I don't believe it.

Swineherd 2 Come on. Let's go tell everyone in the field and the village.

Swineherds run to Persons 1, 2, 3.

Swineherd 1 The man from the tombs is cured.

Swineherd 2 A stranger sent the demons out of him.

Swineherd 1 They went into our pigs.

Swineherd 2 The pigs charged into the lake and were drowned.

Swineherds with Persons 1, 2, 3 return to Jesus.

Person 1 Look at the man from the tombs. He's wearing clothes.

Person 3 And he's talking calmly. Wow!

Swineherd 1 (*pointing to Jesus*) He's the one who ordered the demons out of him.

Man Yes, they went from me into the herd of pigs.

Swineherd 2 You should have seen those pigs squealing and stampeding into the water.

Person 2 (*to Person 1*) If this man has such power over demons, what will he do next? I'm scared.

Person 3 So am I.

Person 1 (*to Jesus*) Please leave.

Person 3 Yes, go to some other town.

Jesus (*to Disciples*) Let's go. Get into the boat.

Jesus and Disciples walk away. Man follows.

Man (*to Jesus*) Please, let me go with you.

Jesus No, return to your home and friends. Tell what God in his mercy has done for you.

Jesus and Disciples exit. Man returns to Persons 1, 2, 3.

Man (*to Person 1*) God did a great thing for me today. Let me tell you about it.

A Possessed, Blind, Mute Man

FOURTH SUNDAY IN ORDINARY TIME: YEAR B

Background Notes

The exorcisms of Jesus were not like those of common magicians who were thought to act with the help of demons. His exorcisms were accomplished by a simple command, sometimes combined with a touch. The point of this account was that Jesus' actions signal the presence of the reign of God. He worked not by the power of Beelzebul (Jewish name for an evil spirit), but by the power of the Spirit of God. Jesus did not perform miracles for popularity or profit, to satisfy curiosity, or even to save his own life. His miracles were usually a response to someone's misery or someone's faith.

The miracle Jesus worked for the suffering man didn't satisfy the Pharisees. When they requested a miracle, they meant one in line with their concept of a messiah: a military victory. Jesus didn't grant their request. The arguments of Jesus against the accusations of these Pharisees were logical. He won the case.

For Discussion

Before the play: What do you learn about Jesus from his miracles?

After the play: How can you help someone who can't see, hear, or speak well or who has mental problems?

Activity

Make a get-well card for a parishioner, friend, or relative that includes a promise of prayer. If possible, deliver the card personally.

Prayer

Breathe in me, O Holy Spirit,
that my thoughts may all be holy.
Act in me, O Holy Spirit,
that my work, too, may be holy.
Draw my heart, O Holy Spirit,
that I only love what is holy.
Strengthen me, O Holy Spirit,
to defend all that is holy.
Guard me, then, O Holy Spirit,
that I always may be holy. Amen.

—St. Augustine

CAST: JESUS, POSSESSED MAN, PERSONS 1, 2, 3, 4, PHARISEES 1, 2, CROWD (+)

A POSSESSED, BLIND, MUTE MAN   MATTHEW 12:22–28, LUKE 11:14–20

Jesus is with Persons 3, 4, Pharisees 1, 2, and the Crowd. Persons 1 and 2 lead the Man, staggering, to him.

Person 1   Jesus, this man is possessed by a devil.

Person 2   He can't see or talk.

Man grunts. Jesus puts his hand on the man's shoulders.

Jesus   Be healed.

Man   (*excitedly*) I see. I see again. Oh, thank you, Master.

Person 3   (*to Person 4*) Did you hear him? It's amazing.

Person 4   Incredible!

Person 3   Can this fellow be the Son of David?

Pharisee 1   This man drives out demons only by the power of Beelzebul, the ruler of the demons.

Pharisee 2   Jesus, work a miracle to show that God approves of you.

Jesus   Any country divided against itself will not last. A town or family divided against itself will fall apart. If Satan drives out Satan, he is divided against himself. How will his kingdom stand? You say that it is by Beelzebul that I drive out demons.

Pharisees   (*nodding*) Yes, yes.

Jesus   Then how do your followers drive them out? But if it is by the Spirit of God that I drive out demons, then the kingdom of God has come upon you.

Pharisees exit.

Peter's Mother-in-Law

FIFTH SUNDAY IN ORDINARY TIME: YEAR B

Background Notes

When friends interceded for Peter's mother-in-law, Jesus healed her. Homey details make this miracle story seem like an eyewitness account. On a deeper level certain features hold a message for Christians. Jesus rebuked the fever as though conquering a demon. The mother-in-law was "raised up," an expression that pointed to Jesus' resurrection. After she was restored, the woman waited on the people gathered there. An implication is that we who have been saved by Christ have a responsibility to serve.

For Discussion

Before the play: Who are some sick people you know who are in need of prayer? How did you feel when you were sick?

After the play: How can you show love and care for the sick?

Activity

Like Peter's mother-in-law we have been healed by Jesus. Plan how you can prepare a meal or part of a meal for others. You might volunteer at a soup kitchen, make a meal or dessert, and take it to someone, or have everyone participate in preparing a family meal.

Prayer

Think about this reflection:

Two seas lie in Palestine. In the north is the Sea of Galilee. Its fresh, blue waters teem with fish; trees spread their branches over it and stretch out roots to sip its waters; along its shores children play. Jesus could look across its silver surface as he taught. People build their homes near it, and birds their nests; and every kind of life is happier because it is there. The Jordan River makes this sea with sparkling water from the hills. The Jordan River flows on south into another sea. Here there is no splash of fish, no fluttering leaf, no song of birds, no children's laughter. Travelers choose another route. Dead trees coated with salt jut out of it. The air hangs heavy above it, and no creature drinks its brackish waters filled with mineral deposits. It is the lowest point on the earth's surface. What makes the difference in the seas? The Sea of Galilee receives but does not keep the Jordan. For every drop that flows into it another drop flows out. The other sea gives nothing. It is named the Dead Sea.

—adapted from Bruce Barton

CAST: NARRATOR, JESUS, JAMES, JOHN, PETER, ANDREW, MOTHER-IN-LAW, PETER'S WIFE

PROPS: LOAF OF BREAD; MAT, CARPET, OR TABLE FOR BED

PETER'S MOTHER-IN-LAW MATTHEW 8:14–15, MARK 1:29–31, LUKE 4:38–39

Mother-in-Law is in bed. Peter, Peter's Wife, and Andrew sit around her. Jesus, James, and John are some distance away.

Narrator One day Jesus went with some of his disciples to the house of Peter and Andrew.

Jesus, James, and John go to Peter's house.

Jesus Peter, Andrew. Are you home?

Peter comes to door.

Peter Come in. Come in. We're worried about my mother-in-law.

Andrew She has such a high fever.

Peter's Wife She doesn't even recognize me—her own daughter. Won't you please help her, Jesus?

Peter Yes, you can make her better if anyone can, Master.

Jesus takes the Mother-in-Law's hand.

Jesus (*to fever*) Leave the body of this woman.

Mother-in-Law sits up.

Peter's Wife Mother, are you all right?

Mother-in-Law I feel wonderful. Very rested. What are you all staring at? (*gets up*) You men look hungry. Jesus, what can I fix for you to eat? I've got some fresh bread, dates, and fish.

Jesus Anything will be fine.

Peter Thank you, Jesus.

A Leper

SIXTH SUNDAY IN ORDINARY TIME: YEAR B

Themes

- evangelization
- conversion
- faith

Background Notes

The leper's highly contagious skin disease (called Hansen's disease today) cut him off from the community. He approached Jesus with faith in his power to heal his leprosy and his loneliness. With pity for the man and anger at the cause of his suffering, Jesus answered his plea to be made clean. Stretching out his hand, a gesture of saving that recalls God's help during the Exodus, Jesus healed the leper. By touching him, Jesus made himself unclean. He then had the leper comply with the Mosaic law which required that a leper with an offering appear before a priest in order to be declared clean. Despite Jesus' orders to keep the miracle quiet, the man spread the news of his good fortune.

Especially in Mark's gospel Jesus asked those who experienced a miracle to keep it a secret. It could be that he did this to discourage people from acclaiming him as the Messiah. He was not the kind they expected: a political savior who would overthrow Rome and establish Israel as a world power. Another explanation why Jesus kept his miracles quiet was he wanted to teach us that in his value system miracles are not as important as loving others, living justly, and converting one's heart.

For Discussion

Before the play: When have you asked Jesus to heal something in your life?

After the play: Who are the people in our communities who need help and how can you reach them?

Activity

On large sheets of paper draw or paste pictures to represent groups that are on the edges of society today. Punch holes in the side of the pages and tie them together with yarn to form a booklet. Use the booklet to pray for these people. Alternate activity: Decide on a way you will reach out to a marginalized person or group.

Prayer

ACT OF FAITH

O my God, I firmly believe that you are one God in three divine persons: Father, Son, and Holy Spirit; I believe that your divine Son became man and died for our sins, and that he will come to judge the living and the dead. I believe these and all the truths which the Holy Catholic Church teaches, because you revealed them, who can neither deceive nor be deceived.

CAST: NARRATOR, JESUS, LEPER, PERSONS 1, 2

A LEPER MATTHEW 8:1–4, MARK 2:40–45, LUKE 5:12–15

Narrator As Jesus went through Galilee, a man covered with leprosy, a terrible skin disease, came to him. The man longed to be made clean so he could come back into contact with other people.

Jesus walks slowly. Leper hobbles up to him and kneels.

Leper Lord, if you choose, you can make me clean.

Jesus (*stretching out his hand and touching him*) Of course I want to. Be made clean.

Leper (*staring at his hands*) I'm cured. I'm clean. Oh, thank you, thank you!

Jesus See that you say nothing to anyone about this. Go show yourself to the priest and let him examine you. Then offer for your cure the sacrifice that Moses ordered. This will prove to everyone that you are cured.

Leper rises and walks toward Persons 1, 2. Jesus walks in the opposite direction.

Leper You won't believe what just happened to me. I was a leper, but a man named Jesus healed me. He touched me and said, "Be made clean," and I was.

Person 1 Where is he?

Person 2 I'd like to meet this man.

Leper (*gestures toward Jesus*) Back there.

Persons 1, 2 run after Jesus.

Narrator So large crowds continued to follow Jesus.

The **Paralytic**

SEVENTH SUNDAY IN ORDINARY TIME: YEAR B

Background Notes

In Jesus, God was with his people even more visibly than God had been with their ancestors. God's goodness was manifest in Jesus' compassionate and loving deeds. Jesus responded to the plight of the paralytic because of his faith and the faith of his friends. In their desire to reach Jesus, they came in through the roof. The entrance was easily made because the roof was just clay and straw.

In curing the man the first step Jesus took was to forgive his sins. The paralytic's act of faith implied repentance. Once the root of all evil had been destroyed, Jesus dealt with one of its side effects—illness. The story presents the healing as proof that Jesus had divine power and authority to forgive sins. It illustrates that his role as Savior went beyond the physical.

For Discussion

Before the play: Where do you find the effects of sin in the world?

After the play: How can friends bring one another closer to Jesus? How can you receive Jesus' forgiveness today? What are some reasons you have to praise and thank God for his goodness?

Activity

Involve young learners in this activity. Make a mat by pasting burlap, felt, or other material onto popsicle sticks or tongue depressors. Let it remind you to help your friends by bringing them to Jesus.

Invite older learners to prepare a reconciliation service.

Prayer

Pray the Confiteor from the Mass or another Act of Contrition.

CAST: NARRATOR, JESUS, PARALYZED MAN,
         FRIENDS 1, 2, 3, 4,
         TEACHERS OF THE LAW 1, 2, PERSONS 1, 2

PROPS: MAT OR CARPETING

THE PARALYTIC MATTHEW 9:1–8, MARK 2:1–12, LUKE 5:17–26

Jesus, Teachers, and Persons sit on the floor. Jesus teaches quietly. At a distance the Paralyzed Man is on a mat with Friends around him.

Narrator	One day Jesus was teaching in a house in Capernaum. A paralyzed man was brought to the house. His friends hoped Jesus would cure him.
Friend 1	Look at all the people.
Friend 2	They're even packed together outside in front of the door.
Friend 3	We'll never get in to see Jesus.
Friend 4	We've carried our friend this far. (*nodding to Paralyzed Man*) We can't give up now.
Friend 1	You're right. We must find a way. Think hard.
Friend 2	I've got it. Let's climb up on the roof and break through right above where Jesus is.
Friend 3	Yes, then we can lower our friend down to Jesus.
Friend 4	Everyone will move out of the way for him then. Good thinking.

While the Narrator speaks, Paralyzed Man moves so that his mat is in front of Jesus. Friends step back.

Narrator	So the men made a hole in the flat roof and carefully lowered the Paralyzed Man on his mat. Jesus was glad to see how much faith the men had.
Jesus	(*looking at Paralyzed Man*) Take heart, son. Your sins are forgiven.
Teacher 1	(*aside*) How dare he talk like that? This is blasphemy!
Teacher 2	(*aside*) Who can forgive sins but God alone?
Jesus	(*to Teachers*) Why do you think evil in your heart? Which is easier to say to the paralytic, "Your sins are forgiven," or to say, "Stand up, pick up your mat and walk"? To show that I have authority on earth to forgive sins...(*to Paralyzed Man*) I say to you, stand up, pick up your mat, and go to your home.
Man	(*picking up mat*) Blessed be God! (*exits*)
Person 1	We have never seen anything like this!
Person 2	How kind and merciful God is to give authority like this to a man!

The Man with a Withered Hand

Ninth Sunday in Ordinary Time: Year B

Themes

- opposition to Jesus
- Sabbath cures
- value of life

Background Notes

Jesus taught through his miracles. Those he worked on the Sabbath illustrated his lesson that the Sabbath was for the sake of people and not vice versa. This lesson was directed to the Pharisees, those zealous laymen who stressed the keeping of the law and its multiple prescriptions more than love of neighbor.

Jesus' healing of the man with the withered hand sparked another confrontation with some Pharisees about the Sabbath. Jesus pointed out that if a person could help a sheep on a Sabbath, certainly it would be lawful to help a human being. Unwilling to admit that good could be performed on the Sabbath, the Pharisees were silent and incurred Jesus' anger for their hard hearts. As a result of Jesus' controversial words and actions, the Pharisees began to plot how to put him to death.

For Discussion

Before the play: What parts of your life are "withered" and in need of Jesus' healing?

After the play: What good acts could you do to make Sunday holy?

Activity

Plan a calendar of fun activities you can do with your family on Sunday for the coming month.

Prayer

Lord, we stretch out our hands to you.
(stretch out hands)
Make them strong in doing good.
Make them gentle in dealing with others.
Keep them from doing anything wrong.
We lift our hands in prayer and praise.
(raise hands)
We offer you our hands and everything
we do.
With gratitude we receive your grace
and your love. (drop open hands to sides)

CAST: Narrator, Jesus, Man, Pharisees 1, 2, 3, Crowd (+)

The Man with a Withered Hand
Matthew 12:9–14, Mark 3:1–6, Luke 6:6–11

Jesus stands before a seated Crowd that includes the Man and the Pharisees. He mimes teaching them.

Narrator   One Sabbath Jesus went to a synagogue and taught. A man with a withered hand was in the crowd.

Pharisee 1   (*to Pharisee 2*) Watch him closely. If he heals on the Sabbath, he is breaking the Law.

Pharisee 2   Right.

Jesus points to Man.

Jesus   Come up and stand here.

Man goes to Jesus.

Jesus   (*to Crowd*) I ask you, what does our Law allow us to do on the Sabbath? To help or to harm? To save a man's life or to kill? Suppose one of you had only one sheep and it falls into a pit on the Sabbath? Will you not take hold of it and lift it out? How much more valuable is a human being than a sheep! So, it is lawful to help someone on the Sabbath.

Jesus looks around at the Crowd with anger and sadness.

Jesus   (*to Man*) Stretch out your hand.

Man stretches out hand.

Man   Why, it's as good as the other one. Thank you, Master.

Crowd oohs and ahs. Man flexes hand and shows it to them. Pharisees 1, 2, 3 leave Crowd and meet at a distance.

Pharisee 1   We have to kill that man Jesus.

Pharisee 2   Yes, but how?

Pharisee 3   I have an idea....

The Centurion's Servant

NINTH SUNDAY IN ORDINARY TIME: YEAR C

Themes

- praise of faith
- universal salvation

Background Notes

The focus of this miracle is the Gentile's faith, which results in Jesus curing someone at a distance. The centurion's young slave, whom he loved, was gravely ill. Wishing to spare Jesus the inconvenience and ritual uncleanness that a visit would cause, the Gentile declared his belief that Jesus had only to speak to perform a miracle. Jesus praised the man and predicted that people from East and West would partake in the feast of the kingdom. The servant was restored to perfect health. The faith-filled words of the centurion are incorporated into our eucharistic liturgy before communion.

In Jesus Christ, God breaks through all barriers. Who would have imagined that almighty God would become a human infant, that God would die for his creatures, or that God would remain with us in the forms of bread and wine? Yet, through Jesus, God does these wonder-full things.

For Discussion

Before the play: What are some small miracles in your life? Do you have faith that Jesus can help you?

After the play: What do you think the feast of heaven will be like?

Activity

On a rock with a flat bottom use permanent marker to write about God as our healer. Add decorations if you wish. Trace the rock on felt and then cut out and glue the felt to the bottom. Possible phrases:

Jesus saves. Jesus heals. Jesus is life.

You show me the path of life (Psalm 16:11).

I love you, O Lord, my strength (Psalm 18:1).

You are the God of my salvation (Psalm 25:5).

O guard my life and deliver me (Psalm 25:20).

You have healed me (Psalm 30:2).

Save me in your steadfast love (Psalm 31:16).

With you is the fountain of life (Psalm 36:9).

You are my help and my deliverer (Psalm 40:17).

He alone is my rock and my salvation (Psalm 62:2).

Your right hand upholds me (Psalm 63:8).

You have delivered my soul from death (Psalm 116:8).

Prayer

Sing a song of praise to our saving God. This might be a responsorial psalm that you know from the Sunday liturgy.

CAST: NARRATOR, JESUS, CENTURION, CROWD (+), JEWISH ELDER, MESSENGER

THE CENTURION'S SERVANT   MATTHEW 8:5–13, LUKE 7:1–10

Jesus walks with Crowd and Jewish Elder.

Narrator One day when Jesus entered Capernaum, a Roman officer came to him. The officer was a centurion, which meant that he commanded about a hundred soldiers. Since he was not Jewish, entering his house would make Jesus unclean by Jewish law.

Centurion enters and goes to Jesus.

Centurion Sir, my servant boy, who is very dear to me, is sick. He is lying at home, paralyzed and in great pain.

Jewish Elder (*to Jesus*) He is worthy of having you do this for him. He loves our people. It is he who built the synagogue for us.

Jesus (*to Centurion*) I will come and cure him.

Centurion Lord, do not trouble yourself. I am not worthy to have you come in my home. But only say the word and my servant will be healed. I am under authority myself, with soldiers under me. I say to one, "Go," and he goes. I say to another, "Come," and he comes. If I order my servant, "Do this," he does it.

Jesus (*to Crowd*) Truly I tell you, I have not found such faith among the people of Israel. Many will come from the east and the west and sit down with Abraham, Isaac, and Jacob at the feast in the kingdom of heaven. But those who should be in the kingdom will be turned out into the dark where they will cry and grind their teeth. (to Centurion) Go home. Let this be done for you because you have believed.

Centurion Thank you, sir.

Jesus and Crowd exit. Centurion walks on. Messenger enters and runs toward him.

Messenger Sir, sir. Your servant boy is cured. He's walking around and talking as if nothing has happened.

Centurion Thank God!

The Canaanite Woman

TWENTIETH SUNDAY IN ORDINARY TIME: YEAR A

Background Notes

The theme of universal salvation predominates in this story. Jesus worked a miracle for the benefit of a Gentile woman. Moreover, she was identified as one of the Canaanites, whom the Jews at that time considered wicked pagans. As with other cures for Gentiles, Jesus worked this one at a distance.

Jesus' first response to the woman's plea seemed brusque and even rude. Commentators propose that Jesus might have been quoting a proverb. The children were the Jewish people, while the Gentiles were the dogs. The Jews sometimes referred to Gentiles as dogs. Some scholars think that the word Jesus used for dog was a gentler term such as pup. The woman's quick retort was witty. Because of it and because of her faith, Jesus extended his ministry to the Gentiles. Both Jews and Gentiles are fed in the Father's house. The Church of Jesus is Catholic—for all.

For Discussion

Before the play: Do you believe God answers our prayers? Why?

After the play: How can you express gratitude to God for our salvation? Who are people you might bring to Jesus?

Activity

Ask younger learners to carry out this activity. Fold a piece of construction paper in half. Place your hand alongside the fold and trace it. Cut out the picture of your hand with the paper folded, careful not to cut along the fold, so that you have a pair of hands that opens. Inside these praying hands list things you want to ask Jesus to do. These can be world intentions or personal intentions.

Older learners might videotape the playlet, then discuss the figures in the story.

Prayer

Jesus, you said, "Ask and you shall receive, seek and you will find, knock and the door will be opened to you." Today we ask you to hear our prayers for things that we need.

(State petitions and conclude each with "Lord, hear our prayer.")

CAST: NARRATOR, JESUS, DISCIPLES 1, 2, WOMAN, DAUGHTER

PROP: MAT OR CARPETING FOR BED

THE CANAANITE WOMAN   MATTHEW 15:21–28, MARK 7:24–30

In the far background Daughter is running about wildly. Jesus and Disciples walk along.

Narrator   One day Jesus was walking with his disciples near non-Jewish cities. A woman came to him who was a Canaanite, a Gentile who worshiped pagan gods.

Woman comes toward Jesus and Disciples.

Woman   (*crying out*) Lord, Son of David!

Jesus walks on.

Woman   Have mercy on me, Lord, Son of David. My daughter is tormented by a demon and is terribly sick.

Jesus walks on.

Woman   (*shouting*) Have mercy, sir.

Disciple 1   (*to Jesus*) Jesus, please give her what she wants and send her away.

Disciple 2   She's following us and making all this noise!

Jesus   (*turning to Woman*) I was sent only to the lost sheep of the people of Israel.

Woman catches up and falls at his feet.

Woman   Lord, help me.

Jesus   It isn't right to take the children's food and throw it to the pups.

Woman   Yes, sir, yet even the dogs eat the crumbs that fall from their master's table.

Jesus   Woman, great is your faith! Let it be done for you as you wish. The demon has left your daughter.

Daughter lies calmly on bed. Woman rises and walks toward Daughter. Jesus and Disciples exit.

Woman   (*seeing Daughter*) She's well. (*raises her arms*) Thanks be to God!

Cure of a Man Who Was Deaf and Mute

TWENTY-THIRD SUNDAY IN ORDINARY TIME: YEAR B

Background Notes

Jesus effected the healing of the deaf mute through gestures and a strange word, rituals that were characteristic of contemporary healers including pagan magicians. In those days saliva was believed to have medicinal power. Jesus' intimacy with God was symbolized by his looking up to heaven.

The messianic secret (Jesus asking people not to reveal his identity) that distinguishes Mark's gospel occurs twice in this miracle account. Not only did Jesus call the man apart from the crowd to cure him, but after the miracle he told the crowd not to speak of it.

An optional "ephphatha" rite, prayer over ears and mouth, is part of our baptism ceremony. The priest or deacon prays that the candidate be open to God's word and proclaim the faith.

For Discussion

Before the play: What rituals and traditions do you practice in your own home? How do they help you grow in faith?

After the play: When do you hear God's word? How do you show that you are open to God's word?

Activity

Learn to sign a religious song, such as "O, How I Love Jesus," or make up your own gestures or sign language for it.

Prayer

My Father, I give myself to you. Do with me as you will.
Whatever you ask me to do, I thank you.
I am prepared for anything, I accept everything.
I ask for nothing more, dear God.
I place myself in your hands.
I give myself to you, my God, with all the love of my heart because I love you.

—adapted from Charles de Foucauld

CAST: NARRATOR, JESUS, DEAF MUTE, PERSONS 1, 2, 3, 4, CROWD (+)

CURE OF A MAN WHO WAS DEAF AND MUTE MARK 7:31-37

Narrator As Jesus entered the district of the Ten Cities, some people brought to him a deaf man with a serious speech defect.

Persons 1, 2, 3 bring Deaf Mute to Jesus.

Person 1 He can't hear at all.

Person 2 And he can hardly speak.

Person 3 Please lay your hands on him and cure him.

Jesus (*to Deaf Mute*) Come with me.

Jesus takes Deaf Mute away from Crowd. Deaf Mute's back is to the audience. Jesus mimes the actions while the Narrator describes them.

Narrator Jesus put his fingers into the man's ears. Then he spat and touched the man's tongue.

Jesus looks up to heaven and sighs.

Jesus Ephphatha. Be opened.

Deaf Mute I heard you speak!

Person 1 Listen. He spoke plainly!

Deaf Mute I can hear them, too.

Jesus (*to all*) Do not tell anyone what has happened here.

Jesus exits. Person 4 enters. Persons 1, 2, 3 and Deaf Mute run to meet Person 4.

Person 1 Jesus cured this man who was deaf.

Person 2 He also made him speak clearly.

Person 3 He has done all things well! He makes the deaf hear and the mute speak.

Person 4 Let's go tell our friends and relatives.

All exit.

A Boy with **Epilepsy**

Background Notes

This miracle illustrates Jesus' messianic power. Jesus, not the apostles, was strong enough to drive out the demon that possessed the boy. The detailed symptoms emphasize the seriousness of the disease and therefore the greatness of the miracle.

Faith is a key theme in the story. Jesus encouraged the father to believe. When Jesus stated that anything is possible with faith, the father prayed for stronger faith. At the end Jesus explained the unlimited power of faith. The boy's exorcism symbolized the resurrection, the sign of Jesus' complete triumph over Satan.

Miracles are in keeping with the extraordinary mission of Jesus. He proclaimed a kingdom that is here, but not yet. He overturned accepted social and religious codes. He invited people to go beyond what was normal to a new moral system, new dreams, and new hopes. In all spheres he exploded the parameters of the present reality. Little wonder then that for Jesus the impossible became possible.

For Discussion

Before the play: Who in your family and among your friends have been examples of faith?

After the play: What means do you use to strengthen your faith?

Activity

Write a personal creed, stating what you believe about Jesus and his teachings. Print it on good paper and glue the paper to a colored backing. You might use calligraphy (stylized lettering) when you print your creed.

Prayer

Response: *Lord, I believe; help my unbelief.*

When life is hard to understand...
When suffering comes to me...
When people I love suffer...
When I am in trouble...
When I don't know what to do...
When trials or tragedies happen...
When the innocent suffer...
When I am discouraged...
When my faith is tested...

CAST: JESUS, FATHER, BOY, DISCIPLES 1, 2, 3, 4, CROWD (+), PERSON

A Boy with Epilepsy Matthew 17:14–20, Mark 9:14–29, Luke 9:37–43

Jesus and Disciples 1, 2, 3 join Crowd, who are talking excitedly to Disciple 4.

Jesus (*to Disciple 4*) What are you arguing about with them?

Father (*kneeling at Jesus' feet*) Lord, have pity on my son—my only child. I brought him to you because he has an evil spirit that makes him unable to speak. The spirit throws him to the ground and he foams at the mouth, grinds his teeth, and becomes rigid. I asked your disciples to cast it out, but they couldn't.

Jesus You faithless generation, how much longer must I be among you? How much longer must I put up with you? Bring the boy to me.

Father brings Boy. Boy falls to the ground.

Jesus How long has this been happening to him?

Father From childhood. The demon has often cast him into the fire and into the water, to destroy him. If you are able to do anything, have pity on us and help us.

Jesus If you are able? All things can be done for the one who believes.

Father (*crying out*) I believe! Help my unbelief!

Jesus (*to Boy*) You, the spirit that keeps this boy from speaking and hearing, I command you! Come out of him and never enter him again!

Boy screams and then lies still.

Crowd (*to one another*) He is dead.

Jesus takes Boy by the hand and helps him up. He puts Boy's hand into the Father's hand. Crowd gasps.

Father Son. My son. You're going to be all right.

Person How great and mighty is our God!

Crowd closes in around Father and Boy. Jesus and Disciples walk away.

Disciple 1 Why couldn't we cast out this evil spirit?

Jesus Because you do not have enough faith. If you have faith the size of a mustard seed, you will say to this mountain, "Move from here to there," and it will move. Nothing will be impossible for you.

The **Infirm Woman**

Background Notes

In this miracle account Jesus takes the initiative. The woman did not request a cure, nor did she demonstrate faith. Yet Jesus called her to him to be cured. This sign could be considered an essential part of his teaching in the synagogue. The chief of the synagogue criticized Jesus indirectly by telling the people not to come to be cured on the Sabbath. But Jesus retorted with a new, more humane teaching. Of course, good may be done on the Sabbath. God's laws are more reasonable than human laws.

The burst of miracles described in the gospels cannot just be dismissed. Oral tradition and literary devices might have modified the original happenings. The Christians who composed the gospels lived on the other side of Easter. As a result, their accounts of the miracles are influenced by their new insights into Jesus. According to William Barclay, the stories are not tall but deep.

For Discussion

Before the play: How do you keep Sunday holy?

After the play: How can you imitate Jesus' concern for the unfortunate and the outcast? What other teachings of Jesus stress love of neighbor?

Activity

Do the following activity with young learners. Draw Jesus on one side of a sheet of paper. On another sheet of paper draw a longwaisted woman dressed in the veil and robes of Jesus' time. Cut her out and cut her in two parts at the waist. Place the top half so that it overlaps the bottom and insert a brass brad through it. Then attach the brad to the paper next to Jesus. The woman will be able to bend over, then stand straight.

Older learners might research who acted as physicians during that time and how they practiced their skills.

Prayer

Jesus, Divine Physician, heal those who suffer from bodily or mental illness. Cure persons who are blind, the deaf, paralyzed, those who have had injuries and accidents, those who have diseases, and those who have chronic illnesses. Give persons who suffer the patience and courage to endure their sickness, accept it in faith, and offer their pain and discomfort for the good of others. Amen.

CAST: NARRATOR, JESUS, WOMAN, CROWD (+), PERSONS 1, 2, CHIEF OF SYNAGOGUE, OPPONENTS (+)

PROP: CANE FOR WOMAN

THE INFIRM WOMAN Luke 13:10–17

Jesus is standing and teaching Crowd. Woman is in Crowd. Chief of Synagogue and Opponents watch.

Narrator One Sabbath Jesus was teaching in the synagogue. A woman was there who for eighteen years had been possessed by a spirit that crippled her. She was bent over and couldn't stand up straight.

Jesus notices Woman.

Jesus Come to me.

Woman hobbles over to Jesus.

Jesus Woman, you are free of your infirmity.

Jesus lays his hands on her shoulders. Immediately she stands up straight.

Woman Thanks be to God. He's cured me in his great mercy.

Chief (*to Crowd*) There are six days on which work ought to be done. Come on those days to be cured, not on the Sabbath day.

Jesus You hypocrites! Does not each of you on the Sabbath untie his ox or his donkey and lead it out of the stall to give it water? Satan has kept this daughter of Abraham bound for eighteen long years. Shouldn't she be set free on the Sabbath day?

Chief and Opponents shake heads, shrug shoulders, and move back.

Person 1 Isn't it marvelous what Jesus does?

Person 2 He brings happiness wherever he goes.

The Man **with Dropsy**

Background Notes

Today dropsy is called edema. It is a swelling of the body resulting from an accumulation of fluid. This condition causes poor circulation and makes moving painful.

Even in the social setting of a banquet, some Pharisees watched Jesus. Aware of their scrutiny, Jesus asked outright if curing on a Sabbath was lawful. When the Pharisees did not respond, Jesus healed a man with dropsy. Jesus appealed to the reason of these Pharisees by asking if they would rescue a son or an ox from a pit on the Sabbath. To this, too, they were silent. They refused to admit that Jesus was right.

For Discussion

Before the play: What is it like to be in pain? What is it like to be cured?

After the play: Give some examples of someone having courage to do what is right even if it means being different.

Activity

Compose a prayer for the sick and for their caregivers.

Prayer

Lord of Life, help us respect all life, nurture it, protect it, and care for it. While we treasure our own lives, we pray for the grace to stand up for the rights of others to live. May we work to eliminate situations where life is threatened, diminished, or extinguished. You said you came to give life and give it abundantly. May we take up your mission that life may flourish.

CAST: **NARRATOR, JESUS, PHARISEES 1, 2, GUESTS 1, 2 (+), MAN**

THE MAN WITH DROPSY LUKE 14:1–6

Narrator One Sabbath day Jesus went to eat at the house of one of the leading Pharisees. A man whose arms and legs were swollen with dropsy was also there.

Pharisees, Guests, and Man are gathered together. Jesus enters.

Pharisee 1 Jesus, welcome. Please come in.

Jesus Thank you.

Jesus stands opposite Man.

Pharisee 1 (*to Pharisee 2*) Watch him closely.

Pharisee 2 I intend to.

Jesus (*to Pharisee 1, 2*) Is it lawful to cure people on the Sabbath or not?

Silence

Jesus (*taking Man by the shoulders*) Be healed.

Man (*looking at his hands*) I'm cured. I'm cured. Thank you.

Jesus Go on your way.

Man exits happily.

Jesus (*to Pharisees*) If one of you had a child or an ox that fell into a well, wouldn't you immediately pull him out on a Sabbath day?

Silence

Narrator The Pharisees were unable to answer. They knew Jesus was right. Human life should be protected by laws, not hindered by them.

The Ten Lepers

TWENTY-EIGHTH SUNDAY IN ORDINARY TIME: YEAR C

Themes
■ gratitude
■ prejudice

Background Notes

The miracle focuses on the importance of gratitude to God. The faith of the lepers is praiseworthy. They trusted in Jesus to deliver them from their dread disease, which isolated them and made them outcasts. He sent them to have their cure verified by the priests. On the way, when the lepers realized they were clean, only one decided to return and thank Jesus for his kindness. The others were either too caught up in their joy to think of returning or they did not wish to spend the time and energy it would take to return.

The hero of the story, the leper who gave thanks, was a Samaritan, a traditional enemy of the Jewish people. Samaritans were regarded as impure because they had intermarried, did not accept all of Hebrew Scriptures, and worshiped in their own temple. Jesus' attention to lepers and Samaritans illustrated his acceptance of all people.

For Discussion

Before the play: What are some reasons you have to be thankful to God?

After the play: How do you show your gratitude to God and others in concrete ways?

Activity

Ask younger learners to carry out this activity. Make a grace mat for meals. Decorate a sheet of heavy paper by dipping a toothbrush in paint, holding it face down over the paper, and rubbing a stick over it or by blowing bubbles over the paper using bubble liquid with food coloring added to it. When your mat is dry, print "Thank you, God" on it.

Invite older learners to celebrate their unique and cultural differences in a practical way.

Prayer

Hail! O Christ, the Word and Wisdom and Power of God. What can we give you in return for all these good gifts of yours? Everything is yours. You ask nothing from us except our love. We are grateful for your unlimited goodness. Thanks be to you who gave us life and granted us the grace of a happy life here and in eternity.

—adapted from St. John of Damascus

CAST: NARRATOR, JESUS, LEPERS 1 TO 9, SAMARITAN LEPER

PROP: CANE

THE TEN LEPERS LUKE 17:11–19

Lepers stand at one side of room. Jesus at the other.

Narrator Leprosy is a terrible disease that is easily spread. Lepers, people with leprosy, lived together outside of town. They were not allowed to come into contact with others. Lepers who thought they were cured went to the priests. If the priests declared that they were perfectly healed, then they could return home. One day Jesus was on his way to Jerusalem. (*Jesus walks toward Lepers*) As he entered a village, ten lepers approached.

Leper 1 There he is. I see him. Come on.

Lepers go forward a little and call from a distance.

Lepers 2, 3 Jesus!

Lepers 4, 5 Master!

Lepers 6, 7, 8, 9 Have mercy on us!

Jesus Go to the priests and let them examine you.

Lepers Yes, Master.

Lepers turn back. Jesus walks on.

Leper 6 Say, my back doesn't hurt anymore.

Leper 7 And my legs are straight again. (*tosses cane aside*)

Leper 8 Look at my hands. The skin is like new.

Leper 9 (*to Samaritan Leper*) Your face is as fresh and clear as a young man's.

Ten Lepers We're healed! We're healed!

Lepers move on quickly.

Samaritan Leper Jesus cured us. (*turns from group and walks back toward Jesus*) Praise God! Blessed be the Lord who healed me. God is my strength and my salvation. (*falls at Jesus' feet*) Thank you, Jesus, for making me whole again.

Jesus You're welcome. But weren't ten made clean? Where are the other nine? Has only the foreigner returned to thank God? Get up and go on your way. (*helps Samaritan Leper up*) Your faith has made you well.

Samaritan Leper follows the other Lepers.

Narrator The man who came back to thank God was a Samaritan, not a Jewish person. Jesus invites all people into the kingdom of his Father.

Blind Bartimaeus

THIRTIETH SUNDAY IN ORDINARY TIME: YEAR B

Themes
- praise of faith
- perseverance in prayer
- courage

Background Notes

This last miracle story before Jesus goes to Jerusalem is unique for three reasons: the beggar is named, Jesus is acclaimed by a messianic title, and the beggar becomes a disciple. Ironically the blind man had the spiritual insight to see Jesus for who he was. In response to the man's faith, Jesus had pity on him and healed him. For the beggar it was a case of love at first sight. Having been gifted with perfect vision, Bartimaeus then followed Jesus as a disciple. Although his name means "son of fear," Bartimaeus showed courage.

The healing of Bartimaeus was another sign heralding the coming of God's kingdom. When John the Baptizer had sent his disciples to ask Jesus, "Are you the one who is to come, or are we to wait for another?" Jesus replied, "Go and tell John what you have seen and heard: the blind receive their sight, the lame walk, the lepers are cleansed, the deaf hear, the dead are raised, the poor have good news brought to them" (Luke 7:20–22).

Matthew's gospel has two versions of this story, and in both he represents the blind man as two men, something he does in other stories.

For Discussion

Before the play: How is faith a matter of spiritual vision?

After the play: How are courage and risk involved in going to Jesus?

Activity

Write a letter to Jesus answering his question, "What do you want me to do for you?"

Prayer

Invite the children to close their eyes and enter into this prayer of the imagination:

Imagine you are Bartimaeus sitting at the side of the road with your eyes closed, hoping someone will put a coin in your cup. You hear a crowd coming and ask what's happening. When they tell you that Jesus is passing, your heart leaps. You know he has cured many people. You don't know exactly where he is, but you shout for him to have mercy on you. People tell you to be quiet. You shout even louder. Now people say to you, "Get up. He's calling you." You throw off your cloak so that nothing holds you back. You jump up and feel hands helping you stagger to Jesus. You hear a voice asking, "What do you want me to do for you?" You say, "Teacher, I want to see." The voice says, "Go. Your faith has made you well." Suddenly you see the face of Jesus looking lovingly at you. You see the crowd around you, the trees, the blue sky. You are overwhelmed with joy and gratitude. Forgetting your cloak, you join the crowd following Jesus down the road.

Think now if there's anything keeping you from Jesus. Is it blindness, other people, things you own? Ask for the grace to run to Jesus and never leave him.

CAST: NARRATOR, JESUS, CROWD (+), BARTIMAEUS, BYSTANDERS 1, 2, 3

PROP: CLOAK (OR JACKET)

BLIND BARTIMAEUS   Matthew 9:27–31, 20:29–34, Mark 10:46–52, Luke 18:35–43

Bartimaeus is seated. Bystanders 1, 2, 3 are around him.

Narrator   As Jesus and his disciples left Jericho, a large crowd followed them. Bartimaeus, a blind beggar, was sitting at the side of the road.

Jesus and Crowd enter and walk toward Bartimaeus and Bystanders 1, 2, 3.

Bartimaeus   (*to Bystanders*) Alms. Alms for the poor. I hear a great crowd coming. What's going on?

Bystander 1   Jesus of Nazareth is passing by.

Bartimaeus   (*shouting*) Jesus! Son of David! Have mercy on me!

Bystander 1   Be quiet.

Bystander 2   Don't make such a scene!

Bystander 3   You're embarrassing us.

Bartimaeus   (*more loudly*) Son of David, have mercy on me!

Jesus   (*to Bystanders*) Bring him here.

Bystander 1   (*to Bartimaeus*) Don't be afraid.

Bystander 2   Take heart. Get up. He's calling for you.

Bartimaeus throws off cloak, jumps up, and walks blindly toward Jesus.

Jesus   What do you want me to do for you?

Bartimaeus   Lord, let me see again.

Jesus   Receive your sight. Go your way. Your faith has made you well.

Bartimaeus   (*excitedly*) I can see you! I can see! Praise God!

Crowd cheers. Jesus, Crowd, and Bartimaeus move on together.

The Nobleman's Son

Themes

- healing resulting from faith
- love for family

Background Notes

The royal official, who probably served Herod, apparently knew of Jesus' power to heal. When his son was very sick, he sought out Jesus and implored him to come cure him. Jesus warned against a faith based on miracles, but then granted the man's request. The correspondence in time between Jesus' assurance that the boy would live and the boy's actual recovery was proof of the miracle. The sign led to faith for the man and his whole house.

For Discussion

Before the play: Why do you believe in Jesus?

After the play: What part of this gospel passage strikes you most?

Activity

Ask younger learners to draw their own idea of what the gospel scene would look like.

Challenge older learners to find out about the sacrament of the anointing of the sick. They might read about it, find out about it on the Internet, or talk to someone who has experienced it.

Prayer

A Prayer of Trust

*For though the fig tree blossom not
nor fruit be on the vines,
Though the yield of the olive fail
and the terraces produce no nourishment,
Though the flocks disappear from the
fold
and there be no herd in the stalls,
Yet will I rejoice in the Lord
and exult in my saving God.
God, my Lord, is my strength;
he makes my feet swift as those of hinds
and enables me to go upon the heights.*

—Habakkuk 3:17–19

CAST: NARRATOR, JESUS, NOBLEMAN, SERVANTS 1, 2

THE NOBLEMAN'S SON JOHN 4:46–54

Narrator When Jesus was in Cana, a royal official in Capernaum had a son who was sick. On hearing that Jesus was nearby, the man went to him for help.

Nobleman walks up to Jesus.

Nobleman Please, Jesus, I beg you come down to Capernaum and cure my son. He is near death.

Jesus Unless you people see signs and wonders, you will not believe.

Nobleman Sir, come down before my little boy dies.

Jesus Return home. Your son will live.

Nobleman walks away. Jesus exits.

Narrator The next day as the nobleman was on his way home, his servants met him.

Servants enter.

Servant 1 Master, master!

Servant 2 Your boy is going to live.

Nobleman What time did he begin to recover?

Servant 1 Yesterday about one in the afternoon the fever left him.

Nobleman That's the very hour Jesus told me he would live.

The Nobleman and Servants exit excitedly.

Narrator The nobleman and his whole household became believers.

Cure at the Pool of Bethesda

Twenty-Second Sunday in Ordinary Time: Year B

Themes

- Sabbath cures
- sin
- perseverance in prayer
- mercy

Background Notes

Evidently the pool in this miracle was fed by an underground spring with curative powers. John gives it the Hebrew name, Bethesda, which means "house of mercy." Without benefit of the water, but merely by the force of his word, Jesus healed a man who had been paralyzed for thirty-eight years.

A specific law forbade carrying a bed on the Sabbath. When the man obeyed Jesus, his healer, and carried his mat away, he was rebuked by Pharisees. This led to further controversy between Jesus and some Pharisees.

When Jesus warned the man not to sin lest something worse befall him, he was not implying that the man's disease was the result of his sin. Rather, he was referring to the eternal consequences of wrong choices.

For Discussion

Before the play: What are some things you couldn't do if you were paralyzed?

After the play: How does the Church exercise the gift of healing today?

Activity

Invite young learners to make simple puppets to act out the gospels.

Older learners can design a baptismal font, and decorate it with symbols of the life Jesus brings. They might draw one or make it out of clay.

Prayer

*God, grant me the serenity
to accept the things I cannot change;
courage to change the things I can;
and wisdom to know the difference.*

—attributed to Reinhold Niebuhr

CAST: Narrator, Jesus, Man, Pharisees 1, 2, Sick People (+), Crowd (+)

PROPS: Mats for the sick

CURE AT THE POOL AT BETHESDA John 5:1–18

Man and Sick People are on mats. Crowd is nearby.

Narrator One day Jesus went up to Jerusalem for a Jewish feast. By the Sheep Gate was a pool called Bethesda. It had five porches crowded with the blind, the lame, and the paralyzed. They were waiting there for the movement of the water, for after the water moved, the first person to go into it was cured. One man lying there had been sick for thirty-eight years. Jesus knew this.

Jesus enters and goes to Man.

Jesus Do you want to be made well?

Man Sir, I have no one to put me into the pool when the water is stirred up. While I am making my way, someone else steps down ahead of me.

Jesus Stand up, take your mat, and walk.

Man stands, picks up mat, and walks. Jesus disappears into Crowd. Pharisees 1, 2 enter and stop Man.

Pharisee 1 It is the Sabbath.

Pharisee 2 It is not lawful for you to carry your mat on the Sabbath.

Man But the man who made me well said to me, "Take up your mat and walk."

Pharisee 1 Who is the man who told you to take it up and walk?

Man I have no idea. I don't see him now in this crowd.

Man moves on and stands alone. Pharisees stand some distance away.

Narrator Later, Jesus found the man in the Temple.

Jesus goes to Man.

Jesus See, you have been made well! Do not sin any more, so that nothing worse happens to you.

Man Yes, sir. Thank you, sir. What is your name?

Jesus I am Jesus. (*exits*)

Man goes to Pharisees.

Man The one who made me well is Jesus.

Pharisee 2 Jesus again. We might have known.

The Man Born Blind

FOURTH SUNDAY OF LENT: YEAR A

Themes

- healings from faith
- opposition to Jesus
- sacrament of baptism
- Sabbath cures

Background Notes

This miracle story traces the path of a person who encounters and follows Jesus, the Light. It has a definite sacramental dimension. The beggar had been in darkness from birth until Jesus cured him without being asked. The healing was brought about by "anointing" with mud and washing with water from the pool of Siloam, which means "sent."

Because it was the Sabbath, some Pharisees challenged and questioned the man. Through the process the man who now had sight grew in understanding of Jesus. He defended the one who healed him even when his own parents deserted him. His arguments revealed that he saw much more clearly than the blind Pharisees. Unable to disprove the miracle, the Pharisees cast the man out. Eventually, Jesus sought out the cured man and called him to the fullness of faith.

For Discussion

Before the play: What do you think it's like to be blind? Close your eyes, try to find your paper and pencil, and to write something.

After the play: What does your baptismal commitment mean to you?

Activity

Younger learners might read a story about someone who is blind, for example, Helen Keller.

Invite older learners to work together on two posters, one with the caption "We Are Blind," the other with the caption "The Eyes of Faith." On the first one list ways in which we can be spiritually blind, for example, not seeing the poor people on the street. On the other one list things that our faith helps us to see, such as the hand of God in coincidences. Draw one of the examples on each poster.

Prayer

Holy God, holy strong One,
holy immortal One, have mercy on us.

—Byzantine Catholic prayer

CAST: NARRATOR, JESUS, MAN, MESSENGER, DISCIPLES 1, 2, PHARISEES 1, 2, 3, NEIGHBORS 1, 2, 3 (+)

PROPS: BOWL OR PAN OF WATER

THE MAN BORN BLIND John 9:1–41

Blind Man is seated on the ground. Jesus and Disciples enter.

Narrator   One Sabbath as Jesus walked along with his disciples, he saw a man who had been blind from birth.

Disciple 1   Rabbi, who sinned, this man or his parents, that he was born blind?

Jesus   Neither. He is blind so that God's works might be revealed in him. I am the light of the world.

Jesus helps Man stand. Then he mimes the actions as the Narrator describes them.

Narrator   Jesus spat on the ground, made some mud, and rubbed the man's eyes with it.

Jesus   (*to Man*) Go, wash in the pool at Siloam.

Man goes to side and splashes water on his face.

Man   I can see! I can see!

Jesus and Disciples exit. Man walks along. Neighbors enter.

Neighbor 1   Isn't this the man who used to sit and beg?

Man   I am the man.

Neighbor 1   Then how were your eyes opened?

Man   The man called Jesus made mud and spread it on my eyes. Then he told me, "Go to Siloam and wash." So I went there and washed and received my sight.

Neighbor 2   Where is the man who put mud on your eyes?

Man   I don't know.

Pharisees and Messenger enter. Neighbors take Man to them.

Neighbor 2   This man was blind, but Jesus made him see.

Pharisee 1   How did he do it?

Man   He put mud on my eyes, I washed it off, and now I can see.

Pharisee 2   That man is not from God for he does not observe the Sabbath law.

Pharisee 3   How can a man who is a sinner perform such miracles?

Pharisee 2   Since it was your eyes he opened, what do you have to say about him?

Man   He is a prophet.

Pharisee 2   (*to Pharisee 1*) He probably wasn't blind from birth.

Pharisee 1 (*to Messenger*) Bring the man here.

Messenger exits and returns with Man.

Pharisee 2 Give glory to God by telling the truth. We know the man called Jesus is a sinner.

Man I do not know whether he is a sinner. One thing I do know is that I was blind and now I see.

Pharisee 3 What did he do to you? How did he open your eyes?

Man I told you already, and you would not listen. Why do you want to hear it again? Do you also want to become his disciples?

Pharisee 1 You are his disciple, but we are disciples of Moses! We know that God has spoken to Moses, but as for this man, we do not know where he comes from.

Man Here is an astonishing thing. You do not know where he comes from, yet he opened my eyes. We know that God does not listen to sinners, but he does listen to one who worships him and obeys his will. Never since the world began has it been heard that anyone opened the eyes of a person born blind. If this man were not from God, he could never have done such a thing.

Pharisees 1, 2, 3 What!

Pharisee 1 You were born entirely in sin, and are you trying to teach us?

Pharisees grab Man and throw him out. Man walks away. Pharisees talk in circle. Neighbors go to Jesus.

Neighbor 1 (*to Jesus*) The Pharisees threw the man you healed out of the synagogue.

Neighbors exit. Jesus looks for Man and catches up to him.

Jesus Do you believe in the Son of Man?

Man Who is he, sir? Tell me, I am he.

Jesus You have seen him. I am he.

Man (*bowing low*) Lord, I believe.

Pharisees 2, 3 walk by.

Jesus I came into this world for judgment, so that those who do not see may see, and those who do see may become blind.

Pharisee 3 Surely, you are not calling us blind, are you?

Jesus If you were blind you would not have sin. But now that you say, "We see," your sin remains.

The Pharisees exit in one direction; Jesus and Man in another.

Raising the Widow's Son

- Easter/ eternal life
- resurrection

TENTH SUNDAY IN ORDINARY TIME: YEAR C

Background Notes

Jesus is called Lord here for the first time in Luke's gospel. In this miracle he showed himself master of life and death. Jesus and his crowd of followers encountered a woman at the head of a funeral procession. Burying the dead was an important work of mercy. Even the poorest people hired mourners and musicians for a funeral. Jesus was filled with pity for the mother. She was a widow who had lost her only son. As such she prefigured Mary. Through God's power the widow's son, like Mary's, came back to life.

Jesus' handing the young man to his mother recalled Elijah's raising of a widow's son (1 Kings 17:8–24). The people who observed the miracle acclaimed Jesus as a great prophet like Elijah. Raising the dead was a sign that Jesus was "the one who is to come" (Luke 7:20).

For Discussion

Before the play: How can you support and comfort others in their sorrow?

After the play: How does Jesus show compassion for the woman?

Activity

Invite young learners to carry out this activity. Make a wreath as a sign of the life that Jesus brings. Cut a cardboard base in the shape of a ring. From tissue paper of different shades of green, cut 1 inch squares. Stand a pencil eraser-side down on each square and bunch the paper up around it. Put glue on the wreath and attach the center of the squares to it close together to cover the cardboard.

Involve older learners in designing symbols that tell the gospel story.

Prayer

Name friends, loved ones, and others who have died and then pray for them:

Eternal rest grant unto them, O Lord, and let perpetual light shine upon them. May they rest in peace. Amen.

CAST: NARRATOR, JESUS, FOLLOWERS 1, 2 (+), WIDOW, WOMAN, SON, MOURNERS 1, 2 (+), BEARERS 1, 2, 3, 4

PROPS: TABLE OR CHAIRS SIDE BY SIDE FOR BIER (PALLET)

RAISING THE WIDOW'S SON Luke 7:11–17

Narrator Jesus was on his way south to the town of Nain. A great number of disciples and other people were with him. Near the gate of the town they met a large funeral procession coming out from the city.

Jesus and Followers walk toward funeral procession. Man is on bier. If he is not carried, the Mourners move forward only slightly and Bearers only pretend to walk. Widow walks in front, crying and supported by Woman.

Follower 1 (*to Mourner 1*) Who are you burying?

Mourner 1 A young man from our town.

Mourner 2 His mother is a widow. He was all she had.

Jesus (*to Widow*) Do not weep.

Jesus goes to the bier and puts his hand on it. The Bearers stop.

Jesus (*to Man*) Young man, I say to you, rise.

Man sits up. Crowd gasps and steps back in awe.

Man (*rubbing eyes*) Where am I? What's going on?

Jesus helps Man off bier.

Jesus (*to Widow*) Here is your son back.

Widow My son! Thanks be to God.

Mourner 1 A great prophet has risen among us.

Follower 2 God has looked favorably on his people.

Raising Jairus' Daughter and Healing the Sick Woman

Theme

■ healings from faith

THIRTEENTH SUNDAY IN ORDINARY TIME: YEAR B

Background Notes

These two stories of Jesus' healing of women are presented as a unit. The healing of the sick woman is sandwiched within the story of Jairus' daughter. In both accounts faith is underlined. Jairus knelt before Jesus, believing that Jesus' touch would cure his daughter. The woman secretly touched the tassel on Jesus' cloak, believing that this contact would heal her. Both acts of faith were rewarded.

The two miracles pointed to Jesus as Savior. The woman's condition made her unclean for twelve years; it also made her poor. Jesus was her salvation. The raising of Jairus' daughter from death prefigured Jesus' resurrection. The girl passed from death to new life, and the mourners' wails were in vain.

The cloak Jesus wore had a tassel on each corner as prescribed by law. However, he stepped outside the law when he let the unclean woman touch him and when he touched the girl's corpse. His love went beyond the law.

For Discussion

Before the play: What does Jesus' power over death mean for you?

After the play: How would you feel if you were in the place of the sick woman?

Activity

Involve the younger learners in this activity. Make an accordion storybook. Fold three sheets of drawing paper in half. Tape the backs of the three sheets together to form a row of frames. In each of the six frames draw a scene from the story of Jairus' daughter: Jairus and Jesus, the woman touching Jesus' cloak, messengers and Jairus, Jesus and the mourners, Jesus and the dead girl, the girl and her parents. Fold the papers so that they open like an accordion.

Invite older learners to choose a person or phrase from the reading that struck them. Ask them to write or draw their own story, centered on that element.

Prayer

You, Eternal Trinity, are like a deep sea. The deeper I enter in, the more I find. The more I find out about you, the more I seek you. For no matter how much we learn about you, we continue to thirst for you. Holy Trinity, give me your light.

—adapted from St. Catherine of Siena

CAST: JESUS, MESSENGER, PETER, JAMES, JOHN, JAIRUS, WOMAN, GIRL, MOTHER, MOURNERS 1, 2 (+), CROWD (+), PERSONS 1, 2

PROPS: CLOAK, MAT FOR BED

RAISING JAIRUS' DAUGHTER AND
HEALING THE SICK WOMAN MATTHEW 9:18–26, MARK 5:21–43, LUKE 8:40–56

Jesus is seated teaching Crowd. Peter, James, John, and Persons 1, 2 are there. Jairus enters and falls at Jesus' feet.

Jairus   Please, sir, come to my house. My little girl, who is only twelve, is dying. Come lay your hands on her so that she may be made well and live.

Person 1   Who is that man?

Person 2   Jairus, the official of the synagogue.

Jesus stands and moves with Jairus and Disciples. Crowd surrounds them. Woman enters, goes through Crowd, and comes behind Jesus.

Woman   If I can just touch the fringe of his clothes, I shall be cured.

Woman touches the edge of Jesus' cloak, Jesus stops.

Jesus   (*looking around*) Who touched me?

Peter   Master, all the crowds surround you and press on you. How can you say, "Who touched me?"

Jesus   Someone touched me, for I noticed that power had gone out from me.

Woman, trembling, kneels at his feet.

Woman   I did it. For twelve years I've been suffering from bleeding. No doctor has been able to help me. The instant I touched your cloak, I was healed.

Jesus   Take heart, my daughter; your faith has made you well. Go in peace.

Woman   (*rising*) Thank you, Master.

Messenger enters and goes to Jairus.

Messenger   Jairus, your daughter is dead. Do not trouble the Teacher any longer.

Jesus   (*to Jairus*) Do not fear. Only believe and she will be saved.

Mourner 1   (*mocking*) Sure she's sleeping. Everyone stops breathing when they're sleeping.

Mourner 2   (*laughing*) Hope you don't plan to stay around until she wakes up.

Crowd exits. Mourners enter, crying and wailing. Jesus, Jairus, Peter, James, and John go to them. Mother enters. Girl enters and lies on mat.

Jesus   (*to Mourners*) What's all this noise? Stop crying. The girl is not dead but sleeping. (*takes Girl by the hand*) Little girl, get up.

Girl gets up and walks around.

Girl   (*rubbing her eyes*) What happened? I must have fallen asleep. Mother, Dad, who are these people?

Jairus   Friends, dear.

Mother   (*to Jairus*) What power this Teacher has! (*goes to Girl and hugs her*)

Jesus   Do not tell anyone what happened here. Now give her something to eat.

The Raising of Lazarus

FIFTH SUNDAY OF LENT: YEAR A

Background Notes

The raising of Lazarus is a preparation for the resurrection of Jesus. When Jesus received the message that his friend was ill, he did not go to him immediately. Lazarus' death was part of a plan to reveal Jesus' power. When Jesus arrived, Martha remarked that if he had been there, Lazarus would not have died. This led to a conversation on the resurrection.

A group gathered at Lazarus' house because mourning rites usually continued for seven days. Jesus was truly grieved at the death of his friend. At Lazarus' tomb he prayed aloud so that the people knew that the Father had sent him. Then at Jesus' command, Lazarus stepped out of the tomb and was freed from his burial cloths. The gospel provides no further details. Ironically, Jesus' miracle of restoring Lazarus to life precipitated the Pharisees' plot to kill him.

For Discussion

Before the play: What would give you the most comfort if you lost someone close to you?

After the play: How would you have felt if you had witnessed the miracle described in this gospel?

Activity

Invite your young learners to carry out this activity. Plant seeds in a small flowerpot and water them. On the pot or on a sign to stand by it, print "I am the resurrection and the life." Watch the pot as the seeds die and the flowers or plants gradually grow.

Ask older learners if they would like to form a prayer hotline for persons who lose a loved one. You might obtain names from the Bereavement Ministry in your parish.

Prayer

You are medicine for me when I am sick;
You are my strength when I need help;
You are life itself when I fear death;
You are the way when I long for heaven;
You are light when all is dark;
You are my food when I need nourishment!

—St. Anselm

CAST: NARRATOR, JESUS, THOMAS, DISCIPLES 1, 2, 3, LAZARUS, MARTHA, MARY, MESSENGER, MOURNERS 1, 2 (+), MEN TO MOVE STONE (+)

PROPS: CLOTHS OR TOWELS FOR LAZARUS, LARGE BOX OR CART

THE RAISING OF LAZARUS   JOHN 11:1–44

Jesus is seated with Disciples. Martha, Mary, and Mourners are seated in a far corner. Lazarus is behind the large box some distance away. Messenger runs to Jesus.

Messenger	Jesus, I have a message for you from Martha and Mary at Bethany. They say, "Lord, he whom you love is ill."
Jesus	Let us go back to Judea again.
Disciple 1	Rabbi, a little while ago the people there were trying to stone you. And you are going there again?
Jesus	Our friend Lazarus has fallen asleep, but I am going there to awaken him.
Disciple 2	Lord, if he has fallen asleep, he will be all right.
Jesus	Lazarus is dead. For your sake I am glad I was not there, so that you may believe. Let us go to him.
Thomas	(*to other Disciples*) Let us also go, that we may die with him!

Group walks toward Mourners.

Narrator	When Jesus and disciples arrived in Bethany, they find out that Lazarus has already been in the tomb for four days. Friends and relatives were still at the house of Mary and Martha comforting them. When Martha heard that Jesus was coming, she left the house to meet him.

Martha gets up and walks to meet Jesus.

Martha	(*to Jesus*) Lord, if you had been here, my brother would not have died. But even now I know that God will give you whatever you ask of him.
Jesus	Your brother will rise again.
Martha	I know that he will rise again in the resurrection on the last day.
Jesus	I am the resurrection and the life. Those who believe in me even though they die, will live, and everyone who lives and believes in me will never die. Do you believe this?
Martha	Yes, Lord, I believe that you are the Messiah, the Son of God, the one coming into the world.
Jesus	Where's Mary?
Martha	She's at home. I'll get her.

Martha runs back to the house. Jesus stays where he is.

Martha	Mary, the Teacher is here, and is calling for you.

Mary gets up and goes quickly to Jesus.

Mourner 1	She must be going to the tomb to weep there.

Mourner 2   Let's go with her.

Mourners follow Mary. Mary throws herself at Jesus' feet. She and Mourners are crying.

Mary   Lord, if you had been here, my brother would not have died.

Jesus   (*sighing*) Where have you laid him?

Mourner 1   Lord, come and see.

Group stops a little way from Lazarus. Jesus goes toward tomb. He wipes his eyes.

Mourner 2   See how he loved him.

Jesus   Take away the stone.

Men push stone away. Jesus looks up to heaven.

Jesus   Father, I thank you for having heard me. I know that you always hear me, but I have said this for the sake of the crowd standing here, so they may believe that you sent me. (*loudly*) Lazarus, come out!

Lazarus comes forth. Mourners gasp.

Jesus   Unbind him, and let him go.

Men unwrap Lazarus. Mary, Martha, and Jesus go up to him and hug him.

Martha and Mary   Lazarus! Lazarus!

The Lost Sheep

TWENTY-FOURTH SUNDAY IN ORDINARY TIME: YEAR C

Themes

- forgiveness of sin
- sacrament of reconciliation

Background Notes

Jesus' stories known as parables are the chief characteristic of his teaching style. The word parable is from the Greek for "comparison." In parables Jesus illustrates supernatural truths by means of natural images.

In this parable Jesus compared a sinner to a lost sheep, and God to the concerned shepherd who goes after it. Just as the shepherd misses his stray sheep, God longs to have the sinner safe back home. A lost sheep is easy prey for wolves or could die of hunger or thirst. A sheep that has lain down and rolled over is unable to get up. In such "cast sheep" circulation is cut off. The shepherd has to carry the sheep back on his shoulders, but the shepherd rejoices. Similarly, God has more intense happiness at the return of a sinner than at people who are righteous.

This parable is another attempt to make the Pharisees see others, particularly sinners, in a different light. Jesus did not condemn sinners, but lovingly worked for their well-being. He said, "Those who are well have no need of a physician, but those who are sick.... I have come to call not the righteous, but sinners" (Matthew 9:12–13).

For Discussion

Before the play: Have you ever been lost? How did you feel?

After the play: How does reconciliation help you grow closer to God and others?

Activity

Have young learners do the following activity. Draw a sheep on heavy paper and cut it out. Glue cotton on for wool, covering the sheep. Add black eyes and hooves made from felt or construction paper. Play a game of hiding the sheep for others to find.

Invite older learners to share in Jesus' ministry. If they know persons who no longer participate at Mass, they might try to bring them back.

Prayer

The Lord is my shepherd,
*   I shall not want.*
He makes me lie down
*   in green pastures;*
he leads me beside still waters;
he restores my soul.
He leads me in right paths
for his name's sake.

Even though I walk through
*   the darkest valley,*
I fear no evil;
For you are with me;
your rod and your staff—
they comfort me.

You prepare a table before me
In the presence of my enemies;
You anoint my head with oil;
my cup overflows.
Surely goodness and mercy
shall follow me
all the days of my life,
and I shall dwell in the house of the Lord
my whole life long.

—Psalm 23

CAST: JESUS, SHEPHERD, SHEEP (+), LOST SHEEP, FRIENDS (+)

THE LOST SHEEP   MATTHEW 18:12–14, LUKE 15:3–7

Shepherd is with Sheep. Lost Sheep is alone in corner of the floor.

Jesus   Suppose a man has a hundred sheep.

Shepherd   (*counting sheep*) 96, 97, 98, 99. Uh, oh. One's missing. I bet he wandered off and got lost. I'll have to go after him. These others will be safe enough as they graze in the pasture. (*searches for Lost Sheep*)

Lost Sheep   Baaaa.

Shepherd   I hear him. (*spots Lost Sheep*) Oh, there he is, too scared to move. I'll have to pick him up and carry him home. (*to Lost Sheep*) I'm so happy I found you. Don't be afraid now. You'll be all right.

Shepherd and Lost Sheep exit. Friends enter.

Jesus   When the shepherd has his lost sheep back with the flock again, he calls his friends.

Shepherd   Joseph, Matthew, Judith, Anna, everybody! Come on over. Celebrate with me because I have found my lost sheep.

Friends joyfully surround Shepherd, shake his hand, slap him on the back.

Jesus   In the same way, there will be more joy in heaven over one sinner who repents than over ninety-nine righteous people who do not need to repent. It is the will of your Father in heaven that not one of those little ones should be lost.

The Lost Coin

TWENTY-FOURTH SUNDAY IN ORDINARY TIME: YEAR C

Themes

- forgiveness of sin
- sacrament of reconciliation
- the kingdom

Background Notes

This parable is one of the simplest. The setting of the story is a house, and the main character is a housewife. Homely as it is, it turns the Pharisees' concept of God upside-down. In the first place, God is compared to a woman. Secondly, the common experience of looking for a lost object and finding it is used to explain God's attitude toward sinners.

The lost coin has some special meaning for the woman. Scholars suggest that it was one of the coins that were her personal property worn in her headdress or necklace and marking her as a married woman. In any case, she desperately searches her house and holds a celebration when she finds the coin. The parable implies that sinners catapult God into the same frustration and distress that the missing coin caused the woman. God took the initiative in seeking out the lost. Once they were recovered, all heaven rejoiced. This picture of a God who is loving and compassionate toward sinners was quite new to those Pharisees who were righteous and rigid.

For Discussion

Before the play: When have you ever lost and then found something precious?

After the play: In this story God is presented as a woman. What are other images of God?

Activity

Review the steps in preparing for and celebrating the sacrament of reconciliation.

Prayer

PRAYER BEFORE THE CRUCIFIX

O kind and most sweet Jesus, I kneel before you. I pray that you will fill my heart with faith, hope, and charity, true sorrow for my sins, and the will to change. With deep affection and sorrow, I think about your five holy wounds. David the prophet said about you: "They have pierced my hands and my feet; I can count all my bones."

CAST: JESUS, MARY, JAMES, SARAH, RACHEL, WOMAN, NEIGHBORS (+)

PROPS: TEN SILVER COINS, CONSTRUCTION PAPER CANDLE WITH FLAME, BROOM, POT AND LADLE, TABLE

THE LOST COIN LUKE 15:8–10

Woman is in the center. Sarah is on one side in the next house, stirring something. Rachel is beyond her in the next house, sleeping in a chair. On the other side of Woman, Mary and James are seated talking quietly. Jesus speaks from the side of the stage.

Jesus   Once there was a poor woman who had ten silver coins.

Woman   (*counting coins*) One, two, three, four, five, six, seven, eight, nine. Nine? Let me count again. Two, four, six, eight, nine. Oh, no! One is missing. Where could it be? (*looks around room*) Maybe some light will help. (*lights a "candle" and searches room*) I know. I'll sweep the house. I might hear it clink against the hard, dirt floor. (*sweeps*)

No luck. I'll just have to search every inch of this house. (*searches carefully and spots the coin against a table leg*) Aha! Here it is. Thank goodness. (*goes to Sarah's house and knocks*)

Sarah, rejoice with me. I've been looking everywhere for one of my coins. I just found it. Come on over and celebrate with me.

Sarah   Sure. I'm always glad to celebrate.

Woman   Would you run over to my cousin Rachel and invite her, too? Thanks.

Sarah goes to Rachel. Woman goes to Mary and James, knocks, and calls out.

Woman   Mary? James? Can you come to my house a while? I just found a coin I had lost. I'm so happy I have to celebrate. Bring all your children, too.

James   Great. We'll be right over.

All gather at Woman's house.

Jesus   I tell you, the angels of God rejoice the same way over one sinner who repents.

The Prodigal Son

FOURTH SUNDAY OF LENT: YEAR C, TWENTY-FOURTH
SUNDAY IN ORDINARY TIME: YEAR C

Themes

- forgiveness of sin
- sacrament of reconciliation
- conversion
- love

Background Notes

This parable might more aptly be named the forgiving father. The hero of the story is the father of two sons who was indulgent, generous, and forgiving. He exhibited an unconditional love that embraced both his weak, foolish son and his resentful, obedient son. The father is a reflection of God who does more than tolerate our foolishness. God longs for us to come to our senses and to trust his love enough to go to him in our need.

The younger son wasted his inheritance and ended up feeding pigs. This job was the lowest for Jews, who regarded pigs as unclean. So the son was cut him off from his people. He decided to apply for a job at home as a hired servant, the lowliest type of servant. The father must have been looking for his son. When the father saw him, he ran to his son, even though this was beneath the dignity of a Near Eastern man. The father did not lecture or punish his son—just hugged him, reinstated him as a son, and prepared a celebration. The ring the father gave his son symbolized authority.

As the firstborn, the older son would receive two-thirds of the father's estate. He should have been satisfied and happy. Because he sulked at his father's loving reception of the returned prodigal, he represented those righteous ones who begrudge others God's mercy.

For Discussion

Before the play: Have you ever felt like giving up? What did you do?

After the play: How was the father like God? How can we help sinners?

Activity

Invite young learners to do their own version of the gospel story.

Older learners might write a poem about this parable, using any form, perhaps rap.

Prayer

Seek the Lord while he may be found,
call upon him while he is near;
let the wicked forsake their way,
and the unrighteous their thoughts;
let them return to the Lord,
that he may have mercy on them,
and to our God, for he will
abundantly pardon.
For my thoughts are not your thoughts,
nor are your ways my ways,
says the Lord.
For as the heavens are higher
than the earth,
so are my ways higher than your ways
and my thoughts than your thoughts.

—Isaiah 55:6–9

CAST: JESUS, FATHER, YOUNGER SON, OLDER SON, EMPLOYER, SERVANTS 1, 2

PROPS: TWO SCROLLS OF PAPER, BAG OF MONEY, SACK OF CORN, ROBE, RING, SHOES, MUSIC

THE PRODIGAL SON LUKE 15:11–32

Jesus is off to the side. Father is seated. Employer is seated at a distance.

Jesus   There was a man who had two sons.

Younger Son enters and goes to Father.

Younger Son   Father, let me have my share of the property that is coming to me.

Father   (*sadly*) If that's what you really want. Call your brother here.

Younger Son leaves. Father writes on two scrolls. Younger Son returns with Older Son.

Father   (*to Older Son*) Your brother wants his share of the inheritance now, so you might as well have yours, too. I have divided the property between you. Here. (*gives each a scroll*)

Sons   Thank you, Father.

All exit.

Jesus   The younger son went to a distant land. There he wasted all his money on drinking, gambling, and women. When a famine came to that country, the boy had nothing left to buy food.

Younger Son walks alone. He shakes the empty money bag upside-down and tosses it away.

Younger Son   Guess I don't need that anymore. I'll have to get a job. (*goes to Employer*)

Younger Son   Pardon me, sir. Can you use some help on your property?

Employer   As a matter of fact, I can. I need someone to take care of the pigs on my farm.

Younger Son   I can do that.

Employer   Fine, you can start now. They're down the road. (*points and exits*)

Younger Son walks to farm, takes sack, and feeds pigs.

Younger Son   I'm so hungry I could eat this pig food. No one said anything about my supper. My father's hired hands have more food than they can eat, and here I am dying of hunger. I will get up and return to my father and say, "Father, I have sinned against heaven and before you. I am no longer worthy to be called your son. Treat me as one of your hired workers."

Son drops sack and walks toward home. Father enters with Servants 1, 2 and, shading his eyes, peers down road.

Father   That looks like my son. (*runs to Younger Son and embraces him*)

Younger Son   Father, I have sinned against heaven and before you; I am no longer worthy to be called your son.

Father   (*gesturing for Servants to come*) Quickly, bring out a robe—the best one—and put it on him. Put a ring on his finger and sandals on his feet. And get the fatted calf and kill it. Let us eat and celebrate. For this son of mine was dead and is alive. He was lost and is found!

Servants exit. Father and Younger Son walk to house. Servants 1, 2 bring robe, ring, and shoes and put them on Younger Son. All exit except Servant 1. Music plays. Older Son enters.

Older Son   (*to Servant 1*) Come here. Tell me, what's the reason for the music and dancing?

Servant 1   Your brother has come. Your father has killed the fatted calf because he has his son back safe and sound.

Older Son   (*folding arms and sitting*) Well, don't think I'm going to celebrate that.

Servant 1 exits. The Father enters and goes to Older Son.

Father   Son, please come in and join the celebration.

Older Son   (*angrily*) Listen! For all these years I have worked like a slave for you. I never disobeyed your commands. Yet you have never given me even a young goat so that I might celebrate with my friends. But when this son of yours comes back after wasting all your money—he and his women—you kill the fatted calf for him!

Father   My son, you are always with me. All that is mine (*hands to chest*) is yours. (*hands out to Older Son*) But we had to celebrate and rejoice, because your brother was dead and has come to life. He was lost and has been found. Come on in.

Older Son rises and both exit.

The Weeds

SIXTEENTH SUNDAY IN ORDINARY TIME: YEAR A

Background Notes

The parables employ simple language, ordinary objects, and familiar situations. Consequently, they charmed listeners of all ages and levels of intelligence, were easy to relate to, and left a lasting impression.

This parable, along with the parables of the Mustard Seed and the Yeast, is known as the Great Assurance. It occurs after accounts of some Pharisees' attacks on Jesus. Through parables Jesus explained how the kingdom of God would be spread through the world gradually. In this parable, the weeds sown by the enemy were darnel, a type of weed that resembles wheat in its early stages. At harvest time the wheat and weeds would look different and be easily separated.

Jesus explained that good people, children of God, and sinners, children of Satan, lived together on earth. The separation of good and evil would not occur until the end of the world. Jesus associated with tax collectors and sinners. His disciples then should not exclude sinners from their ministry or judge them. At the final coming Jesus will separate the unrepentant from the saints. The parable of the Net has the same message. See Matthew 13:47–50.

For Discussion

Before the play: Name two important ways in which you use your ability to choose.

After the play: What do you think Jesus might be asking you to change in your life?

Activity

Involve young learners in a simple activity to benefit the care of creation.

Invite older learners to complete this activity. Fold a sheet of white drawing paper four times to make sixteen sections. On practice paper make a design of wheat and a design of dandelions. On the good paper copy these designs in alternating squares to create a repeat pattern. You might draw the designs with black and yellow to reflect the theme of good and evil. Alternate activity: Read the parables of the Mustard Seed and the Yeast in Matthew 13:31–33.

Prayer

Keep me, O Lord, from all pettiness.
May I be generous in thought and word
and deed.
Help me to be honest that I may meet
my neighbor face to face without self-
pity and without prejudice.
May I never be hasty in my judgments
but generous to all and in all things.
Help me be calm, serene, and gentle.

—adapted from Mary Stuart

CAST: JESUS, SOWER, ENEMY, SERVANTS 1, 2

PROPS: TWO BASKETS

THE WEEDS MATTHEW 13:24–30

Jesus The kingdom of heaven is like this. Someone sowed good seed in his field.

Sower enters casting seeds from basket. Servants 1, 2 enter. They and Sower stretch, yawn, and sleep.

Jesus One night while everybody was asleep, an enemy came and sowed weeds among the wheat. Then he went away.

Enemy enters casting seeds from basket where the Sower did. Exits.

Jesus When the plants came up and bore grain, then the weeds appeared as well. The servants noticed there was a problem.

Servant 1 (*to Sower*) Master, didn't you sow good seed in your field? Where then did these weeds come from?

Sower An enemy has done this.

Servant 2 Do you want us to go and pull up the weeds?

Sower No, because if you pull up the weeds, you would uproot the wheat along with them.

Servants You're right.

Sower Let the wheat and weeds grow together until harvest. Then at harvest time I will say to the reapers, "Collect the weeds first and tie them in bundles to be burned. Then gather the wheat and put it in my barn."

Servants Good idea, Master.

The Hidden Treasure

SEVENTEENTH SUNDAY IN ORDINARY TIME: YEAR A

Theme

■ value of the kingdom

Background Notes

This parable is one of the seven parables of the kingdom in Matthew 13. It focuses on the great joy of the person who comes upon the reign of God. This joy is compared to the joy of someone who unexpectedly finds a treasure. In Palestine at that time when there were frequent wars, people kept their valuables safe by burying them in the ground. When the owners were killed, the valuables remained hidden.

In the parable the man who discovered the treasure had a legal right to it, if the land was his. He prized the treasure so much that he was willing to trade everything he owned to possess it. Similarly, people who understand the value of the kingdom of heaven gladly give up everything to possess it. They strive for this magnificent goal with eager determination, although in the eyes of the world they may be considered reckless or foolish.

For Discussion

Before the play: Who helped you learn about the happiness of Jesus' kingdom?

After the play: When have you had a taste of the peace, joy, and love that characterize the kingdom? Who are some people who have sacrificed earthly goods for heaven?

Activity

Read the story of a saint who gave up much in order to gain eternal life. Some suggestions are St. Francis of Assisi, St. Katherine Drexel, St. Maximilian Kolbe, St. Thomas More, St. Elizabeth of Hungary, St. Clare, St. Teresa of Avila, and St. Francis Xavier.

Prayer

Invite the children to listen to or sing a hymn about loving God above everything. At the end teach them to pray the short prayer "My God and my all."

CAST: JESUS, MAN, BUYERS 1, 2, 3, OWNER

PROPS: TREASURE CHEST, PAPER DIRT, COINS

THE HIDDEN TREASURE MATTHEW 13:44

Jesus is at one side. Buyers 1, 2, 3 and Owner stand off to the side.

Jesus The kingdom of heaven is like this.

Man walks along and stumbles.

Man (*stooping*) What's this? Hmmm. It looks like the corner of a chest. (*digs up chest and opens it*) Wow, it's a treasure chest full of coins and jewelry! (*puts it back and covers it with dirt*) I must buy this field. First, I'll have to get some money. (*walks near Buyers 1, 2, 3*) House for sale! House for sale!

Buyer 1 I'm looking for a house. How much does yours cost?

Man Five thousand silver coins.

Buyer 1 This must be my lucky day. Here's your money. (*gives coins to Man and exits*)

Man (*loudly*) Donkey and sheep for sale.

Buyer 2 I'd like a donkey. How old is yours?

Man Only two years old and he's healthy. You can have him for one thousand silver coins.

Buyer 2 It's a deal. (*hands over coins and exits*)

Buyer 3 How many sheep do you have?

Man Five beautiful sheep.

Buyer 3 I'll give you one thousand silver coins for them.

Man Three thousand.

Buyer 3 Two thousand.

Man They're yours.

Buyer 3 hands coins to Man and exits.

Man Now I have enough money to buy that field. (*goes to Owner*) I'd like to buy your north field. I'll give you ten thousand silver coins for it.

Owner Are you crazy? It's only worth half that much.

Man Not to me.

Owner All right. You can have it.

Man gives Owner the coins.

Owner Thank you! (*exits*)

Man Thank you. (*goes to field, digs up treasure, and hugs it*) Ah, you're mine. All mine.

The Pearl of Great Price

SEVENTEENTH SUNDAY IN ORDINARY TIME: YEAR A

Background Notes

As we read or listen to a parable, it is good to ask what God is saying to us personally, as a community and as individuals. If we open our hearts and respond to his message, then we will know how alive and transforming God's word is.

The supreme worth of the kingdom of heaven is taught by the story of a purchase. To the Jewish people a pearl was the most precious jewel. In the parable a pearl merchant searched for an exceptionally large and lovely pearl. He didn't just stumble over it unexpectedly, as the man who found the treasure in the field. Finally, the merchant's efforts were rewarded. He recognized a priceless pearl and sold all he had to possess it. Heaven is like this pearl. Those who realize its true value will do anything to obtain it. No matter how high the price, it is always a bargain.

For Discussion

Before the play: How do you "picture" heaven?

After the play: Why don't people always recognize the value of heaven? What "pearls" are you willing to sacrifice to reach heaven?

Activity

Use this activity with young learners. Buy some plastic pearls at a craft shop. Then hide them around your meeting space and hold a "pearl hunt."

Ask older learners to write or draw a modern version of this parable.

Prayer

ACT OF HOPE

O my God, relying on your infinite goodness and promises, I hope to obtain pardon of my sins, the help of your grace, and life everlasting, through the merits of Jesus Christ, my Lord and Redeemer.

CAST: JESUS, MAN, SALESMAN

PROPS: DESK FOR SALESMAN, BEADS OR MARBLES FOR PEARLS (ONE LARGER THAN OTHERS), COINS

The Pearl of Great Price   Matthew 13:45–46

Jesus is off to the side. Salesman is at desk.

Jesus   The kingdom of heaven is like this.

Man enters and approaches Salesman.

Salesman   Hello. Can I help you?

Man   Yes. I've been looking everywhere for a beautiful pearl.

Salesman   We have an excellent collection of pearls. (*takes out pearls*) See what you think of these.

Man looks at pearls for a short time.

Man   These are nice, but I'm looking for something special.

Salesman   We do have one rare pearl. It's very expensive.

Man   Let me see it.

Salesman   (*taking out large pearl*) Here it is. Isn't it lovely?

Man   (*with admiration*) I have never seen such a pearl. It is so large and perfect. How much is it?

Salesman   Actually it's priceless, but we're selling it for twenty thousand silver coins.

Man   I can give you ten thousand for it.

Salesman   Eighteen and no lower.

Man   Twelve thousand.

Salesman   Fifteen thousand and that's final.

Man   I'll buy it. Would you hold it for me until I return tomorrow?

Salesman   I'd be glad to.

Jesus   The man went home and had a large sale. He sold his house, his livestock, and everything he owned. Finally, he had enough money to buy the pearl.

Man returns to store.

Man   (*to Salesman*) Hello. I came for my pearl. (*puts down money*)

Salesman   (*counts money, then hands over pearl*) Congratulations!

Man   Thank you! This is the happiest day of my life.

The Great Banquet

Background Notes

Jesus was dining at the home of a leading Pharisee. When someone remarked, "Blessed is the one who will dine in the kingdom of God," Jesus responded with the parable of the great banquet. Obviously the banquet represented the kingdom of heaven and the host, God.

During the time of Jesus people received two invitations to feasts. Those who said yes to the first one were invited again when everything was ready. In the parable the first guests invited were very rude. Not only did they fail to keep their first commitment, but their excuses were ridiculous. These guests were like the people of Israel who refused Jesus' invitation to the kingdom.

The second group in the parable, the beggars and outcasts of society, were the sinners who recognized their need for salvation. The third group of guests were hobos and strangers on the roads outside the city walls. They were the Gentiles. In essence, Jesus revealed that everyone is invited to the kingdom of heaven.

For Discussion

Before the play: Have you ever been at a big party? Why do you think Jesus compares God's kingdom to a banquet?

After the play: What are some excuses people give for not trying to get into God's kingdom?

Activity

Design an invitation to the wedding feast of heaven that Jesus might send. Include time, required dress, possible gift, and similar information.

Prayer

Glory to the Father, and to the Son, and to the Holy Spirit. As it was in the beginning, is now, and will be forever. Amen.

CAST: **JESUS, MASTER, POOR COUPLE, SERVANT, CRIPPLED WOMAN, BLIND MAN, GUESTS 1, 2, 3, OTHER GUESTS (+)**

THE GREAT BANQUET LUKE 14:16–24

Jesus is at far side. Master and Servant are at one side of stage, and Guests 1, 2, 3 are on opposite side.

Jesus There was once a man who gave a great dinner. He invited many people.

Master (*to Servant*) It's time for the feast. Go to my guests. Say to them, "Come, everything is ready now!"

Servant goes to Guest 1.

Servant It's time for my master's feast. Come. Everything is ready.

Guest 1 I have bought a piece of land and must go out and see it. I'm sorry.

Servant goes to Guest 2.

Servant It's time for my master's feast. Come. Everything is ready.

Guest 2 I have bought five pairs of oxen and am going to try them out. Please accept my regrets.

Servant goes to Guest 3.

Servant It's time for my master's feast. Come. Everything is ready.

Guest 3 I've just been married, and therefore I cannot come.

Servant returns to Master. Guests 1, 2, 3 exit. Poor Couple, Crippled Woman, Blind Man enter.

Servant Sir, none of your guests can come. They are all too busy.

Master (*angrily*) What! After all the trouble I went to, they can't come! Go out at once into the streets and lanes of the town and bring in the poor, the crippled, the blind, and the lame.

Servant goes to Poor Couple, Crippled Woman, and Blind Man.

Servant (*to Poor Couple*) My master is giving a grand feast. Come. (*to Blind Man*) Come to my master's feast. (*to Crippled Woman*) You're invited to my master's house for supper.

All go to Master.

Servant (*to Master*) Sir, what you ordered has been done. And there is still room for more.

Master Go out to the roads and lands and compel people to come in so that my house may be filled. For I tell you that none of those who were invited will taste my dinner.

Servant Yes, sir. It shall be done.

Other guests enter.

The Wicked Vinedressers

TWENTY-SEVENTH SUNDAY IN ORDINARY TIME: YEAR A

Background Notes

Vineyards were a familiar sight on the hillsides of Israel. Jesus knew that the people were protected by walls and watchtowers. He also knew about the winepress, rocks on which the grapes were squeezed to yield the juice that would become wine. Already in Isaiah, chapter 5, a vineyard stands for the House of Israel. In Jesus' parable, the history of Israel is presented. The man who plants a vineyard represents God who carefully tended the people Israel. Just as the parable's tenants do not hand over the produce to the servants, the leaders did not yield good works at the prophets' pleadings.

The tenants in the parable threw the son out of the vineyard and killed him because by Jewish law if a man had no heirs his property went to his tenants. Tradition holds that Jesus, the Son of God, was killed outside the city walls of Jerusalem. In telling the story the "son" (Jesus) announced, to the "tenants" that God would give the kingdom of heaven to a new people: believers, whether Israelites or Gentiles. The king's lack of retaliation mirrors God's goodness in dealing with us.

For Discussion

Before the play: How can you tend your part of the "vineyard" carefully?

After the play: What harvest are you expected to produce? Who are prophets that speak to us?

Activity

Involve young learners in this activity. Make a study of different types of crosses, such as the Jerusalem cross, the Greek Orthodox cross, and the Celtic cross. Choose one to illustrate. Draw it on black construction paper and cut it out. Cover it with triangles cut from bright paper. Alternate activity: You might cover the cross with bits of Easter egg shells.

Older learners might enjoy learning more about the process of growing grapes and making the wine.

Prayer

AN ACT OF SPIRITUAL COMMUNION

My Jesus, I believe that you are in the Blessed Sacrament. I love you above all things, and I long for you in my soul. Since I cannot now receive you in the Eucharist, come at least spiritually into my heart. As though you have already come I embrace you and unite myself entirely to you. Never permit me to be separated from you. Amen.

CAST: JESUS, LANDOWNER, TENANTS 1, 2, SERVANTS 1, 2, 3, SON

THE WICKED VINEDRESSERS
MATTHEW 21:33–41, MARK 12:1–12, LUKE 20:9–16

Jesus is off to the side. Tenants 1, 2 are on one side. Landowner is on the other side. Servants 1, 2, 3 are near him.

Jesus   Listen to another parable. A man planted a vineyard on his land. Then he leased it to tenants. They were to care for it while he was out of town. At harvest time he expected the tenants to give him his grapes.

Landowner gestures for Servant 1 to come.

Landowner   (*to Servant 1*) It's harvest time. Go to the tenants and collect my grapes from them.

Servant   (*goes to Tenants*) My master sent me to collect his grapes.

Tenant 1   Is that so? Well, he can't have them.

Tenants "beat" Servant 1. He returns to Landowner.

Landowner   What happened?

Servant 1   The tenants attacked me when I asked for the grapes.

Landowner   Take care of your wounds.

Servant 1 exits. Landowner gestures for Servant 2 to come.

Landowner   Go to the tenants on my land and ask for the harvest.

Servant 2   Yes, Master. (*goes to Tenants*) I've come to collect my master's grapes.

Tenants "beat" Servant 2. He returns to Landowner.

Servant 2   They will not give you your grapes.

Landowner   Take care of your wounds.

Servant 2 exits. Landowner gestures for Servant 3 to come.

Landowner   What shall I do? I will send my beloved son. Perhaps they will respect him. (*to Servant 3*) Tell my son to come here.

Servant 3 exits and returns with Son.

Landowner   Son, please go to the tenants and collect the grapes that belong to us.

Son   Yes, Father. (*walks toward Tenants*)

Tenant 1   (*to Tenant 2*) Say, this is the heir coming.

Tenant 2   Come on, let's kill him so that the inheritance may be ours.

Tenants grab the Son, take him off to the side and "kill" him. Servants 1, 2 enter and stand by Landowner. Then Servant 3 runs in.

Servant 3 (*to Landowner*) Sir, I bring you bad news. Your son's body has been found outside the vineyard. He's been killed.

Landowner My son, my son! (*to Servants*) Come with me. We'll put an end to this.

Servants 1, 2, 3, and Landowner go to Tenants, grab them from behind.

Landowner (*to Servants*) Take these men away and see that they get what they deserve. I'll find tenants who will give me grapes at harvest time.

Jesus The kingdom of heaven will be given to people who produce the fruit of good works.

The Workers
in the Vineyard

TWENTY-FIFTH SUNDAY IN ORDINARY TIME: YEAR A

Background Notes

Jesus used parables to communicate the mystery of God and God's kingdom. They show God acting in unexpected ways and teach lessons that turn common notions upside-down. Through parables Jesus led people to a new way of thinking and acting.

At first glance the employer in this parable might seem unjust, or at least a bit crazy. Actually he is just very benevolent. The focus of the parable is the employer who rewards all his workers equally—even those who come at the last minute. With incredible loving mercy God grants heaven to people who repent late in life as well as people who have been faithful all their lives. God is free to do this.

The Law of Moses stipulated that day laborers were to be paid before sundown. Holy people who resent the good fortune of repentant sinners—the way the first workers resented the generous pay given to the last workers—are not so holy after all. Law conscious Jewish Christians needed this lesson in regard to sinners and Gentiles who joined the Church of Jesus.

For Discussion

Before the play: Have you ever felt that you were not treated fairly? What did you do?

After the play: How would you feel if you were one of the first workers? How has God shown kindness to all?

Activity

List ways that God has been merciful to you, and then write a prayer of gratitude to God for his great mercy.

Prayer

O God, help us always treat others fairly and with mercy, as we would wish to be treated. Amen.

CAST: JESUS, EMPLOYER, FIRST WORKERS 1, 2,
SECOND WORKERS 1, 2,
THIRD WORKERS 1, 2,
FOURTH WORKERS 1, 2,
LAST WORKERS 1, 2, FOREMAN

PROPS: FIVE BASKETS FOR GRAPES, TEN SILVER COINS

THE WORKERS IN THE VINEYARD MATTHEW 20:1–16

Jesus is to the side. Workers stand in pairs.

Jesus   The kingdom of heaven is like this. Once there was a man who went out early in the morning to hire workers for his vineyard.

Employer enters and goes to First Workers.

Employer   I need help in my vineyard. I'll pay you the usual day's wage, a silver coin. How about it?

First Workers   Great.

Employer   You know where my place is. Go to my vineyard and my foreman will tell you what to do.

First Workers exit. Employer exits in the opposite direction.

Jesus   At nine o'clock the employer again went to the marketplace.

Employer enters and goes to Second Workers.

Employer   You look like you need work. Go and work in my vineyard, and I'll pay you a fair wage.

Second Workers   All right.

Second Workers exit. Employer exits in the opposite direction.

Jesus   At twelve o'clock the employer returned to the marketplace.

Employer enters and goes to Third Workers.

Employer   Would you like a job in my vineyard? Go now and I'll pay you tonight.

Third Workers   Sure.

Third Workers exit. Employer exits in the opposite direction.

Jesus   At three o'clock the employer again hired workers.

Employer enters and goes to Fourth Workers.

Employer   I'm hiring workers for my vineyard. Would you like a job?

Fourth Workers   Yes.

Fourth Workers exit. Employer exits in the opposite direction.

Jesus   It was almost five o'clock in the evening when the employer came again to the marketplace.

Employer enters and goes to Last Workers.

Employer   Why are you wasting the whole day here doing nothing?

Last Workers   No one hired us.

Employer   Well, then, go work in my vineyard.

All exit.

Jesus   At six o'clock in the evening the owner of the vineyard spoke to his foreman.

Employer and Foreman enter.

Employer   Call the workers and give them their pay, beginning with the last and ending with the first.

Foreman   (*shouting*) The day's over. Come for your pay. Those who came last stand in line first.

Workers enter and set down baskets. They go to Foreman and stand two by two from Last Workers to First Workers hired. Employer stands nearby.

Foreman   (*giving Last Workers each a coin*) Here's your silver coin.

First Worker 1   (*to First Worker 2*) Wow! Imagine what we'll get.

Foreman   (*giving each of the others a silver coin*) And here's yours...and yours...and yours...and yours...and yours...and yours...and yours...and yours.

First Worker 1   (*to Employer*) These workers who were hired last worked only one hour, while we did a hard day's work in the hot sun. Yet you paid them the same as you paid us!

Employer   Friend, I am not cheating you. You agreed to do a day's work for one silver coin, didn't you? Now take what belongs to you and go. If I choose to give the person hired last as much as I gave you, don't I have the right to do as I choose with what is mine? Or are you envious because I am generous?

Jesus   So those who are last will be first, and those who are first will be last.

The Wedding Feast

TWENTY-EIGHTH SUNDAY IN ORDINARY TIME: YEAR A

Themes

- members of the kingdom
- readiness for the kingdom

Background Notes

In the ancient Near East the initial invitation to a wedding feast was followed by a second invitation immediately before the celebration. To refuse to go to the feast after first accepting was the height of discourtesy. Since going to a feast for a king's son was a chance to pay homage, the refusal in this parable was also insulting on the political level.

The wedding feast is a symbol of heaven. This parable shows how Israel, the chosen people, sometimes rejected salvation and even killed the prophets who invited them to it. Then all people are welcome. But the man who came later without a wedding garment, a clean white robe, was also rude, especially if, as some scholars think, wedding clothes were provided at the feast. Through laziness or pride he did not put one on. Similarly, we can only enjoy the eternal feast if we are clothed with good deeds. We, too, might miss salvation.

The building of the city in the parable may have been added as a reference to the destruction of Jerusalem in AD 70.

For Discussion

Before the play: Have you ever been to a wedding and the party after the wedding? What was it like?

After the play: Why do you think Jesus compared heaven to a wedding feast? What are some good deeds we can "clothe" ourselves with to be ready for the feast?

Activity

Invite young learners to each design a wedding garment for heaven. On them they can write virtues needed to enter heaven.

Invite older learners to talk about concrete ways they can bring the good news of the "feast"—the kingdom of heaven—to others.

Prayer

Lord, help me obey you in the little
things that come up each day:
the requests of parents and other family
members, teachers, those we work with,
all those in authority.
Multiply our good works for your glory.
Amen.

CAST: JESUS, KING, SERVANTS 1, 2, 3, 4, GUESTS 1, 2, 3, 4, PERSONS 1, 2, 3 (+), MAN

PROPS: OLD SHIRT OR JACKET FOR WEDDING GUEST

THE WEDDING FEAST   MATTHEW 22:1–14

Jesus is at the far side. King and Servants are at one side. Guests are at the other side.

Jesus   The kingdom of heaven is like this. Once there was a king who prepared a wedding feast for his son.

King   (*to Servants 1, 2*) Go, tell the people invited to our wedding feast to come now.

Servants 1, 2 go to Guests.

Servant 1   Come. It's time for the wedding feast at the palace.

Guest 1   I don't feel like going today.

Servant 2   What about you?

Guest 2   We're too busy. (*Servants return to King*)

Servant 1   Your Highness, the guests do not want to come.

King   Maybe they didn't understand. (*to Servants 3, 4*) Come here. Go to my guests. Tell them I have prepared my dinner. My oxen and my fat calves have been slaughtered, and everything is ready. Come to the wedding banquet.

King, Servants 1, 2 exit. Servants 3, 4 go to Guests.

Servant 3   The king has this message for you: My dinner is ready now. My oxen and my fat calves have been slaughtered. Everything is ready. Come to the wedding banquet.

Guest 1   (*leaving*) So long. I'm going to my farm.

Guest 2   (*leaving*) I have to get to my business.

Guests 3, 4 grab Servants 3, 4 and beat them to death.

Guest 3   There. I don't think they'll ever bother anyone again.

Guests exit.

Jesus   When the king heard that his servants had been killed, he sent his soldiers to kill the murderers and burn down their city. Then he called for his servants again.

Persons 1, 2, 3 enter and go to the far side of stage. King, Servants 1, 2 enter.

King   (*to Servants 1, 2*) My wedding feast is ready, but the people I invited did not deserve it. So go out into the streets and invite everyone you can find, good or bad.

Servants   Yes, Your Highness.

Servants go to Persons 1, 2, 3.

Servant 1 (*to Person 1*) Come to the King's wedding feast.

Servant 2 (*to Person 2*) Stop your gambling a while and come to the palace for a feast.

Servant 1 (*to Person 3*) You're invited to a royal wedding feast.

All move to palace, including Man.

King (*walking among people*) Welcome. Welcome to our feast. Come in. Ah, it's good to have the hall filled. (*sees Man without a wedding robe*) Friend, how did you get in here without a wedding robe?

Man is silent.

King (*to Servants 1, 2*) Tie him up hand and foot and throw him into the darkness outside where there will be weeping and gnashing of teeth.

Servants take Man out.

Jesus Many are called, but few are chosen.

A House Built on Rock

Themes
- hearing God's word
- spiritual life

Background Notes

Some parables describe the qualities expected in those who follow Jesus. Often he challenged listeners to take a new look at themselves and their attitudes.

Jesus drew on his experience as a craftsman to teach a lesson about listening to God's word. He knew that a house built on a rock foundation is more secure than one resting on sand. God's word is as strong and bracing as solid rock. A person who acts on it can weather all storms. In contrast, a person who chooses not to live according to God's word eventually finds his or her life in shambles. Wise persons heed God's words; fools ignore them. Wise persons plan for the future; fools live only for the day.

For Discussion

Before the play: How do you receive the message of God's word? What are some of your favorite words of God from Scripture?

After the play: What are some words of God that you use to lead a good life?

Activity

Young learners might draw a house on top of a rock. On the rock they can print things that Jesus told us to do.

Have older learners write a news report of the storm and what it did to the house. Include quotations from the two men.

Prayer

Lord, give us a pure spirit so we can see you,
a humble spirit so we can hear you,
a loving spirit so we can serve you,
a believing spirit so we can live with you. Amen.

—Dag Hammarskjöld

CAST: JESUS, MAN 1, 2

PROPS: TWO CHAIRS, SOUND EFFECTS FOR STORM AND COLLAPSE OF HOUSE

A House Built on Rock   Matthew 7:24–27, Luke 6:47–49

Jesus   Two men were building houses.

Man 1 is digging. Man 2 comes to him.

Man 2   Are you still digging? My house is almost finished, and I started the same time you did.

Man 1   Well, I'm laying a deep foundation. I want my house to be founded on rock.

Man 2   Why bother? My house is built on sand and it looks great, if I do say so myself.

Man 1   I think my extra time and effort will pay off someday. If a storm comes up, my house will be stronger.

Man 2   Good luck.

Man 1 and Man 2 set chairs some distance apart and sit down.

Jesus   The two men were in their finished houses when a fierce storm arose. Rain poured down, flood waters rose, and the wind beat against the houses.

Sounds of a storm.

Man 2   (*jumping up*) Oh, no! The walls are shaking. My house is going to collapse. I had better get out. (*runs outside and turns to watch house*) Oh no...it's falling apart!

Man 1 and Man 2 put their hands over their ears. Sound of house falling.

Man 1   What was that?

Man 2   Now the flooded river is carrying away every piece. I'm ruined! (*goes to home of Man 1, pounds on door*) Help! Help!

Man 1   What's wrong?

Man 2   My house is completely destroyed. Can I stay with you for a while?

Jesus   Anyone who hears my words and obeys them is like a wise man who built his house on rock. The rain fell, the floods came, and the winds blew on that house, but it did not fall because it had been founded on rock.

The Sower

FIFTEENTH SUNDAY IN ORDINARY TIME: YEAR A

Themes

- hearing God's word
- need for faith

Background Notes

Coming from Galilee, a highly agricultural society, Jesus finds in a sower and seed a natural image of God and God's word. In those days farmers planted seeds by casting huge quantities on the ground and then plowing. Footpaths ran through the fields, and slabs of limestone lay close to the surface in some areas. The fate of seeds in different environments corresponded to the fate of God's words in people's lives. In some people the word never has a chance at all. It is immediately destroyed. In stone-hearted people, it does not take root, and it withers at the first challenge. Sometimes the word is choked by life's cares, activities, and pleasures. But some people are like rich soil where the seed produces a great harvest. In the parable much seed is wasted, but what does grow produces an amazing abundance. The reign of God will prevail, despite obstacles.

For Discussion

Before the play: Where do you hear God's word?

After the play: What can you do to let God's word make a bigger difference in your life?

Activity

Involve younger learners in the following activity. Make a story wheel of the parable. Divide a paper plate into four parts. In the sections draw these pictures facing the center of the plate in order: seeds on a path with birds, seeds on rocks withering in the sun, and seeds among thorns, and good seeds that yield crops. Take another paper plate and cut away a wedge not quite to the center and as wide as the original plate's parts. Fasten the second plate to the first plate with a brass fastener so that as you turn one plate the story is revealed.

Invite older learners to choose their favorite saying(s) from the gospels. Type these on the computer, make copies, and put together a booklet for each learner.

Prayer

"When I found your words, I devoured them. They became my joy and the happiness of my heart" (Jeremiah 15:16). Lord, let your words touch my heart. May they guide my life. I want to always remember your words and listen to them. Then my life will be fruitful, and I will also bring life to others. Amen.

CAST: JESUS, FARMER, TWO SEEDS FOR PATH, TWO SEEDS FOR ROCKS, TWO SEEDS FOR THORNS, THREE GOOD SEEDS, TWO BIRDS, TWO THORNS, SUN, CROWD (+)

PROPS: FLASHLIGHT FOR SUN, NINETEEN PAPER EARS OF CORN, BASKET

THE SOWER Matthew 13:3–9, 18–23, Mark 4:2–9, 14–20, Luke 8:4–8, 11–15

Jesus and Crowd are to the side. Thorns stoop in place. Three Good Seeds offstage have three, six, and ten ears of corn respectively, but out of sight.

Jesus   (*to Crowd*) One day a farmer went out to sow some seeds.

Farmer enters followed by nine Seeds. He takes the first three pairs of Seeds by the hand and flings them to their places where they stoop: the path, the rocks, the thorns. He flings the three Good Seeds. Farmer exits.

Jesus   (*pointing to Seeds on path*) Some seeds fell on the path and were trampled on. The birds came and ate them up.

Birds fly in and take away Seeds on path.

Jesus   (*pointing to Seeds on rocky ground*) Other seeds fell on rocky ground where they had little soil and water. They sprang up right away since the soil was not deep.

Two Seeds stand.

Jesus   But as soon as the sun came up...

Sun "shines."

Jesus   They were scorched and, not having roots, they withered away.

Seeds sink to ground.

Jesus   (*pointing to Seeds in thorns*) Other seeds fell among thorns. The thorns grew up and choked them, and they produced no crops.

Thorns and Seeds rise. Thorns wind arms around necks of Seeds. Seeds fall.

Jesus   (*pointing to Three Good Seeds*) Still other seeds fell on rich soil and, growing tall and strong, produced their crop.

Good Seeds stand, smile, and flex arms.

Jesus   Some thirty.

One Good Seed holds out three ears.

Jesus   Some sixty.

One Good Seed holds out six ears.

Jesus   Even a hundredfold.

One Good Seed holds out ten ears. Farmer returns with basket and gathers corn from Three Good Seeds.

Jesus   Listen, anyone who has ears to hear. The seed is the word of God. The seed on the edge of the path (*walks to where they were and gestures*) are people who hear the word, but Satan comes and takes the word from their hearts.

Those who received the seed on rocky ground (*moves to rocky ground and gestures*) are those who first hear the word with joy and believe for a while. But they have no root in them. If a trial comes or some persecution because of the word, they fall away.

Then there are those who receive the word in thorns. (*moves to Thorns and gestures*) These, too, have heard the word, but the worries and riches and pleasures of life choke the word, so they produce nothing.

(*moves to Good Seeds*) And there are those who have received the seed in rich soil. They hear the word and accept it and yield a harvest thirty, sixty, and a hundredfold.

The Good Samaritan

Themes
- love of neighbor
- prejudice
- generosity

Background Notes

This classic story of human mercy is actually Jesus' commentary on the law. The Teacher of the law correctly identifies the path to eternal life as the two greatest commandments: love of God (in the words of the Shema, the Jewish prayer prayed twice a day) and love of neighbor. Jesus illustrates the preeminence of love by a story about a person whose love is stronger than religious taboos, prejudices, and concern for self. The priest and Levite do not assist the victim perhaps because contact with him would make them unclean, and they would not be able to perform their functions at the temple. Perhaps they thought the man was a decoy for bandits who worked the dangerous route. In any case, the priest and Levite avoid carrying out God's law.

In contrast, the Samaritan ministers to the Jewish man in need, even though the Jews considered his people impure—traitors and heretics. Moreover, the Samaritan does so with unusual generosity, sacrificing his time, his goods, his money, and a night's sleep. Besides teaching that love is superior to legalism, Jesus' parable teaches that love must be practical, manifested in deeds. Furthermore, the Good Samaritan story clarifies that the neighbor we are to love is everyone, including our enemies.

For Discussion

Before the play: Talk about a time when you or another person did a generous act for someone.

After the play: What would you do for someone who was hurt, whether physically or emotionally?

Activity

Make a good Samaritan board game. On a large sheet of paper draw a man and a donkey in one corner and an inn in the corner diagonally opposite. Connect the two with a winding path. Separate the path into about 20 sections. Play the game by rolling dice and moving a marker the number of blocks shown on the dice. Before moving, the player must name a good deed. The one to the inn first wins.

Prayer

Jesus, you ask us to love our neighbor as ourselves. Help us put aside prejudice and selfishness, and serve others as you would.

CAST: JESUS, CROWD (+), TEACHER OF THE LAW, MAN, SAMARITAN, ROBBERS 1, 2, PRIEST, LEVITE, INNKEEPER

PROPS: WALLET, TWO SILVER PIECES, TWO JARS FOR OIL AND WINE, WHITE CLOTH FOR BANDAGE

THE GOOD SAMARITAN Luke 10:25–37

Jesus and Crowd are at the side. Teacher of the Law enters and comes to Jesus.

Teacher of the Law Master, what must I do to inherit eternal life?

Jesus What do the Scriptures say? What do you read there?

Teacher of the Law You shall love the Lord your God with all your heart, with all your soul, and with all your strength, and with all your mind, and your neighbor as yourself.

Jesus You have given the right answer. Do this and you will live.

Teacher of the Law But who is my neighbor?

Jesus A man was going down from Jerusalem to Jericho and was attacked by robbers. They took all he had, beat him, and left him half dead.

Man walks alone. Robbers "beat" him, take his money, and leave him lying on the ground.

Jesus A priest came by.

Priest enters, sees Man, moves to other side of road, and continues on.

Jesus A Levite also came there.

Levite enters, sees Man, moves to other side of road, and continues on.

Jesus But a Samaritan who was traveling that way also came upon the man.

Samaritan enters and stops next to Man.

Samaritan Poor fellow. Some oil and wine should help.

Samaritan rubs oil and wine on Man. Takes out cloth and ties it around Man's head.

Jesus The Samaritan lifted the victim onto his own animal and brought him to an inn where he cared for him all night.

Samaritan helps Man up. They exit. Innkeeper enters.

Jesus The next morning the Samaritan went to the innkeeper.

Samaritan enters.

Samaritan (*giving money to Innkeeper*) Here are two silver pieces for that man I brought in. Take care of him. When I come back, I will repay you whatever else you spend.

Jesus Which of the three travelers do you think was neighbor to the man attacked by robbers?

Teacher of the Law The one who showed him mercy.

Jesus Go and do likewise.

The **Persistent Friend**

SEVENTEENTH SUNDAY IN ORDINARY TIME: YEAR C

Background Notes

The Jewish people considered hospitality a sacred duty. The man in this parable was bound to serve his unexpected guest. When he disturbs his neighbor for help, not only is it in the middle of the night, but to open the door the friend has to remove a heavy wooden or iron bar. No doubt the whole family was awakened since they all slept on mats on the floor of the one-room house. Nevertheless, the neighbor responds to the man's pleas because of his friend's persistence. This is a lesson in perseverance in prayer. Of course, God, who is more than friend to us, will answer our cries for help. As a loving parent, God is at our service any time. All we have to do is trust and knock.

For Discussion

Before the play: How do you feel when someone asks you a favor at a bad time? What do you do?

After the play: When should we pray? What might keep us from praying?

Activity

Cover a box with paper. On the paper on all sides of the box write prayer intentions you have. Add pictures and decorations if you wish. Keep the box in your room as a reminder to pray for these intentions.

Prayer

Lord, you say in Scripture, "When you call upon me and come and pray to me, I will hear you. When you search for me, you will find me; if you seek me with all your heart, I will let you find me" (Jeremiah 29:12–13). Today we call to you, come to you, and search for you. Please listen to our prayers. (Invite all to pray in the silence of their hearts, in particular for special intentions they may have.)

CAST: JESUS, DISCIPLES (+), SAM, TRAVELER, FRIEND, CHILDREN 1, 2

PROPS: MAT OR CARPETING FOR BED, THREE LOAVES OF BREAD, CHAIR

THE PERSISTENT FRIEND LUKE 11:5–8

Jesus is off to the side with Disciples. Sam is seated on left side. Friend and Children are sleeping on the floor in the center. Traveler enters and knocks at Sam's house.

Traveler   Sam, Sam. It's me, Joseph.

Sam   (*going to door*) What a surprise! It's good to see you, old friend. Come in.

Traveler   Sorry it's so late. I never thought I'd be getting here at midnight.

Sam   No problem. Just have a seat. I'll be back in a minute.

Traveler sits. Sam goes to Friend's house and knocks.

Sam   Friend, are you awake?

Friend   (*sitting up and rubbing eyes*) Huh? Who's there?

Sam   It's me. Lend me three loaves of bread. A friend of mine on a journey has just arrived at my house, and I have no food to offer him.

Friend   Don't bother me. The door has already been locked, and my family and I are in bed. I can't get up to give you anything.

Sam   Please—just this once.

Friend   Leave me alone!

Sam   Friend, what am I to do if you don't help me?

Friend   Oh, all right. How many loaves do you want?

Sam   Three.

Friend gets loaves, unbolts door, and hands them to Sam.

Sam   Thanks so much.

Jesus   (*to Disciples*) I say to you, ask and you shall receive, seek and you shall find, knock and the door will be opened to you.

The Rich Fool

EIGHTEENTH SUNDAY IN ORDINARY TIME: YEAR C

Background Notes

Jesus put this world's goods in proper perspective in this story. As the rich man solved his problem, his thoughts centered around "I." He seemed to have forgotten about God and his neighbor as he planned for the future. He had a rude awakening. Unfortunately, he hadn't planned for the ultimate future and faced judgment unprepared. The money and property we accumulate in this life mean nothing when we die. In the words of a Spanish proverb: "There are no pockets in shrouds." On the other hand, we will have to give an account of our spiritual wealth. Those who spend their life seeking natural goods rather than spiritual goods will someday regret their mistaken values. As Jesus asks, "What good is it if a person gains the whole world but loses life?" (Matthew 16:26).

For Discussion

Before the play: Why are people greedy? What are some people greedy about?

After the play: What can you do to be less concerned about having material goods?

Activity

Plan a project to share earth's goods with the poor. You might, for example, hold a fundraiser and send the profits to Catholic Relief Services or a local organization that helps the needy.

Prayer

Lord, may I be rich in friends,
rather than money,
rich in peace, rather than fine clothes,
rich in mercy, rather than power,
rich in goodness, rather than gadgets,
rich in courage,
rather than investments,
rich in humility, rather than property,
rich in health, rather than fine foods,
rich in charity, rather than jewels.
Then not only will I be more like you,
but I will enjoy a full and happy life
and nurture life in others.

CAST: JESUS, RICH MAN, SERVANT, VOICE OF GOD

THE RICH FOOL LUKE 12:16–21

Rich Man is center of stage. Jesus stands to the side.

Jesus There was a rich man who had a good harvest.

Servant enters.

Servant Sir, you have never had such good crops.

Man rubs hands together greedily.

Servant Acres and acres of land are ready to be harvested, but the workers will never fit all the grain into the bins.

Rich Man Wonderful! Go now and let me think.

Servant leaves.

Rich Man What should I do? I have no place to store my crops. (*paces floor, thinking*) I know! (*snaps fingers*) I will tear down my barns and build larger ones where I will store all my grain and my goods. Then I will say to myself, "You have plenty of good things for years to come. Relax, eat, drink, and be merry."

God's Voice You fool!

Man gasps.

God's Voice This very night your life is being demanded of you. And the things you have piled up—whose will they be?

Jesus This is how it is with those who store up treasures for themselves but are not rich in the eyes of God.

The Barren Fig Tree

THIRD SUNDAY OF LENT: YEAR C

Themes

- good deeds
- use of gifts
- virtue

Background Notes

In this parable Jesus draws a comparison from nature to encourage his followers to put their faith into action. Just as a fig tree is expected to yield fruit, we sons and daughters of God are expected to produce good deeds. Ordinarily a fig tree needs no extra care. The gardener takes unusual measures to get the barren tree to bear fruit. He does not give up on it. Similarly God endeavors to cultivate virtue in us through grace. Although God is patient, eventually people who do not act like the holy children of God they were meant to be will be deprived of eternal life.

For Discussion

Before the play: How would you feel if you put a lot of effort into something and it didn't work?

After the play: Which virtues are your strong points? (e.g., kindness, honesty, courage)

Activity

Make a tree of good works. Stand a branch in clay or plaster of paris. On small slips of paper write good works. Make a hole in each slip, put an opened paper clip or a piece of string through it, and hang it on the tree. You might fold the slip in half so it can't be read and have family members take one from the tree to practice each day.

Prayer

Have the children think of saints and the good fruit (good deeds) they were known for. Then invite them to pray to the saint, asking for the grace to imitate him or her. For example, St. Peter Claver, pray that we may have a heart for the poor. St. Frances Cabrini, pray for us that we may help the persons working in the missions.

CAST: JESUS, MAN, GARDENER

PROPS: TREE (A PLANT OR A DRAWING ON THE BOARD), TOOLS FOR GARDENER: HOE, RAKE

THE BARREN FIG TREE LUKE 13:6–9

Jesus is to the side. Gardener is working some distance from the tree.

Jesus A man had a fig tree planted in his vineyard, and he came looking for fruit on it.

Man enters and searches tree for fruit.

Jesus But he did not find any.

Man (*shaking head*) Again no fruit? What's wrong with this tree? (*calling to Gardener*) Gardener, see here. For three years I have come looking for fruit on this fig tree, and still I find none. Cut it down! Why should it be wasting the soil?

Gardener Sir, let it alone for one more year. I will dig around it and fertilize it. If it bears fruit next year, well and good. But if not, you can cut it down.

Man Oh, all right. But tend it well.

The Crafty Steward

TWENTY-FIFTH SUNDAY IN ORDINARY TIME: YEAR C

Background Notes

A steward in charge of finances is about to be fired for squandering his employer's money. As preparation for the future when he will need friends, the shrewd agent does a favor for his employer's debtors: He reduces the amount they owe. The steward is praised not for his crooked acts, but for his ingenuity in managing his life. This parable concretizes Jesus' advice to his disciples, "Be shrewd as serpents and simple as doves" (Matthew 10:16).

The struggle between good and evil demands clever strategies on our part. It may even require sacrificing material goods. If people in the business world apply themselves earnestly to gain material goods, shouldn't we devote our energy and intelligence to working for heavenly goods?

For Discussion

Before the play: What do you do to live your faith as hard as you try to succeed in school, sports, work, etc.?

After the play: What can you learn from this parable about the importance of trying hard to be good Christians?

Activity

Name five characters from literature or from the movies. Work out a salvation strategy for each one. Pinnochio, for example, would have to obey Gepetto, tell the truth, stay away from bad companions, and listen to his conscience.

Prayer

*Jesus, help me plan one way to be a better follower. (*Time for reflection when the children think of how they can love God or others better.*) Holy Spirit, give me the grace to follow my plan.*

CAST: JESUS, RICH MAN, REPORTER, STEWARD, MESSENGER, DEBTORS 1, 2

PROPS: TWO SCROLLS FOR INVOICES, DESK AND CHAIR

THE CRAFTY STEWARD LUKE 16:1–9

Rich Man is seated at desk. Reporter enters.

Reporter Excuse me, sir. I think you should know that the fellow who is managing your property is wasting it.

Rich Man Thank you for the news. Please have him come here.

Reporter leaves. Enters with Steward.

Rich Man What is this I hear about you? Draw up an account of your management, for you can no longer be my manager.

Rich Man exits.

Steward What will I do, now that my master is taking the position away from me? I am not strong enough to dig. I am ashamed to go begging. Ah, I know what to do to make sure that when I am unemployed people will welcome me into their homes. Messenger!

Messenger enters.

Steward Have Jonah and Matthew come here.

Messenger exits. Debtors 1, 2 enter.

Steward (*to Debtor 1*) How much do you owe my master?

Debtor 1 One hundred jugs of olive oil.

Steward (*giving him a scroll*) Take your bill, sit down quickly, and write down fifty.

Debtor 1 Say, thanks!

Debtor 1 sits and writes, then exits.

Steward (*to Debtor 2*) How much do you owe?

Debtor 2 A hundred containers of wheat.

Steward (*handing him a scroll*) Here is your bill. Make it eighty.

Debtor 2 Great!

Debtor 2 and Steward exit. Rich Man enters.

Reporter Do you know what your clever manager did? He called in your debtors and let them reduce the amount they owed.

Rich Man Well, I have to give him credit. He certainly is smart.

Jesus enters.

Jesus The children of this world are more clever than the children of light in making use of their skills.

The Rich Man and Lazarus

TWENTY-SIXTH SUNDAY IN ORDINARY TIME: YEAR C

Themes

- hearing God's word
- love of neighbor
- materialism
- riches
- virtue

Background Notes

This parable in Luke is the story form of a beatitude from the Sermon on the Plain (6:20–26): Those who are hungry now will be satisfied, and those who are filled now will be hungry. The rich man (sometimes called Dives) and Lazarus (the only person given a name in Jesus' parables) were at extreme ends of the economic scale. The rich man wore purple robes and linen undergarments, the clothes of the elite, while Lazarus longs for even the scraps from the table. Someone suggests that these scraps were hunks of bread that the diners, who had no silverware, used to wipe their fingers.

Being rich is no sin, but the selfish use of riches is. The rich man's crime was that he ignored the human being in need on his doorstep. He received his just deserts in hell, while Lazarus rested with Abraham, which meant the highest level of bliss. When the rich man tried to prevent his brothers from repeating his mistake, he was told that they had had enough warning. Abraham's ending statement was prophetic. Although Jesus did rise from the dead, people continued in their selfish, uncaring ways.

For Discussion

Before the play: What do you do to help your needy brothers and sisters?

After the play: Who are the poor in our lives and how we can help them? How can you become more aware of others' needs?

Activity

Learn about the poor in one section of the world, perhaps your own town. Read articles, watch a video, or invite a speaker. Your diocesan mission office might give you ideas. Decide how you can help others who are less fortunate than you.

Prayer

Have the children think of different countries and pray for the poor people in them using the form "For the poor people in _____, let us pray to the Lord."

CAST: JESUS, RICH MAN, LAZARUS, SERVANT, ABRAHAM, ANGELS (+)

PROPS: PLATE, CUP, DESK FOR TABLE

THE RICH MAN AND LAZARUS LUKE 16:19–31

Jesus stands off to the side. Lazarus lies at gate. Rich Man is seated at table. Servant stands behind him. Abraham stands at a distance.

Jesus Once there was a rich man who dressed in purple garments and fine linen. He ate magnificent meals every day. There was also a poor man named Lazarus, who was covered with sores. He lay at the rich man's gate. Dogs even came and licked his sores.

Servant leaves Rich Man and goes to Lazarus.

Servant What are you doing here?

Lazarus Food, please. I'm starving. Are there any pieces that have fallen from your master's table?

Servant No. The dogs eat the scraps. (*exits*)

Jesus Lazarus died and angels took him to the bosom of Abraham.

Angels enter and take Lazarus next to Abraham.

Jesus The rich man also died and was buried.

Rich Man slumps at table.

Jesus He was punished in the land of the dead.

Angels take Rich Man some distance from Lazarus and Abraham.

Rich Man Father Abraham, have mercy on me. Send Lazarus to dip the tip of his finger in water to cool my tongue, for I am in agony in these flames.

Abraham My child, remember that during your lifetime you received all good things and Lazarus suffered. Now he is comforted here, while you are in pain. Besides all this, between you and us there is a great pit. (*spreads arms wide*) Those who want to cross from our side to yours cannot do so. Nor can anyone cross from your side to ours.

Rich Man (*pleading*) Then, Father, I beg you to send Lazarus to my father's house. I have five brothers. Let Lazarus warn them so that they do not end up in this place of pain.

Abraham They have Moses and the prophets. They should listen to them.

Rich Man That is not enough, Father Abraham. But if someone goes to them from the dead, they would turn from their sins.

Abraham If they will not listen to Moses and the prophets, neither will they be convinced if someone rises from the dead.

Rich Man covers face and groans.

Rich Man What a blind fool I was!

The Judge and the Widow

TWENTY-NINTH SUNDAY IN ORDINARY TIME: YEAR C

Themes

- perseverance in prayer
- courage

Background Notes

In the natural world, even a rock-like resistance is eroded by constant pounding. Jesus illustrated this by the story of a woman who hounded a tough, unjust judge for her rights. Weary of her persistent nagging, the judge finally agreed to use his power to give her what she wanted. Jesus assures us that in the same way God will respond to our cries for justice. Not a grasping, selfish judge, but a generous Father, God hears us when we call. With confidence, trust, and patience we can turn to the Lord, our just and merciful judge, for help. If we never give up asking, God will reward us with the good we desire.

For Discussion

Before the play: Can you tell a story about prayers that were eventually answered?

After the play: What are some things that are worth praying for? How can you pray repeatedly for something?

Activity

Thanksgiving is the best petition. Think of one way God has answered your prayers. Design a thank-you card and then write a thank-you note to God inside.

Prayer

Decide on a certain intention and pray a decade of the rosary for it.

CAST: JESUS, JUDGE, PERSON, WIDOW, VISITOR

THE JUDGE AND THE WIDOW LUKE 18:1–8

Jesus It's important to pray always and not get discouraged. In a certain city there was a judge.

Judge passes by, followed by Widow. Person and Visitor stand talking.

Person (*to Visitor*) There's our judge. He's a real crook. You can't trust him.

Visitor I wonder what that woman wants.

Person She's a widow who lives here, too. The poor woman has been cheated by someone. Everyday she begs the judge to act in her favor. She might as well forget it, if her enemy has bribed the judge.

Widow (*to Judge*) Sir, give me justice against my enemy.

Judge You've been bothering me for days now. When will you stop?

Widow When you stand up for my rights.

Judge (*sighing*) All right. All right. I'll take care of your case tomorrow.

Widow (*leaving*) Thank you, Your Honor.

Judge (*shrugging*) Though I have no fear of God and no respect for anyone, yet because this widow keeps bothering me, I will grant her justice. If I don't, she will wear me out by continually coming.

Jesus Won't God give justice to his chosen people who call out to him day and night? Will he be slow to answer them? I tell you, he will quickly grant justice to them.

The Pharisee and the Tax Collector

Thirtieth Sunday in Ordinary Time: Year C

Themes

- self-righteousness
- humility
- virtue

Background Notes

A Pharisee, an expert in religion, was meticulous in keeping the laws. On the other hand, a tax collector had the reputation of being dishonest. Tax collectors in Palestine were despised because they collected money for Rome, the oppressor, and pocketed whatever was above their quota.

Through two brief prayers Jesus sketches the pictures of a proud, holy man and a humble sinner. This self-righteous Pharisee's prayer was a list of his own accomplishments. He did more than was required in fasting and tithing. Jews were only required to fast one day a year, the Day of Atonement, while the Pharisee fasted twice a week. However, this man gives the impression that he has earned God's love. On the other hand, the tax collector's prayer was an admission of guilt and a plea for help. In fact, he called himself "the sinner." The Pharisee had done everything perfectly, but he was obnoxious in his smugness. The tax collector, relying on God for salvation rather than himself, was a better candidate for sainthood.

For Discussion

Before the play: How do you feel when a person tells everyone about all the good he or she does?

After the play: Share some examples of persons who do good works without making a show.

Activity

Long ago repentant sinners wore sackcloth and sprinkled ashes on their heads as a sign that they were truly sorry for their sins. Cut a shirt shape out of burlap or brown paper and mark it with a black cross to represent ashes. Keep it near your bed to remind you to ask forgiveness for any sins you committed that day.

Prayer

Invite the children to think of one of their sins or faults and then pray:

> Lord, have mercy. Lord, have mercy.
> Christ, have mercy. Christ, have mercy.
> Lord, have mercy. Lord, have mercy.

CAST: JESUS, PHARISEE, TAX COLLECTOR, CROWD (+)

THE PHARISEE AND THE TAX COLLECTOR LUKE 18:9–14

Jesus and Crowd are off to the side.

Jesus Some people are proud of their virtue and look down on everyone else. Once two people went up to the Temple to pray. One was a Pharisee, and the other was a tax collector.

Pharisee enters, faces audience, arms raised and head unbowed. The Tax Collector enters and stays far back and to the side. He kneels, keeping his head and eyes down.

Pharisee God, I thank you that I am not like other people: thieves, criminals, and adulterers—or even like this tax collector here. (*gestures to Tax Collector*) I fast twice a week. I give a tenth of all my income.

Tax Collector (*beating breast*) God, be merciful to me, a sinner.

Jesus (*pointing to Tax Collector*) This man, I tell you, went home from the Temple at rights with God. The other did not. For everyone who exalts himself will be humbled, but all who humble themselves will be exalted.

The Unforgiving Servant

TWENTY-FOURTH SUNDAY IN ORDINARY TIME: YEAR A

Background Notes

Jesus' disciples should be distinguished by their readiness to forgive one another. The Lord's Prayer reminds us of this when we pray, "Forgive us our trespasses as we forgive those who trespass against us." Through the parable of the unforgiving servant, we come to realize that mercy toward others is a logical response since God has forgiven us what we could never make up for.

In those days it was the practice of higher servants to borrow their rich employer's money for private investments of their own. The servant in the parable owed the king an exorbitant amount of money, which he could never repay. The oriental king unexpectedly waived the entire debt for his servant. Then when this servant met someone who owed him only a paltry sum, he dared to treat him harshly for not being able to repay him. The servant's action is obviously outrageous. The parable makes plain why we ought to be willing to forgive our brothers and sisters seventy-seven times, which means an indefinite number of times.

For Discussion

Before the play: When are times that you have forgiven others? When have you been forgiven?

After the play: How can you express gratitude to God for forgiving you? How can you show others that you forgive them?

Activity

Invite young learners to carry out this activity. On one half of a sheet of drawing paper draw something to show how you feel when you need to be forgiven. On the other half draw something to show how you feel after you've been forgiven.

Older learners might write short, modern scenarios where one person has to forgive another.

Prayer

Jesus, you said that we should forgive seventy times seven, in other words, always. Make my heart to be like yours so that I can forgive those who hurt me. May I forget about getting even, seeking revenge, and telling others about the injustice. Instead, let me show kindness to those who harmed me and accept them as friends so that I may promote peace and love. Amen.

CAST: JESUS, PETER, KING, SERVANTS 1, 2, 3, 4

PROP: A SCROLL, CHAIR

THE UNFORGIVING SERVANT MATTHEW 18:21–35

Jesus is off to one side. King is seated in center with scroll. Peter enters and goes to Jesus.

Peter   Lord, if another member of the Church sins against me, how often should I forgive? As many as seven times?

Jesus   Not seven times, but, I tell you, seventy-seven times. The kingdom of God is like this. Once there was a king who decided to check on his servants' accounts.

King looks at scroll. Servant 1 is brought in by Servants 2, 3.

Servant 2   Your Highness, here is the man who owes millions of dollars.

Servant 1   Your Excellency, I do not have enough money to pay off this debt.

King   (*to Servants 2, 3*) Take him away and have him sold as a slave, and his wife and children, too. Sell all he owns in order to pay the debt he owes.

Servant 1   (*breaking away and falling on his knees*) Have patience with me, and I will pay back everything.

King   Very well. I'll cancel your debt. You may go free.

Servant 1   How can I ever thank you?

Servants 2, 3 walk to other side. King reads scroll. Servant 4 enters. Servant 1 starts shaking Servant 4. Servants 2, 3 watch.

Servant 1   I loaned you a little money, remember? Pay back what you owe.

Servant 4   (*kneeling*) Have patience with me, and I will pay you back.

Servant 1   No way. You're going to jail until you pay your debt.

Servant 1 takes Servant 4 out.

Servant 2   (*to Servant 3*) How can he do that when the king just cancelled his debt?

Servants 2, 3 go to King.

Servant 3   Your Highness, the servant whose debt you cancelled is an ungrateful wretch.

Servant 2   He is taking one of your men to jail because that man owes him a few dollars.

King   Call that servant here.

Servants 2, 3 exit and return with Servant 1.

King   (*to Servant 1, angrily*) You wicked servant! I cancelled your entire debt, because you pleaded with me. You should have had mercy on your fellow servant, just as I had mercy on you. (*to Servants 2, 3*) Take him out of my sight. Let him suffer in jail until he pays back the whole amount.

Servants 2, 3 take out Servant 1.

Jesus   That is how my heavenly Father will treat you, if you do not forgive your brother or sister from your heart.

The Two Sons

TWENTY-SIXTH SUNDAY IN ORDINARY TIME: YEAR A

Background Notes

On one level this parable instructs us to act according to our words. Mere lip service is worthless. If we say we are Christians, our lives should show it. We should not be like the older son who says one thing and does another. Better to be like the younger son who has a change of heart and carries out the father's will after all. On another level, since Jesus was speaking to the chief priests and elders, this parable is seen as a condemnation of them. The older son represented the religious leaders. They originally bound themselves to follow God's law as the chosen people, but then did not accept the prophet John and Jesus. The younger son stood for the religious outcasts who repented and the Gentiles who received salvation. Someone once pointed out that Jesus is the third son who both said yes and lived yes.

For Discussion

Before the play: How would you feel if someone promised to do something for you and then didn't? Why is it important to keep promises and resolutions?

After the play: What responsibilities flow from our baptismal commitment? Being a Christian means we always have the chance for conversion. How can we say yes to God by our actions?

Activity

Invite young learners to do this activity. Make a doorknob hanger to remind you to say yes and follow through with your promise. Cut a sheet of paper in half. At the center of one short end of the rectangle about an inch from the edge draw a circle about two inches wide. Slit the paper from the circle to the edge of the paper so it can be put around a doorknob. Print "Yes, Lord!" on the paper and draw pictures or designs around the words. Keep it on the door of your room.

Older learners might design their own symbols for the virtues.

Prayer

Mary, when God asked you to do something, you answered, "Behold, I am the servant of the Lord." For the rest of your life you lived out these words. Pray for me that I may live out my baptismal commitment. May I have the courage and love to follow the teachings of your Son, Jesus, all my life.

CAST: JESUS, RELIGIOUS LEADERS (+), FATHER, SONS 1, 2

THE TWO SONS   MATTHEW 21:28–32

Jesus is off to the side with the Religious Leaders. Sons 1, 2 are some distance apart.

Jesus   What do you think of this? There was once a man who had two sons. One day he went to the older son.

Father enters and goes to Son 1.

Father   Son, go and work in the vineyard today.

Son 1   I can't go, Father. I have other things to do.

Father leaves.

Son 1   (*to self*) Now why did I say no? Here my father needs help and I have time. I think I'll go work in the vineyard after all.

Son 1 leaves. Father enters and goes to Son 2.

Father   Son, go and work in the vineyard today.

Son 2   I will go, Father.

Father exits.

Son 2   (*to self*) I think I'll go see my friend Jacob. I'm sure Father doesn't really need me in the vineyard.

Son 2 exits.

Jesus   Which of the two sons did what the father wanted?

Leaders   The older one.

Jesus   Truly I tell you, tax collectors and sinful women are going into the kingdom of God ahead of you. For John the Baptist came to you showing you the right path and you did not believe him. But the tax collectors and the sinful women believed him. Even when you saw it, you did not change your minds and believe him.

The Ten Bridesmaids

THIRTY-SECOND SUNDAY IN ORDINARY TIME: YEAR A

Background Notes

This is one of the crisis parables that show how we must act immediately to choose salvation. Through lack of planning and foresight, the five foolish bridesmaids missed the wedding feast. Jesus wants us to be prepared with good deeds since we do not know when the kingdom will come. Just as the bridegroom in the parable did not come on schedule, the kingdom did not arrive when the Israelites had expected. Now two thousand years later, we still await it. When the divine bridegroom arrives to take us into the eternal feast, we should be ready with our lamps burning brightly. Those who are not caught by surprise will be admitted to the joys of heaven.

For Discussion

Before the play: How can you prepare for meeting Jesus?

After the play: What oil should you have ready for Christ's coming? How do you make sure the bridegroom recognizes you?

Activity

Invite young learners to draw an oil lamp with rays of light coming forth from it. On each ray write a virtue needed to enter the kingdom of heaven.

Have older learners write an interview with one of the wise or foolish virgins.

Prayer

Teach me, Lord, to be sweet and gentle in all the events of life, in disappointments, in the thoughtlessness of those I trusted, in the unfaithfulness of those I relied on. Let me think of the happiness of others. Teach me to learn from the suffering that comes across my path. May I be generous in my forgiveness. May no one be less good for having come within my influence. No one less pure, less true, less kind, less noble for having been a fellow traveler in our journey toward Eternal Life. Amen.

CAST: JESUS, WISE BRIDESMAIDS 1, 2, 3, 4, 5, FOOLISH BRIDESMAIDS 1, 2, 3, 4, 5, BRIDEGROOM, ANNOUNCER, SERVANT, CROWD (+)

PROPS: TEN LAMPS: FIVE WITH LARGE FLAMES, FIVE WITH SMALL FLAMES; FIVE CONTAINERS OF OIL

THE TEN BRIDESMAIDS MATTHEW 25:1–13

Jesus and Crowd are off to the side. The Wise and Foolish Bridesmaids are together, the Wise ones with large flames in their torches and the Foolish with small flames.

Jesus The kingdom of heaven will be like this. Ten Bridesmaids took their lamps and went to meet the Bridegroom for the wedding feast.

Wise Bridesmaid 1 There's no sign of him yet. I'm glad I brought extra oil along to keep my lamp burning.

Wise Bridesmaids 2, 3, 4, 5 I did, too.

Foolish Bridesmaid 1 I hope he comes soon. I didn't bring any extra oil.

Foolish Bridesmaids 2, 3, 4, 5 I didn't either.

Wise Bridesmaid 2 We might as well sit while we're waiting.

Ten Bridesmaids sit down and set their lamps on the ground.

Foolish Bridesmaid 2 (*yawning*) I'm so tired.

Ten Bridesmaids nod and then fall asleep.

Announcer's Voice Look! Here is the bridegroom. Come out to meet him.

Ten Bridesmaids jump up and pick up their lamps.

Wise Bridesmaid 3 It's midnight already.

Five Wise Bridesmaids pour oil into their lamps.

Foolish Bridesmaid 3 Give us some of your oil.

Foolish Bridesmaid 4 Our lamps are going out.

Wise Bridesmaid 4 No, for there will not be enough for you and us.

Wise
Bridesmaid 5   You had better go to the dealers and buy some for yourselves.

Five Foolish Bridesmaids exit. Bridegroom enters with Announcer and Servant.

Bridegroom   Come in. Come in. (*to Servant*) Bar the door.

All go through doorway. Servant bars the door. Foolish Bridesmaids return.

Foolish
Bridesmaid 5   (*pounding on door*) Lord, Lord.

Foolish
Bridesmaid 1   Open the door for us.

Bridegroom   I tell you I do not know you.

Five Foolish Bridesmaids exit sadly.

Jesus   Keep awake therefore, for you do not know when the Bridegroom will come.

The Three Servants and the Money

THIRTY-THIRD SUNDAY IN ORDINARY TIME: YEAR A

Themes

- good deeds
- use of gifts

Background Notes

This parable illustrates the necessity of using whatever gifts we have been given, both spiritual and natural gifts. Two servants put their money to work and increased it. They were handsomely rewarded. The third servant did absolutely nothing with the money entrusted to him. He didn't even put it in the bank. For his lack of initiative he was severely punished. Our sharing of the master's joy depends on our response to his graces and gifts. We can either develop our gifts and share them, or we can bury them and waste them. The choice is ours. The parable can also be taken as a warning to some Pharisees who wanted to keep things as they were.

For Discussion

Before the play: What gifts did God give you and how did you use them?

After the play: What is the meaning of the saying, "What I am is God's gift to me; what I become is my gift to God"?

Activity

Invite young learners to carry out this activity. At the bottom of a sheet of paper trace your open hand face up. Turn the paper so the hand faces you. Draw five circles below the hand to represent the coins. In each circle print a gift that you have.

Have older learners draw or write about themselves, sharing one of their gifts.

Prayer

Holy Spirit, thank you for the gifts you have given me—gifts of body, mind, and spirit. Inspire me to use and not waste these talents and gifts to show that I am truly grateful for them. Let me use them for your greater honor and glory and to further your kingdom here on earth. Amen.

CAST: JESUS, CROWD (+), MAN, BANKER, SERVANTS 1, 2, 3

PROPS: FIVE BAGS OF MONEY: ONE MARKED 1000, TWO MARKED 2000, TWO MARKED 5000; SHOVEL; "BANK" SIGN

THE THREE SERVANTS AND THE MONEY
MATTHEW 25:14–30, LUKE 19:11–27

Jesus is off to the side with the Crowd. Man has three bags: 5000, 2000, and 1000. Servants stand in background. Banker stands by Bank sign.

Jesus The coming of the kingdom is like this. A man about to go on a journey entrusted his property to his servants according to their ability.

Man Come here, please. I have something to say.

Servants go to Man.

Man As you know, I'm going on a long trip. While I'm away, I'd like you to take care of my money. (*hands 5000 bag to Servant 1*) Here are 5000 silver pieces for you. (*Then hands 2000 bag to Servant 2*) Here are 2000 for you. (*Then hands 1000 bag to Servant 3*) Here are 1000 for you. I expect each of you to do your best to increase the amount given to you.

Man exits. Servants 1, 2 go to Banker. Servant 3 takes shovel and goes in the opposite direction.

Servant 1 (*to Banker*) I would like to invest these 5000 silver pieces.

Banker (*taking bag*) Wonderful. An intelligent choice.

Servant 2 (*to Banker*) I would like to invest these 2000 silver pieces.

Banker (*taking bag*) Yes, sir.

Servants 1, 2 and Banker exit.

Servant 3 (*to self while digging*) I'll hide the master's money so no one can steal it.

Servant 3 exits.

Jesus After a long time the master returned.

Man enters. Shortly after, Servant 1 enters with two bags of 5000.

Man Well, give me a report on my funds.

Servant 1 Sir, you gave me 5000. I have made 5000 more.

Man Well done, my good and faithful servant. Since you were faithful in small matters, I will put you in charge of greater. Come, share your master's joy.

Servant 2 enters with two bags of 2000.

Servant 2 Sir, you gave me 2000. I have made 2000 more.

Man Well done, my good and faithful servant. Since you were faithful in small matters, I will put you in charge of greater. Come, share your master's joy.

Servant 3 enters with bag of 1000.

Servant 3   Sir, I knew you were a hard man. You reap where you did not sow, and gather crops where you did not scatter seed. So I was afraid, and I went and hid your money in the ground. Here it is.

Man   You worthless and lazy servant. So you knew I reap where I did not sow and gather crops where I did not scatter seed? Then you ought to have invested my money with the bankers, and on my return I would have received what was my own with interest.

(*to Servant 2*) Take the thousand away from him and give it to the man with 10,000. Those who have will be given more until they are rich, but those who have nothing, even what they have will be taken away.

Servant 2 takes bag from Servant 3 and gives it to Servant 1.

Man   As for this useless servant, throw him into the darkness outside where there will be weeping and gnashing of teeth.

Servants 1, 2 take hold of Servant 3 and exit.

The Entry into Jerusalem

PASSION SUNDAY (PROCESSION): YEARS A, B, C

Themes

- the identity of Jesus
- humility

Background Notes

Jesus entered Jerusalem as Messiah-king. Jerusalem was the holy city where the Temple was located. It was also King David's city. Jesus rode a colt, not a horse, because he was not a military Messiah but a humble one who came in peace. The people who knew about his raising Lazarus from the dead acclaimed him as king and Messiah. They hoped for the restoration of David's kingdom. They laid branches on the ground to make it soft. They spread their cloaks, the red carpet treatment afforded royalty. They greeted Jesus with hosannas, a cry of acclamation that means "Do save us." The Pharisees feared that the procession might attract the notice of the Romans. But their attempts to quell the noisy crowd were futile. They admitted that the whole world was following Jesus.

For Discussion

Before the play: Do you have palm branches in your home? When do you receive this sacramental? Why?

After the play: Why did the people honor Jesus? How do you honor him in your home?

Activity

Compose a song or poem praising Jesus. You might set words to a tune that you know. Alternate activity: Listen to or sing a hymn of praise.

Prayer

Have the learners sing a song acclaiming Christ as king. This could be a hymn sung on Passion Sunday such as "All Glory, Laud and Honor," "Blessings on the King," "Ride On, Ride On," a "Holy, Holy" from the celebration of the Eucharist, or a general hymn of praise.

CAST: NARRATOR, JESUS, DISCIPLES 1, 2 (+), BYSTANDER, CROWD (+), PHARISEES 1, 2 (+), PERSON (+)

PROPS: CHAIR FOR COLT, ROPE AND BLANKET FOR COLT, CLOAKS, BRANCHES

THE ENTRY INTO JERUSALEM
MATTHEW 21:1–11, MARK 11:1–11, LUKE 19:28–40, JOHN 12:12–19

Jesus and Disciples enter. Bystander and "colt" are off to the side.

Narrator   Jesus and his disciples walked toward Jerusalem.

Jesus   (*to Disciples 1, 2*) Go into the village ahead of you. As you enter it, you will find a colt which no one has ever sat on. Untie it and bring it here. And if anyone should ask you, "Why are you untying it?" just say, "The master has need of it."

Disciples 1, 2, walk toward colt.

Disciple 1   There's the colt, just as Jesus said.

Disciple 2 unties the colt.

Bystander   What are you doing? Untying the colt?

Disciple 2   The master has need of it.

Bystander   Oh, all right then.

Disciples 1, 2 and Bystander go to Jesus. Disciple 2 leads colt.

Disciple 1   (*to Jesus*) We found it.

Disciples throw cloaks over the colt, help Jesus mount it. Crowd enters. Some throw cloaks on the ground. Others spread branches. Half the Crowd go before Jesus, and half follow. He rides the colt.

Disciples and Crowd   (*loudly with joy*) Hosanna to the Son of David! Blessed is he who comes in the name of the Lord—the King of Israel! Hosanna in the highest!

Pharisee 1   (*to Jesus*) Teacher, stop them!

Jesus   I tell you, if they keep silent, the stones themselves will shout out!

Narrator   The procession entered Jerusalem.

Person enters.

Person   Who is this?

Crowd   This is Jesus, the prophet from Nazareth in Galilee.

Pharisee 2   (*to Pharisee 1*) Look, the whole world is running after him!

Pharisee 1   (*angrily*) And we can do nothing.

Narrator   The crowd who praised Jesus on Palm Sunday, a few days later was calling for his death. We are called to be faithful to Jesus every day, especially when it is hard.

The **Last Supper**

Themes

- the Eucharist
- service
- love of neighbor

Background Notes

The earliest record of the institution of the Eucharist is in 1 Corinthians 11:23–25. Then in John's account of the Last Supper, the washing of the feet is described but not the institution of the Eucharist. The washing is a parable in action of what the Eucharist stands for. By assuming the role of the lowest servant, Jesus showed his disciples how they were to love one another. The four gospel accounts of the Last Supper differ in other details. In the gospels of Matthew and Mark, the betrayal of Judas occurs before the Eucharist, but in Luke and John, Judas shares the meal with Jesus.

By the time of Jesus, the Jewish people had adapted the Hellenistic custom of eating while reclining on carpets and pillows around a low table. The diners shared large bowls in the center. It is supposed that the Last Supper was the Passover meal. Blessing of the bread and distributing it and the drinking of wine was part of that Jewish ritual. The paschal lamb is the symbol of Christ, the unblemished victim of the sin of humankind. As at the Passover meal, after sharing the bread and wine, Jesus as presider explained their meaning. Unlike the Passover meal, the bread becomes his body and the wine his blood. He was inaugurating a covenant. Just as covenants of the Old Testament were ratified by sprinkling the blood of the sacrificed animal over the people, Jesus sealed his new covenant with his blood—the symbol of life. He was the new Passover victim.

For Discussion

Before the play: What is the greatest gift that anyone can give you? When did Jesus give himself to us?

After the play: Why do we celebrate the Eucharist? How can we participate in the Eucharist fully?

Activity

Plan a simple but special family meal for Holy Thursday, to recall the Last Supper.

Prayer

Lord Jesus Christ, I firmly believe that you are present in the Blessed Sacrament as true God and true man, with your Body and Blood, soul and divinity. My redeemer, I adore you with the angels and saints. I believe, O Lord; increase my faith. Amen.

CAST: Narrator, Jesus, Peter, John, Judas, Apostles (9)

PROPS: Table, bread, cup, bowl, robe for Jesus, basin, pitcher, towel, psalm to sing

THE LAST SUPPER

MATTHEW 26:20–30, MARK 14:17–26, LUKE 22:14–22, JOHN 13:1–30, 31–35, 36—14:3; 25–26

Jesus and Twelve Apostles are eating around table. John is next to Jesus.

Narrator   At Jesus' direction the apostles had prepared for the Passover meal in a large upper room in Jerusalem. When it was evening, he came there with the Twelve.

Jesus stands, removes his robe, and ties a towel around his waist. He pours water into a basin, and "washes" and "dries" the feet of the Apostles except for Peter.

Peter   Lord, are you going to wash my feet?

Jesus   You do not know now what I am doing, but later you will understand.

Peter   You will never wash my feet.

Jesus   Unless I wash you, you will have no share with me.

Peter   (*extending hands*) Lord, then not only my feet, but also my hands and my head!

Jesus "washes" and "dries" Peter's feet. Then he puts on robe and goes to table.

Jesus   Do you realize what I have done for you? You call me "Teacher" and "Lord," and you are right, for that is what I am. So if I, (*points to self*) your Lord and Teacher, have washed your feet, you (*gestures to Apostles*) ought to wash one another's feet. Servants are not greater than their master. Amen, amen, I say to you, one of you will betray me.

Apostles look at one another.

John   Surely not I, Lord?

Apostles   Surely not I, Lord?

Jesus   It is the one to whom I hand the bread after I have dipped it. (*dips bread in a bowl and hands it to Judas*) Do quickly what you are going to do.

Judas exits. All continue eating.

Jesus   (*taking bread*) Blessed are you, O Lord our God, King of the universe. You have made this bread holy. (*breaks bread and passes it to Apostles*) Take and eat. This is my body. Do this in remembrance of me.

(*taking the cup*) Blessed are you, O Lord our God, King of the universe, Creator of the vine. (*gives cup to Apostles*) Drink from it, all of you, for this is my blood of the covenant, which shall be shed for many for the forgiveness of sins.

I am with you only a little longer. I give you a new commandment, that you love one another. Just as I have loved you, you also should love one another. By this everyone will know that you are my disciples, if you have love for one another.

Peter   Lord, where are you going?

Jesus   Where I am going, you cannot follow me now.

Peter   (*with enthusiasm*) Lord, why can I not follow you now? I will lay down my life for you.

Jesus   Very truly, I tell you, before the cock crows you will have denied me three times. (*to all*) Do not let your hearts be troubled. In my Father's house there are many dwelling places. If I go and prepare a place for you, I will come again and will take you to myself, so that where I am, there you may be also.

The Holy Spirit, whom the Father will send in my name, will teach you everything and remind you of all that I have said to you. I am going to the Father. Rise, let us be on our way.

Narrator   Jesus gave us the gift of himself in the Eucharist. Each time we celebrate Mass we remember him and his sacrifice for us. We receive him into our hearts in Communion. Let us celebrate the Eucharist often and with great joy.

All sing a psalm and exit.

The Agony
in the Garden

PASSION SUNDAY: YEARS A, B, C

Themes

- prayer
- the mission of Jesus
- obedience
- the suffering of Jesus

Background Notes

The garden Jesus and his apostles went to was probably the private garden of a friend. Jesus took the favored three and then left them to pray by himself. He was overwhelmed by sorrow. He asked that the Father take the cup of suffering away from him but submitted to the divine plan. When he, the innocent one, took on our sins and accepted the cup of suffering, we were saved.

People retired early in those days, and the apostles fell asleep in the garden instead of being a comfort to Jesus. They are a symbol of those who are not alert to their final test. When the Temple soldiers came to arrest Jesus and Peter tried to prevent them, Jesus stopped him. It was the hour for the climactic struggle between God and Satan.

The kiss of Judas was a normal Near East greeting. It served to identify Jesus in the dark and became a symbol of betrayal.

For Discussion

Before the play: When have you been afraid? What does it feel like?

After the play: How did Jesus show he was obedient to God? When has God called you to do something you were afraid to do?

Activity

Visit Jesus in church.
Pray aloud together or just sit quietly and speak to him in your heart.

Prayer

Invite the children to imagine they were there in the garden during the agony of Jesus:

In your mind's eye picture the dark garden and Jesus on his knees praying. Hear the insects and the breeze blowing through the olive leaves. Think of what might have gone through the mind of Jesus: his love for his Father and for us, his dread of the coming suffering and cruel death, the pain his suffering would cause his mother. (Pause.) Reflect on the ordeal Jesus was going through for you. (Pause.) Now place yourself in the scene next to him. What would you do? What would you say? (Allow time for silent reflection.)

CAST: NARRATOR, JESUS, PETER, JAMES, JOHN, JUDAS, APOSTLES (8), SOLDIERS (+), MALCHUS

PROPS: SWORDS

THE AGONY IN THE GARDEN
MATTHEW 26:36–56, MARK 14:32–52, LUKE 22:39–53, JOHN 18:1–12

Narrator After supper on Thursday evening, Jesus and the disciples went to the Mount of Olives. They stopped at the garden of Gethsemane.

Jesus and Eleven Apostles enter.

Jesus Sit here while I go over there and pray. Peter, James, and John, come with me.

Apostles sit. Jesus, Peter, James and John walk over to side.

Jesus I am sorrowful even to death. Remain here and keep watch with me.

Peter, James, and John sit. Jesus goes forward a little, kneels on the ground, and folds hands. Peter, James, and John close their eyes. Their heads nod.

Jesus My Father, if it is possible, let this cup pass from me. Yet, not what I want but what you want.

Jesus rises and goes to Peter, James, and John.

Jesus (*to Peter*) So, you could not stay awake with me for one hour? Watch and pray that you may not undergo the test. The spirit is willing, but the flesh is weak.

Jesus goes forward, kneels, and prays. Peter, James, and John sleep again.

Jesus My Father, if it is not possible that this cup pass without my drinking it, your will be done.

Jesus rises and goes to Peter, James, and John. He looks at them and shakes his head.

Jesus Can you not keep awake?

Peter, James, and John awake, rub eyes, and look at one another. Jesus goes forward, kneels, and prays.

Jesus My Father, if it is not possible that this cup pass without my drinking it, your will be done.

Jesus rises and goes to Peter, James, and John.

Jesus Are you still sleeping? The hour is come when the Son of Man is betrayed into the hands of sinners. Get up, let us go. See, my betrayer is at hand.

Judas, Soldiers, and Malchus enter.

Narrator Judas had arranged with the soldiers that he would identify Jesus by kissing him.

Judas (*kissing Jesus*) Greetings, Rabbi!

Jesus Friend, do what you are here to do.

Soldiers grab Jesus. Peter draws a sword and swings at Malchus.

Malchus   (*screaming*) Ahhh! My ear.

Jesus touches Malchus's ear.

Malchus   (*amazed*) I'm healed!

Jesus   (*to Peter*) Put your sword back into its sheath. All who take the sword will perish by the sword. Do you think that I cannot call upon my Father and he will at once send me more than twelve legions of angels?

(*to Soldiers*) Have you come out with swords and clubs to arrest me as though I were a robber? Day after day I sat teaching in the Temple, yet you did not arrest me. But this is your hour, the time for the power of darkness.

Apostles exit, running. Soldiers walk Jesus out.

Narrator   Jesus is our model in accepting God's will. When suffering comes into our lives, may we become stronger because of it and use it for good.

The Trial before Pilate

Themes

- the identity of Jesus
- the suffering of Jesus
- the death of Jesus

Background Notes

Jesus' trial before Pilate focused on his innocence and on his identity. The dream of Pilate's wife and the handwashing occur only in Matthew's account. These details underline the innocence of Jesus. The Scripture authors make the Jewish leaders, not Rome, responsible for the death of Jesus. The leaders brought Jesus to Pilate because they did not have the power to crucify. In choosing to free the Zealot, the terrorist Barabbas (whose name means Son of the Father) instead of Jesus, they chose political liberation rather than the true Messiah.

The gospels portray Pilate as fickle and subservient to the Jewish crowd. History, on the other hand, tells us that Pilate was strong-willed and held the Jewish people in contempt. In the gospels, although Pilate found Jesus without blame, he gave in to the pressure of the Jewish crowd when his career was threatened.

Jesus is presented by the evangelists as Messiah and king during the trial. The charge against him was that he said he was king of the Jews. This claim amounted to treason against Rome, a capital offense. Jesus explained to Pilate that his kingdom is not of this world. In the end, the Roman soldiers mocked him as king. They put a crown of thorns on him and a cloak, which was probably the scarlet cloak of the Roman soldiers. Ironically, these Gentiles unwittingly did homage to their real king as he was about to give his life for them and for all his people.

Scourging before crucifixion was routine procedure for the Romans. It was a terrible ordeal performed with a whip of leather strips ending in knots or bits of metal or bone. After this torture, Jesus was led to his throne, the cross.

For Discussion

Before the play: When do you especially think about the suffering Jesus went through? How does his suffering give meaning to ours?

After the play: What sufferings did Jesus endure for us? Why did Pilate order Jesus crucified?

Activity

On a white sheet of drawing paper, draw or paste some black symbols of Jesus' passion. Suggestions: a crown of thorns, the cross, whips, dice, a rooster, cloak, hill, INRI sign, a spear, nails. You might use white or black symbols on a purple sheet instead.

Prayer

*Soul of Christ, sanctify me
Body of Christ, save me.
Blood of Christ, cleanse me.
Water from the side of Christ, wash me.
Passion of Christ, strengthen me.
O good Jesus, hear me. Within your wounds shelter me. At the hour of my death call me and bid me come to you, that I may praise you with all your saints for ever and ever. Amen.*

CAST: NARRATOR, JESUS, PILATE, SOLDIERS 1, 2, 3, 4 (+), JEWISH LEADERS 1, 2 (+)

PROPS: CLOAK, CROWN OF THORNS, CHAIR, BOWL

THE TRIAL BEFORE PILATE
MARK 15:1–20, MATTHEW 27:11–31, LUKE 23:1–25, JOHN 18:28—19:16

Pilate stands on one side of the stage with his back to the other. Soldiers stand in the background, arms crossed.

Narrator On the morning after Jesus was arrested, soldiers brought him from Caiaphas, the high priest, to Pilate, the Roman procurator.

Jesus and Jewish Leaders enter from opposite side. They stop some distance from Pilate.

Jewish Leader 1 Pilate, we cannot enter your building, or we will not be able to eat the Passover meal.

Pilate walks over to Jewish Leaders.

Pilate What charge do you bring against this man?

Jewish Leader 2 If he were not a criminal, we would not have handed him over to you.

Pilate Take him yourselves and judge him according to your law.

Jewish Leader 1 We do not have the right to execute anyone.

Pilate returns to his side of the stage. He turns to face the Jewish Leaders.

Pilate (*beckoning to Jesus*) Come here.

Jesus walks to Pilate.

Pilate Are you the king of the Jews?

Jesus Do you ask this on your own or did others tell you about me?

Pilate I am not a Jew, am I? Your own nation and the chief priests handed you over to me. What have you done?

Jesus My kingdom is not of this world. If my kingdom were from this world, my followers would be fighting to keep me from being handed over to the Jews. But as it is, my kingdom is not from here.

Pilate So you are a king?

Jesus You say I am a king. For this I was born and for this I came into the world, to testify to the truth. Everyone who belongs to the truth listens to my voice.

Pilate What is truth? (*goes to Jewish Leaders*) I find no guilt in him. But you have a custom that I release one prisoner to you at Passover. Do you want me to release to you Barabbas or Jesus, called Messiah?

Jewish Leaders	Barabbas!
Pilate	(*to Soldiers*) Take him away and whip him.

Soldiers and Jesus exit.

Narrator	The soldiers whipped Jesus. They wove a crown of thorns and placed it on his head. They clothed him in a purple cloak and mocked him saying, "Hail, king of the Jews." Then they returned him to Pilate.

Soldiers and Jesus enter. Jesus is wearing the cloak and the crown of thorns. Pilate goes to Jewish Leaders.

Pilate	Look, I am bringing him out to you, so that you may know that I find no guilt in him. Behold the man.
Jewish Leaders	Crucify him. Crucify him.
Pilate	Take him yourselves and crucify him. I find no case against him.
Jewish Leaders	We have a law, and according to that law he ought to die, because he claimed to be the Son of God.

Pilate puts his hand to his face in fear and returns to his side of stage.

Pilate	(*to Jesus*) Where are you from? (*long pause*) Do you not speak to me? Do you not know that I have power to release you and power to crucify you?
Jesus	You would have no power over me if it had not been given to you from above. For this reason the one who handed me over to you has the greater sin.

Pilate goes to Jewish Leaders.

Pilate	This man should be released.
Jewish Leaders	If you release him, you are not a friend of Caesar. Everyone who makes himself a king sets himself against Caesar.

Pilate goes to bowl and washes his hands.

Pilate	I am innocent of this man's blood. See to it yourselves.
Jewish Leaders	His blood be upon us and upon our children.
Pilate	(*to Soldiers*) Take him out and crucify him.

Soldiers go to Jesus and roughly pull him up. Soldiers and Jesus exit. Jewish Leaders cheer.

Narrator	Jesus was condemned to death. By his suffering and death on the cross he saved the world. He saved you. What love and gratitude should fill our hearts when we recall this.

The **Resurrection**

EASTER SUNDAY: YEARS A, B, C

Themes

- Easter
- the resurrection
- women
- Peter
- love for Jesus

Background Notes

No one witnessed the actual resurrection. The first clue that Jesus was risen was the empty tomb. All the gospels record that before dawn women went to the tomb. Although John focuses on Mary Magdalene (or Mary of Magdala), Mary's use of "we" in her report to the disciples indicates that she was with others. John let Peter enter the tomb first. Peter, therefore, predominates in the story. The apostles saw the burial cloths. The wrapping for the head was rolled up and separate. This probably means that it was still in the oval shape it took when it was looped around the head and knotted at the top to keep the jaw from slacking. The presence of the linens discredits the rumor that the body was stolen. Thieves would not leave the wrappings behind. The disciples did not understand the full impact of the scene. They had yet to receive the Holy Spirit.

It is fitting that Mary Magdalene, who faithfully stood at the cross, was the first to see the risen Lord. But because he was so altered in his glorified state or because her vision was so blurred by tears, she mistook him for the gardener. Her love for Jesus prompted her to ask where the body was so that she could take it away. She was oblivious to whether or not she would be able to do this. When Jesus said Mary's name, she recognized him immediately. She called him Rabbouni, a form of rabbi. Jesus told Mary to stop clinging to him. He still had to return to the Father and complete the cycle of his glorification and our salvation.

For Discussion

Before the play: What do we celebrate at Easter? How do you celebrate it at home?

After the play: What difference does the resurrection of Jesus make for us? How can you show from your actions how much you love Jesus?

Activity

Decorate Easter eggs. You might tear or cut out small, shiny pieces of paper from magazines and glue them on overlapping to cover the egg. Then coat the egg with a protective covering.

Prayer

Invite the children to close their eyes and lead them to reflect on Jesus' resurrection:

Because Jesus died and rose from the dead we, too, will have eternal life. Death is not the end for us. A whole new world awaits us. We will have new life. St. Paul wrote that heaven is so wonderful that we can't even imagine what God has prepared there for us. Let us think for a moment what heaven will be like. There will be no more suffering, pain, and worry. We will be with God forever in perfect happiness. We will be with Mary and all the saints and angels in heaven. Many of the people we have loved on earth will be there too. We will see Jesus and be loved by him without end. Let us thank Jesus for making heaven possible for us. (Pause.) Now let's praise God for restoring to us the hope of everlasting life.

Sing an Easter song or an Alleluia.

CAST: NARRATOR, JESUS, PETER, JOHN, MARY, ANGELS 1, 2

PROPS: TWO CLOTHS

THE RESURRECTION John 20:1–18

Peter and John are at the far side of the stage. Mary enters from the other side.

Narrator Early on the first day of the week, while it was still dark, Mary of Magdala came to the tomb. She saw that the stone had been removed.

Mary gasps and puts hands to face in horror. She runs to Peter and John.

Mary They have taken the Lord from the tomb. We don't know where they have laid him.

Peter and John run to the tomb. John arrives first and peers in the tomb. He waits for Peter. Peter arrives.

John I can see the burial cloths.

Peter (*stooping and going in tomb*) Look. The cloth that covered his head is rolled up in a place by itself.

John stoops and goes in tomb. Peter and John exit. Mary stands weeping. Angels 1, 2 enter and sit in the tomb.

Angels 1, 2 Woman, why are you weeping?

Jesus enters behind Mary.

Mary They have taken away my Lord, and I don't know where they laid him.

Mary turns and sees Jesus, but doesn't know who he is.

Jesus Woman, why are you weeping? Whom are you looking for?

Narrator Mary thought Jesus was the gardener.

Mary (*to Jesus*) Sir, if you have carried him away, tell me where you have laid him, and I will take him away.

Jesus Mary!

Mary (*excitedly*) Rabbouni! (*kneels and clasps Jesus' knees*)

Jesus Do not hold on to me because I have not yet ascended to the Father. Go to my brothers and tell them I am going to my Father and your Father, to my God and your God.

Mary rises and exits.

Mary (*shouting offstage*) I have seen the Lord!

Narrator Because Jesus is alive, we can live forever. His rising brought us new life. All our actions ought to show that we are new people in Christ. They should shine forth Christ's love to everyone.

The Appearance to the Women

EASTER VIGIL: YEARS A, B, C

Background Notes

The gospel accounts of the resurrection differ, but all agree that Jesus' tomb was empty and that he appeared to various people. The women were going to anoint Jesus' body. As an afterthought, they wondered how they would move the heavy, flat stone that covered the entrance to the tomb. Their worries were allayed when they discovered that the stone had already been moved for them. The women were full of fear on seeing the angel and the empty tomb. The details in this account of the resurrection highlighted the glory of the event: the angel, the dazzling white clothes, the earthquake, the fainting guards. The disbelief of the disciples was understandable. In the gospels of Mark and Luke, Peter is singled out as the one who learned of the resurrection. Interestingly, it was the women, not the apostles, who were the first heralds of the resurrection.

For Discussion

Before the play: If someone told you that he was going to die and then rise from the dead, would you believe it? Why or why not?

After the play: In this account of the resurrection, what signs are there that it is a glorious event? Why didn't the disciples believe the good news at first? If you believe in the resurrection, how will you live?

Activity

Invite young learners to take part in this activity. Make an Easter lily. Fold a triangle with two equal sides in half. Hold it so that the longest side is up. Fold the two sides in and over each other equally. Turn the figure over and cut a peak to the straight horizontal edge of paper. This will yield six petals when the paper is opened. Curl the petals outward using a scissor blade. Tape the edges of the lily around a green pipe cleaner or green construction paper stem. Cut a few yellow strips with knobs on the end and glue them inside the lily so they show at the top. Add leaves to the stem.

Older learners might like to take some time for prayer.

Prayer

REGINA CAELI

Queen of heaven, rejoice, alleluia.
The Son whom you were made worthy
to bear, alleluia,
Has risen as he said, alleluia.
Pray for us to God, alleluia.

Rejoice and be glad, O Virgin Mary,
alleluia,
for the Lord has truly risen, alleluia.

Let us pray.
God of life,
you have given joy to the world
by the resurrection of your Son,
our Lord Jesus Christ.
Through the prayers of his mother,
the Virgin Mary,
bring us to the happiness of eternal life.
We ask this through Christ our Lord.
Amen.

CAST: JESUS, NARRATOR, ANGEL, MARY, WOMEN 1, 2, GUARD (+), DISCIPLES 1, 2, PETER

PROPS: BAGS FOR SPICES, CHAIR FOR TOMB

The Appearance to the Women

Matthew 28:1–10, Mark 16:1–8, Luke 24:1–12

Stone is before tomb. Guards stand by it.

Narrator Very early when the sun had risen, on the first day of the week Mary of Magdala and other women went to the tomb. They brought spices to anoint Jesus.

Mary and Women enter and walk toward tomb.

Woman 1 Who will roll back the stone for us from the entrance to the tomb?

Women shake.

Woman 2 What was that?

Mary An earthquake.

Angel enters and rolls back stone. Guards fall to ground in a faint.

Angel (*to Women*) Do not be afraid! I know that you are looking for Jesus the crucified. He is not here (*gestures to tomb*) for he has been raised just as he said. Come, see the place where he lay. Then go quickly and tell his disciples, "He has been raised from the dead, and he is going before you to Galilee. There you will see him." This is my message for you.

Women peer into tomb. They begin to run. Jesus enters and meets them.

Jesus Good morning!

Woman 1 (*with joy*) Jesus!

Woman 2 (*excitedly*) Master!

Women kneel and bow to Jesus.

Jesus (*laughing*) Do not be afraid. Go tell my brothers to go to Galilee, and there they will see me.

Jesus exits. Disciples enter. Women go to them.

Woman 1 Jesus is alive!

Woman 2 He is risen.

Disciples 1 That's nonsense!

Woman 1 He spoke to us.

Disciple 2 You're out of your minds!

Group stands arguing. Peter leaves group, goes to tomb, and peers in. He stands up amazed.

Peter The tomb is empty! How can this be?

Narrator The risen Lord is alive in our world today. Be open to the ways he comes to you and be ready to greet him.

The Appearance on the Emmaus Road

THIRD SUNDAY OF EASTER: YEAR A

Themes

- the resurrection
- the identity of Jesus
- the Eucharist

Background Notes

The Emmaus story is the story of all people who come to know Jesus. Two disciples are leaving Jerusalem with their hopes dashed. One is identified as Cleopas; the other could be his wife. They had hoped that Jesus was the Messiah but were discouraged by his death. When Jesus came to them, they did not recognize him. Then they summarized the good news for him. He dispelled their confusion and doubts by explaining how the Scriptures foretold that the Messiah would have to suffer. Their hearts burned within them. When the travelers reached Emmaus, about seven miles from Jerusalem, the two disciples invited Jesus to stay with them. During supper as Jesus was breaking bread, the disciples suddenly realized who he was. He vanished, and they immediately returned to Jerusalem to tell the other disciples what had happened.

This account has the structure of the eucharistic liturgy. First the disciples heard the word, and then they shared a meal with Christ. In the Eucharist, Jesus is present with his people no less than he was before his death. Our hearts, too, should burn within us.

For Discussion

Before the play: Did you ever have the experience of not recognizing someone? Why didn't you recognize him or her? Why do you think some disciples wouldn't recognize Jesus after the resurrection?

After the play: Although Jesus died, he is present with us at the Eucharist. In what ways is he with us? How can listening to God's word proclaimed at Mass bring you closer to Jesus? How does sharing the sacred bread and wine at Mass bring you closer to Jesus and one another?

Activity

Young learners might enjoy this activity. On a sheet of practice paper draw a cup, grapes, stalks of wheat, and a loaf of bread, placing them in an arrangement that looks good. Then on black construction paper copy this picture using colored chalk dipped in water.

Invite older learners to decide on or even write a song that reflects the theme of this gospel passage.

Prayer

Lord, in your sacrament we receive you into our bodies. Make us worthy to experience the resurrection for which we hope. We have held your treasure hidden within us ever since we received baptismal grace. It grows ever richer at the table of the Eucharist.

—adapted from St. Ephrem

CAST: NARRATOR, JESUS, CLEOPAS, DISCIPLE

PROPS: TABLE, THREE CHAIRS, BREAD

THE APPEARANCE ON THE EMMAUS ROAD Luke 24:13–35

Narrator On the day of the Resurrection two disciples were going to a village called Emmaus, about seven miles from Jerusalem.

Cleopas and Disciple enter.

Cleopas I can't believe the Teacher is dead.

Disciple According to those women, he's not.

Jesus enters and joins the Disciples.

Jesus What are you discussing as you walk along?

Disciples stand still.

Cleopas (*sadly*) Are you the only visitor to Jerusalem who does not know of the things that have taken place there in these days?

Jesus What things?

Disciple The things that happened to Jesus of Nazareth. He was a prophet mighty in deed and word before God and all the people. Our chief priests and rulers handed him over to be condemned to death and crucified him.

Cleopas But we had hoped that he was the one to redeem Israel. Yes, and besides all this, it is now the third day since these things took place.

Disciple Moreover, some women from our group have astounded us. They were at the tomb early in the morning and did not find his body. They came back and told us that they had seen a vision of angels who said that he was alive.

Cleopas Then some of those with us went to the tomb and found it just as the women had described, but they did not see him.

Jesus (*shaking head*) Oh, how foolish you are! How slow of heart to believe all that the prophets spoke! Was it not necessary that the Messiah should suffer these things and then enter into his glory? The Scriptures tell you this. Let me explain, beginning with Moses and the prophets.

Jesus, Cleopas, and Disciple walk on, talking.

Narrator Jesus explained to them what referred to him in all the Scriptures until they approached the village.

Cleopas and Disciples stop. Jesus keeps walking.

Cleopas Stay with us.

Disciple It is almost evening and the day is now nearly over.

Jesus All right. I will.

Jesus smiles. He, Cleopas, and Disciple go to the table and sit.

Jesus (*taking bread*) Blessed are you, O Lord our God, King of the universe.

Jesus breaks the bread and passes it to Cleopas and Disciple.

**Cleopas
and Disciple** (*in awe*) Jesus!

Jesus disappears backstage or under the table.

Cleopas He's gone!

Disciple Weren't our hearts burning within us while he talked to us on the road and explained the Scriptures to us?

Cleopas (*excitedly*) Let's go back to Jerusalem and tell the others what happened.

Cleopas and Disciple rise and run off.

Narrator The two disciples recognized Jesus in the breaking of the bread. At Mass we share the sacred bread and wine. Our hearts should burn within us then, for Christ is present.

The Appearance to the Apostles

THIRD SUNDAY OF EASTER: YEAR B; PENTECOST: YEARS A, B, C

Themes

- the resurrection
- evangelization
- the good news
- ministry

Background Notes

The disciples experienced the resurrected Jesus as a human being. He assured them he was not a ghost. He showed them his wounds, asked for food, and ate fish in front of them. Eating was an obvious sign that someone was not a ghost. Jesus was able to eat just as the daughter of Jairus had been able to eat after Jesus raised her from the dead.

The disciples moved from shock, confusion, and fear to peace and joy. Jesus recalled how he had told them about the closing events of his life on earth and how the Scriptures pointed to these events. He foretold that they would witness these things and preach repentance to all nations. The promised Spirit would make things clear to the disciples and empower them to carry out their mission. In the account from the Gospel of John, Jesus breathed on the apostles and gave them the Holy Spirit that day, enabling them to forgive sins.

For Discussion

Before the play: How would you feel if the risen Lord appeared to you?

After the play: In what ways can you proclaim to others the good news that Jesus is risen? How will the Holy Spirit help you?

Activity

Invite younger learners to carry out this activity. The Hebrew word for peace is *shalom*. On a half sheet of stiff paper or cardboard, print the letters for this word so that they are about a half-inch thick. Color the letters by putting glue on them and then filling them in with various seeds, rice, or circles of colored paper made with a hole punch. You may wish to sponge-paint the background first.

Older learners might share their thoughts about the gospel reading. They could decide in what concrete ways they can "share bread" with their needy sisters and brothers.

Prayer

*Lord, make me an instrument
    of your peace.
Where there is hatred, let me sow love;
where there is injury, pardon;
where there is doubt, faith;
where there is despair, hope;
where there is darkness, light;
where there is sadness, joy.*

*O Divine Master,
grant that I may not so much seek
    to be consoled, as to console;
to be understood, as to understand;
to be loved, as to love.
For it is in giving that we receive;
it is in pardoning that we are pardoned;
and it is in dying that we are born
    to eternal life.*

—attributed to St. Francis of Assisi

CAST: NARRATOR, JESUS, DISCIPLES 1, 2 (+)

PROPS: TABLE, FISH

THE APPEARANCE TO THE APOSTLES Luke 24:36–51

Disciples are onstage, talking excitedly.

Disciple 1 How amazing that he walked to Emmaus with those disciples.

Disciple 2 And they didn't know him until he broke bread!

Jesus enters and stands in the middle of them.

Jesus Peace be with you.

Disciples gasp and shrink back, frightened.

Jesus Why are you frightened? And why do doubts arise in your hearts? Look at my hands and my feet. See that it is I myself. Touch me and see, (*extending hands*) because a ghost does not have flesh and bones (*gesturing to feet*) as you can see I have.

Disciples come forward with joy and amazement.

Jesus Have you anything here to eat?

Disciple 1 takes fish from table and gives it to Jesus.

Jesus Thank you.

Jesus "eats" the fish while the Disciples watch.

Jesus These are my words that I spoke to you while I was still with you. Everything written about me in the law of Moses, the prophets, and the psalms must be fulfilled.

It is written that the Messiah would suffer and rise from the dead on the third day and that repentance for the forgiveness of sins, would be proclaimed in his name to all the nations, (*makes a sweeping motion with arm*) beginning from Jerusalem. (*points down*) You (*points to Disciples*) are witnesses of these things. I am sending upon you what my Father promised, so stay in the city until you are clothed with power from on high.

Narrator After the resurrection Jesus did not scold the men who had deserted him. Instead he offered them peace. May we, like Jesus, be quick to forgive and forget.

The Appearance to Thomas

SECOND SUNDAY OF EASTER: YEARS A, B, C

Themes

- the resurrection
- forgiveness
- faith
- Holy Spirit

Background Notes

Jesus was truly resurrected. His entering through locked doors shows that he had not merely survived crucifixion. He had died and risen. He possessed new spiritual qualities. Jesus was, however, the same person the disciples knew and loved. The wounds on his hands and feet identified him. Jesus' first word to his disciples was "Shalom," that is, "Peace be with you." Understandably he had to calm their fears. Not only were the disciples seeing a person they knew had died, but also a person whom almost all of them had abandoned.

Jesus' breathing on his disciples was a sign that he was giving them his Spirit. Breath signifies life. The Spirit of creation brings us new life. Now that Jesus was risen, the Spirit would empower his Church to carry on his mission. His disciples would share in his power to forgive and to reconcile the world through the sacraments. They, too, would bring peace.

Thomas, nicknamed "doubting Thomas," came to believe that the Lord was risen—not on the word of others but by seeing Jesus with his own eyes. He made an act of faith. He called Jesus "Lord" and "God," names that were used for the God of Israel. Unlike Thomas' faith, our faith depends not on sight but on the gospel, the Word.

For Discussion

Before the play: What are some things you find hard to believe? Why do you believe them?

After the play: How can you become stronger in your faith?

Activity

Younger learners can carry out this activity. Make a copy of the Apostles' Creed and paste it on drawing paper. Around the Creed draw symbols of faith, including a candle to symbolize the light of faith.

Older learners might write a personal creed stating what they believe about Jesus.

Prayer

Invite the learners to contribute to a spontaneous litany of faith. Explain that someone will state a truth that we believe and then all will respond, "I believe. Jesus increase my faith." Suggest thinking of the Apostles' Creed to get ideas. You might begin the prayer:

That God exists...

That Jesus loves me...

That I will live forever...

CAST: NARRATOR, JESUS, DISCIPLES (+), THOMAS

THE APPEARANCE TO THOMAS JOHN 20:19–29

Disciples are onstage.

Narrator On the evening of the resurrection, the first day of the week, the disciples were behind locked doors in fear of the Jews.

Jesus enters and stands in the middle of the Disciples. They step back in fear.

Jesus Peace be with you. It is really I, Jesus. See. (*extends his hands*) And see. (*points to his side*)

Disciples 1 Jesus, I'm so happy.

Disciple 2 We thought you were dead.

Disciples laugh, clasp their hands together, and show joy.

Jesus Peace be with you. As the Father has sent me, so I send you. (*breathes on the Disciples gently*) Receive the Holy Spirit. Whose sins you forgive are forgiven them, and whose sins you hold are retained.

Jesus exits. Thomas enters.

Disciple 2 Thomas! You missed it.

Disciple 3 We have seen the Lord.

Thomas (*shaking head*) Unless I see the mark of the nails in his hands (*points to palms*) and put my finger into the nailmarks and put my hand (*holds up hand*) into his side, I will not believe.

Narrator A week later the disciples were again inside behind locked doors, and Thomas was with them.

Jesus enters and stands among the Disciples.

Jesus Peace be with you. (*to Thomas*) Put your finger here (*extending hands*) and see my hands, and bring your hand and put it into my side. Do not doubt but believe.

Thomas (*kneeling*) My Lord and my God!

Jesus Have you believed because you have seen me? Blessed are those who have not seen and yet have come to believe.

Narrator What we believe we take on faith. We have not seen God, or Jesus, or heaven. Our faith can grow stronger through prayer and study.

Jesus and Peter

THIRD SUNDAY OF EASTER: YEAR C

Themes

- the Church
- Peter
- the resurrection

Background Notes

As soon as Peter knew that the Lord was on the shore, he dove into the water and swam to Jesus. That way he would arrive faster than by boat. The Lord cooked breakfast, using some of the fish the disciples caught. After breakfast, the Lord established Peter's roles as shepherd and martyr. Peter had denied Jesus three times. Now Jesus gave him an opportunity to reverse the denial by a triple declaration of love. He commanded Peter to show his love by assuming his own mission. He entrusted Peter with the care of his flock. Peter and his successors, the popes, would be responsible for teaching, governing, and sanctifying the Church.

When Jesus told Peter he would stretch out his hands, he might have been referring to Peter's being taken prisoner or crucified. Peter was crucified under the emperor Nero. He kept the promise he made at the Last Supper that he would lay down his life for Jesus.

Today on the Sea of Galilee the Church of the Primacy stands on the site where it is believed Jesus commanded Peter to lead his Church.

For Discussion

Before the play: What is the role of the pope in the Church?

After the play: What role did Peter have in the early Church? What were his strengths and weaknesses? How do you show love and respect for the Holy Father?

Activity

Invite young learners to compare the Church to a ship with the pope at the helm. Have them draw a picture of this.

Older learners could find out about the present pope and put together a booklet about him.

Prayer

Holy Spirit, guide the leaders of our Church: our Holy Father and bishops. Give them wisdom to make right decisions. Give them compassion to be good shepherds. Give them courage to stand up for what is right. Give them zeal in proclaiming the gospel and the kingdom of God. Make them one as they lead us to the glory of God the Father. Above all, fill their hearts with love so that they truly may be Christ for the world. Amen.

CAST: NARRATOR, JESUS, PETER, THOMAS, NATHANAEL, JAMES, JOHN, APOSTLE 1, APOSTLE 2

PROPS: WOOD FOR FIRE

JESUS AND PETER JOHN 21:13–19

Jesus, Peter, Thomas, Nathanael, James, John, Apostle 1, and Apostle 2 are seated in a semi-circle around wood.

Narrator   The third time Jesus appeared to the apostles after the Resurrection, they were fishing. Although they had caught nothing all night, Jesus helped them catch many fish. When Peter realized that it was Jesus on the shore, he dived into the water and swam to him. There Jesus served the apostles breakfast.

Thomas   That was delicious. I was starved. Thank you.

Apostles   Yes, thank you.

Jesus   My pleasure. (*turning to Peter*) Simon, son of John, do you love me more than these?

Peter   Yes, Lord. You know that I love you.

Jesus   Feed my lambs. (*pause*) Simon, son of John, do you love me?

Peter   Yes, Lord. You know that I love you.

Jesus   Tend my sheep. (*pause*) Simon, son of John, do you love me?

Peter   (*exasperated*) Lord, you know everything. You know that I love you.

Jesus   Feed my sheep. Very truly, I tell you, when you were younger, you used to fasten your own belt and go wherever you wished. But when you grow old, you will stretch out your hands, (*extends hands*) and someone else will fasten a belt around you and take you where you do not wish to go. Follow me.

Peter   (*pointing to John*) Lord, what about him?

Jesus   If it is my will that he remain until I come, what is that to you? Follow me!

Narrator   Peter did feed Jesus' sheep. He became the chief shepherd of Christ's Church. And as Jesus foretold in this story, Peter died for his faith in Jesus. May our love for Jesus make us ready to give everything for him, even our lives.

The **Ascension**

Trinity Sunday: Year B

Background Notes

The ascension is a part of the paschal mystery. In Matthew, Mark, and Luke the Ascension takes place on the day of the resurrection, but in the Acts of the Apostles it occurs forty days after the resurrection.

The story of the ascension foreshadowed the parousia (second coming). Jesus appeared on a mountain and was exalted or taken up into glory. The cloud was a symbol of the divine presence, as it was during the Exodus and the Transfiguration. Jesus is seated at the right hand of the Father. Jesus has authority from God and power over the whole universe. Jesus' ascension is the assurance that someday we too will be taken up into glory.

At the ascension Jesus gave "the great commission" to the eleven apostles. They were to be his personal witnesses and to make disciples of all people, the Jewish people as well as the Gentiles. Jesus promised to still be Emmanuel, God with us. He blessed the apostles. While they were still there in an attitude of worship, they were ordered to go and take the good news to all. Angels explained that Jesus would return the same way they saw him go. They were referring to the final judgment day.

On the top of Mount Olivet in Jerusalem today there is a Shrine of the Ascension. Inside is a rock in the ground which, according to tradition, marks the area from which Jesus ascended.

For Discussion

Before the play: Who carries on Jesus' work for him? How does Jesus help them?

After the play: Who is called to witness to Jesus today? How can you do this in a practical way?

Activity

Write a poem about Jesus being with you always. You might begin each line, "When I'm..." and name a situation or place. Then end, "You are with me."

Prayer

O Lord, teach me to be generous.
Teach me to serve you as you deserve;
to give and not to count the cost;
to fight and not to heed the wound;
to toil and not to seek for rest;
to labor and not to ask for reward
save that of knowing that I am doing
your holy will. Amen.

—St. Ignatius of Loyola

CAST: NARRATOR, JESUS, DISCIPLES (+), MAN 1, MAN 2

PROP: LARGE PAPER CLOUD

THE ASCENSION
MATTHEW 28:16–20, MARK 16:15–20, LUKE 24:50–53, ACTS OF THE APOSTLES 1:6–11

Narrator The eleven disciples went to Mount Olivet as Jesus had directed them.

Disciple 1 Lord, is this the time when you will restore the kingdom to Israel?

Jesus It is not for you to know the times or periods that the Father has set by his own authority. But you will receive power when the Holy Spirit has come upon you. And you will be my witnesses in Jerusalem, in all Judea and Samaria, and to the ends of the earth. (*makes sweeping motion with arm*) All authority in heaven and on earth has been given to me.

Go therefore (*points to distance*) and make disciples of all nations, baptizing them in the name of the Father and of the Son and of the Holy Spirit. Teach them to obey everything that I have commanded you. And remember, I am with you always, to the end of the age.

Narrator As the men were watching, Jesus was lifted up, and a cloud took him out of their sight.

Jesus raises hands over the apostles in blessing. He backs off, and a cloud covers him. Man 1, 2 enter.

Man 1 Men of Galilee, why do you stand looking up toward heaven?

Man 2 This Jesus, who has been taken up from you into heaven, will come in the same way as you saw him go into heaven.

Narrator The apostles returned to Jerusalem where they stayed in an upper room. They prayed and awaited the Holy Spirit. We, who have received the Holy Spirit at baptism, have the power to witness to Jesus. Let us do this in our words and actions.

Disciples exit.

Sunday and Feast Day Gospels that Correspond to Plays in This Book

PLAYLETS CAN HELP PREPARE LEARNERS TO CELEBRATE SUNDAY LITURGIES.

Liturgy	Event
Second Sunday of Advent A, B, C	The Baptism of Jesus (John the Baptist)
Third Sunday of Advent B, C	The Baptism of Jesus
Fourth Sunday of Advent B	The Annunciation of the Lord
Fourth Sunday of Advent C	The Visitation
Christmas Mass at Midnight A, B, C	The Birth of Jesus
Christmas Mass at Dawn A, B, C	The Birth of Jesus
January 1, Octave of Christmas, Solemnity of Mary, Mother of God	The Birth of Jesus
Sunday in the Octave of Christmas B	The Presentation
Sunday in the Octave of Christmas C	The Boy Jesus in the Temple
Epiphany A, B, C	The Visit of the Magi
Sunday after January 6 A, B, C	The Baptism of Jesus
First Sunday of Lent A, B, C	The Temptation of Jesus
Second Sunday of Lent A, B, C	The Transfiguration of Jesus
Third Sunday of Lent A	The Samaritan Woman
Third Sunday of Lent B	The Cleansing of the Temple
Third Sunday of Lent C	The Barren Fig Tree
Fourth Sunday of Lent A	The Man Born Blind
Fourth Sunday of Lent B	Nicodemus
Fourth Sunday of Lent C	The Prodigal Son
Fifth Sunday of Lent A	The Raising of Lazarus
Fifth Sunday of Lent C	The Woman Caught in Adultery
Passion Sunday (Procession) A, B, C	The Entry into Jerusalem
Passion Sunday A, B, C	The Last Supper
	The Agony in the Garden
	The Trial before Pilate
Passion Sunday B	The Anointing at Bethany

Fifteenth Sunday of the Year A	The Sower
Fifteenth Sunday of the Year C	The Good Samaritan
Sixteenth Sunday of the Year A	The Weeds
Sixteenth Sunday of the Year C	Martha and Mary
Seventeenth Sunday of the Year A	The Hidden Treasure
	The Pearl of Great Price
Seventeenth Sunday of the Year B	The Multiplication of Loaves
Seventeenth Sunday of the Year C	The Persistent Friend
Eighteenth Sunday of the Year A	The Multiplication of Loaves
Eighteenth Sunday of the Year C	The Rich Fool
Nineteenth Sunday of the Year A	Walking on the Sea
Twentieth Sunday of the Year A	The Canaanite Woman
Twenty-First Sunday of the Year A	Peter's Profession of Faith
Twenty-Second Sunday of the Year B	Cure at the Pool of Bethesda
Twenty-Third Sunday of the Year B	Cure of a Man Who Is Deaf and Mute
Twenty-Fourth Sunday of the Year A	The Unforgiving Servant
Twenty-Fourth Sunday of the Year B	Peter's Profession of Faith
Twenty-Fourth Sunday of the Year C	The Lost Sheep
	The Lost Coin
	The Prodigal Son
Twenty-Fifth Sunday of the Year A	The Workers in the Vineyard
Twenty-Fifth Sunday of the Year C	The Crafty Steward
Twenty-Sixth Sunday of the Year A	The Two Sons
Twenty-Sixth Sunday of the Year C	The Rich Man and Lazarus
Twenty-Seventh Sunday of the Year A	The Wicked Vinedressers
Twenty-Seventh Sunday of the Year B	The Blessing of the Children
Twenty-Eighth Sunday of the Year A	The Wedding Feast
Twenty-Eighth Sunday of the Year B	The Rich Young Man
Twenty-Eighth Sunday of the Year C	The Ten Lepers
Twenty-Ninth Sunday of the Year A	Paying Taxes to Caesar
Twenty-Ninth Sunday of the Year C	The Judge and the Widow
Thirtieth Sunday of the Year B	Blind Bartimaeus
Thirtieth Sunday of the Year C	The Pharisee and the Tax Collector
Thirty-First Sunday of the Year C	Zacchaeus, the Tax Collector
Thirty-Second Sunday of the Year A	The Ten Bridesmaids
Thirty-Second Sunday of the Year B	The Widow's Offering
Thirty-Third Sunday of the Year A	The Three Servants and the Money

Index of Themes

THE FOLLOWING TOPICS CAN BE ENLIVENED BY A PLAY IN THIS BOOK